Health and Safety
IN
Child Care

SUSAN S. ARONSON, M.D., F.A.A.P.
CLINICAL PROFESSOR OF PEDIATRICS
Hahnemann University

HarperCollins*Publishers*

Dedicated to my mother, who taught me child development from the ground up, and to my daughter, son, and husband, who helped me practice what I preach. I owe special thanks to Jeanne L. Shane, educator, and Bruce J. Aronson, college student, for their patient reading and suggestions for revisions of the manuscript.

Executive Editor:
Christopher Jennison
Project Editor:
Shuli Traub
Design and Cover Coordinator:
Dorothy Bungert
Cover Design:
Kay Canizzaro
Photo Research:
Karen Koblik
Director of Production:
Jeanie Berke
Production Administrator:
Beth Maglione
Compositor:
Bi-Comp, Inc.
Printer and Binder:
R. R. Donnelley & Sons Company
Cover Printer:
The Lehigh Press, Inc.

For permission to use copyrighted material, grateful acknowledgment is made to the copyright holders on page 238, which is hereby made part of this copyright page.

Health and Safety in Child Care
Copyright © 1991 by HarperCollins Publishers Inc.

Library of Congress Cataloging-in-Publication Data

Aronson, Susan S.
   Health and safety in child care / Susan S. Aronson.
      p.   cm.
   Includes bibliographical references and index.
   ISBN 0–673–38911–1
   1. Day care centers—United States.   2. Day care centers—United
States—Safety measures.   3. Day care centers—Health aspects—
United States.   I. Title.
HV854.A83   1991
362.7'12'0289—dc20   90–48682
                                                          CIP

91 92 93 94   9 8 7 6 5 4 3 2 1

Brief Contents

iii

Detailed Contents

vi

Preface

Child care is a multibillion-dollar, rapidly growing industry in the United States. More than half of all mothers with infants and toddlers (children under age 3) are in the labor force. Families with working mothers are the norm.

More than half of the working mothers with children less than age 5 use some form of care outside the family. Nursery schools, Head Start programs, child care centers, group homes or mini-centers (child care with more than one caregiver in a residence), and family day care homes (in which one caregiver takes care of children in her own home) provide out-of-home care. School-age children receive care outside the home in before-and-after-school and recreational programs provided by schools and other community organizations, in family day care, in child care centers, and in latchkey arrangements. Although the specific arrangements differ, children's needs for nurturance and protection are the same in all settings.

Child care is labor-intensive, requiring skilled workers who must augment their experience as caregivers with learning about the special needs of children in group settings. This textbook is written to help child care professionals and students of early childhood education acquire information to manage health and safety issues responsibly in child care settings. The book is intended as an independent text, providing a survey of the relevant topics. At the end of each chapter, additional sources of information are provided for those who wish to read more about specific subjects. Suggested activities are listed as a guide to instructors who are using the book as a course text. The appendixes include practical guides and forms to be used by child care providers.

Reviewers Scott Mies, Fel-Pro Daycare Center, and Karen Stephens, Illinois State University, are gratefully acknowledged.

Susan S. Aronson

Overview

IN THIS CHAPTER:

WHAT ARE THE HEALTH AND SAFETY NEEDS OF ALL CHILDREN?
IDENTIFYING HEALTH AND SAFETY ISSUES FOR CHILD CARE
SETTING PRIORITIES FOR HEALTH AND SAFETY IN CHILD CARE
HOW THIS BOOK IS ORGANIZED

WHAT ARE THE HEALTH AND SAFETY NEEDS OF ALL CHILDREN?

All children need protection from injury and infection, both of which can lead to discomfort, disability, or even death. But children need more than simple protection from hazards. They need activities that promote healthy development and prevent problems with growth, body system functioning, learning, and social and emotional competence. Health promotion includes traditional health care services such as:

- □ check-ups
- □ immunization
- □ screening tests
- □ diagnostic services
- □ treatment.

In addition, health promotion should include:

- □ good nutrition
- □ dental health measures such as fluoridation and dental hygiene
- □ opportunities to develop fitness habits
- □ opportunities to develop mental health skills.

IDENTIFYING HEALTH AND SAFETY ISSUES FOR CHILD CARE

Health and safety issues in child care are identified by looking at the most significant risks to the health of children and adults in the child care setting. Risks can be measured systematically and objectively by looking at how often an undesired outcome occurs, but the acceptability of risk is a value judgment. In the past, children have been knowingly exposed to risks with frequent, undesired outcomes because the economic expense or inconvenience has been judged to outweigh the health benefit. Views about the acceptability of risk change. For example, between 1976 and 1984, laws requiring use of seat belts and car seats for young children traveling in cars were adopted in all 50 states. The adoption of seat restraint laws was the result of advocacy for the right of children to be protected from a known, significant risk that many adults had previously viewed as acceptable.

Health risks are identified by causes of death, disease, disability, and discomfort. Positive health outcomes are longevity, wellness, activity, comfort, resilience, and achievement. The topics chosen for discussion in this book are those that, statistically, have been found to contribute significantly to positive health outcomes for children.

Health and safety issues in child care are developmentally determined. Newborns are nearly completely dependent on adults. Nourishing physical and emotional development and protecting young infants is quite different from the approaches needed for toddlers. Health risks for toddlers are different from those for preschoolers, which in turn are different from those of school-age children. Adults must function as advocates for children of all ages to guide their interactions with the environment, other children, and adults. Child care professionals must simultaneously function as protectors, role models, and teachers for children, as well as look after their own health and safety as adults.

SETTING PRIORITIES FOR HEALTH AND SAFETY IN CHILD CARE

Many health-related activities deserve the time and attention of child care staff, parents, and children, but no child care program can do everything. What can be done is determined by limitations of funds and personnel as well as by physical and curricular constraints. Integration of health and safety in the child care setting requires making choices. Even if resources were unlimited, a completely risk-free, infection-proof, and injury-proof child care program would not meet children's needs because children's cognitive, social, and emotional growth require some controlled risk taking.

How Should Priorities Be Set?

One approach to setting priorities is to give attention to the topic or issue which circumstances bring to the fore. With this approach, a crisis serves as the stimulus for corrective action. Those who use this approach are doomed to suffer. Planning ahead helps avoid crisis.

Risk Management

Risk management efforts in child care programs are focused on three areas: minimizing injuries, preventing and managing infectious diseases, and modifying features of the environment and program to promote health. In all three areas, some data are available from child care settings to assess the magnitude of risk in the child care setting. Risks can be measured by the frequency and severity of harm associated with a given situation. For example, the risk of injury is measured by data on deaths, disability, and the frequency of visits to medical facilities. Preventive efforts can then be focused on those situations in which the probability of injury is greatest. For illnesses, useful data include the number of episodes of disease, the number of days of illness, the frequency of need for professional medical care, the extent of disability, and the number of deaths from the illness. Such data were used to focus the discussion in this book.

HOW THIS BOOK IS ORGANIZED

Chapters 2 through 4 address health and safety related to health promotion in the child care setting. Issues related to promoting child health are discussed in detail in Chapter 2. The key role of nutrition in child care is covered in Chapter 3. Adult health in early childhood programs is addressed in Chapter 4.

Chapters 5 through 7 are devoted to a detailed discussion of significant health and safety concerns in the building and surrounding areas where child care takes place. Chapter 5 focuses on planning for site location and structural design. Chapter 6 reviews safety outdoors, including on the playground and during transportation, pedestrian safety, and seasonal safety. Indoor facility safety, chemical hazards, emergency preparedness, and first aid are covered in Chapter 7.

Chapters 8 and 9 discuss the problems, prevention, and management of infectious diseases in the child care setting. The care of children and families with special problems is discussed in Chapter 10. Child abuse and neglect are covered in Chapter 11.

Finally, all elements of the health component require mechanisms for implementation. These issues are discussed in detail in Chapter 12.

Special Sections about Infants, Toddlers, Preschoolers, and School-Age Children

This book discusses children in child care in general. Some sections apply only to infants, toddlers, preschoolers, or school-age children. Except for those with disabilities, children are considered infants until they can walk, toddlers from the time they can walk until they are toilet trained, preschool age until they attend kindergarten, and school age thereafter. Throughout this book, special concerns that apply to children at one developmental level but not to all are highlighted.

Special Concerns for Child Care Centers/Nurseries or Preschools, Group Day Care Homes, and Family Day Care Homes

For the most part, health and safety issues are child oriented, not setting based. However, there are some issues that must be addressed differently in different settings. For example, the ability to call for help from other adults in an emergency is limited in a family day care home. In center care, reducing the numbers of caregivers with whom any one child has contact requires planning and compromise. This is generally not an issue in family day care. Setting-specific concerns are highlighted where they apply.

The activities listed at the end of each chapter are intended as a guide for instructors who are teaching the material to groups of early childhood education students. These activities are suggested to help students reinforce their learning, and to apply the information covered in the chapter.

Suggested Activities

Many of the references listed in the section headed "For More Information" at the end of each chapter have sample forms and handout material. These forms and materials are intended as start-up and self-improvement tools and may be modified to meet the specific needs of the settings in which they are used.

For More Information

Some sample forms and letters for parents are provided to help both new early childhood professionals and seasoned directors implement some of the recommendations made in the text. These are referred to in the chapters and found together at the end of the book.

Appendixes

CHAPTER

2

Promoting General Health of Children in Child Care

Child care programs have many significant opportunities and reasons to promote the general health of children. Some children spend only 3–5 hours a day in an early childhood program, but many children spend 8–10 hours a day in some form of child care. Whether a child is in an early childhood program or cared for only at home, poor health interferes with communicative, social, and cognitive development. Investment in prevention of physical and mental health problems in early childhood makes children more productive and socially competent adults. Health professionals have begun to recognize that they can make a greater impact with preventive measures by forming partnerships with early childhood educators and parents.

FACTORS THAT RELATE TO THE HEALTH OF CHILDREN IN CHILD CARE

Personnel

Child care staff create the human environment of the child care programs. Affection, warmth, and a positive personal child rearing experience are essential criteria for selection of caregivers. Adults who were themselves well parented as children find it easier to be good caregivers.

Caregivers must learn through training and experience to recognize and respond appropriately to children from moment to moment and to foster their progress along the continuum of development. In addition to having the knowledge and skills required to provide a safe and healthy environment for children, caregivers must be highly motived to continuously integrate health and safety with other aspects of the curriculum. The caregiver is the final common pathway for merging activities that will meet both the physical and psychological needs of children.

While everyone who works in child care should have responsibility for health and safety issues, someone in the program should be designated as the program's Health Advocate. The Health Advocate can be a caregiver, the director, the educational coordinator, or, in large programs, a health professional such as a nurse who works for the program. The Health Advocate is responsible for ensuring that health issues are considered as a part of general planning and as a part of specific activities organized by the program for whatever reason. Some Health Advocates will not have time to carry out all functions of the health

Caregivers should create an environment that satisfies both the psychological and physical needs of children.

component themselves, but they can still act as the spokespersons for health and safety issues in the program.

Facility Use and Maintenance

Numerous features of the facility are related to general health: space, noise control, humidity, pollution, ventilation, odor control, and cleaning routines.

Space Space is a key factor in the comfort, health, and safety of children and adults. When spaces are crowded by people and things, orderly behavior deteriorates. Activity areas help children associate expected behavior with the space, and they create a comfortable, familiar orientation to the child care setting. Just as adults organize household space by function (e.g., living room, bedroom, kitchen, and bath), children and adults are comforted and organized by dividing their work and play spaces by function.

The importance of orientation to space and function is illustrated by the observation that a new child will generally return to the last place of play when returning to the child care setting, as if to pick up where she left off. In work areas, adults complain when someone straightens up their creative clutter. What appears to be disorganization to someone else is another person's filing system.

By using the placement of furniture, the group can be divided into numbers of children who can safely and meaningfully use each area. Changes in the organization of space must anticipate the effect on the group as a whole as well

An activity center in a child care classroom.

as on the activity to be conducted there. Space to be active, space to be quiet, space to be social, and space to be private are all needed in the child care setting. While the traditional housekeeping corner, block area, reading area, circle, and activity tables may be present, how these areas are designated and how they relate to one another are key elements in planning.

Noise Control Noise pollution is a common problem in child care. The joy of play may drown conversational tones and thus interfere with language development and communication. It is often difficult to hear distinct speech sounds amidst the clamor of children at play. Environmental modifications focus on the use of sound-absorbing materials and installation of barriers to sound transmission wherever possible. For example, carpeting can be used as a wall and floor covering except in areas where sanitation dictates otherwise. Lightweight sound sponges are available that can be installed in blocks on ceilings and walls to capture and deaden the din. Contoured surfaces and partitioned areas also help.

Sound engineers can often suggest creative and inexpensive improvements for the child care setting. Free advice on how to obtain help with acoustical and other safety and health problems is available on request from state offices of the Occupational Safety and Health Administration Consultation Project.

Humidity Excessively dry or excessively humid air challenges body defenses. In the winter, outdoor air is cold and can hold little moisture. When this dry air is heated, it can hold more moisture but has few sources for this water. Living plants and animals need moisture to carry out protective functions, especially those that defend against invasion by unwanted infections. When body surfaces

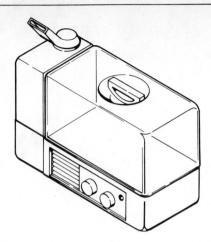

lose moisture into dry air, increased susceptibility to infection may result. On the other hand, with excess humidity, molds and other fungi grow more easily. Sensitive individuals may become infected with mold and fungus infections or become allergic to such substances. Humidity can be controlled by inexpensive equipment that adds or removes water as needed.

Pollution, Ventilation, and Odor Control Many adverse environmental conditions strain body resources. Living where someone smokes or where a kerosene heater or improperly vented wood stove is being used has been found to be associated with increased incidence of respiratory disease. Use of chemical cleaning agents with a residual odor may make those who are sensitive to such agents feel ill. Odor intolerance and allergic diseases affect more than half the population at one time or another.

In the child care setting, every effort should be made to avoid prolonged, repeated, and unnecessary exposure to odorous and noxious substances, including volatile cleaning solutions, pesticides, smoke, and personal perfumes. If odors are offensive, ventilate to remove them; don't spray to cover them up. As a general rule, if something has a strong odor (even a "clean smell"), it probably isn't good to breathe much of it.

Cleaning Routines Cleanliness reduces the opportunities for germs to grow and pests to feed. Aside from the cultural bias toward cleanliness that makes some people more comfortable in an orderly and clean environment, messy, dusty, and dirty settings stress the defense mechanisms of the body and can result in injury and disease. Routine cleaning of all surfaces and sanitization of those that are likely to be contaminated by body fluids requires discipline and a lot of staff time. Separate schedules are required for parts of the facility that need daily, weekly, monthly, and periodic cleaning.

Child care is first and foremost a child development service. A companion and equally important role is to provide support to families so they

Curriculum

can foster healthy psychosocial development of children. Using early intervention, appropriate curriculum, and care, child care can link professional, community, and social supports to benefit families engaged in the critical task of raising the next generation.

The schedule of activities is based on the physical, social, cognitive, and behavioral needs of the children in care. While plans are often made for the group, individualized plans are also needed to reinforce skills and provide new challenges for each child's development. Some children will not be able to do the activities planned for the group; others will need additional, more complicated tasks.

Exercise promotes health in many ways. It builds stamina for stressful situations and, as a lifetime habit, contributes to the prevention of heart dis-

Exercise

ease, high blood pressure, lung disease, and obesity. It also benefits children with chronic illnesses such as asthma, diabetes, and diseases of the nervous system. In addition to its easily measured health benefits, exercise releases tension by providing an outlet for emotional pressure.

The size and development of muscle mass and the amount of body fat are significantly affected by exercise throughout the period of growth. In addition, exercise affects joint mobility and the strength of bones. Children who do not exercise, especially those who watch more than two hours of television per day, are more likely to be overweight than children who exercise regularly and whose television watching is limited.

Fewer than half of the children taking the fitness test of the President's Council on Physical Fitness and Sports pass. The declining levels of fitness among American children is of great concern. Physical inactivity is a risk factor for coronary heart disease and is three to six times more prevalent than any other risk factor. Lifetime habits are set in early childhood.

Infants and Toddlers Infants and toddlers need exercise, but adult manipulation of very young children in structured exercise is not necessary. Infant exercise programs that involve massage techniques, passive exercises, and holding infants in specific positions do not enhance the healthy development of very young children. Infants will naturally exercise in a stimulating environment, and external forces used to coerce activity may result in injury. Infants given opportunities for reaching, touching, and moving without restriction within a safe play area will get the exercise they need. Rolling over, crawling, standing, and walking while holding on to furniture are developmentally appropriate forms of exercise for infants. Step climbing, running, throwing balls, and tumbling are developmentally appropriate forms of exercise for toddlers.

Preschoolers Preschoolers will exercise adequately if given access to gross motor play areas at least twice a day for 30–45 minutes each time. Safe activity that allows freedom of movement without undue waiting time for access to equipment is appropriate. Because preschoolers are poor judges of their motor skills, the gross motor area must be carefully structured and closely supervised to prevent injury. Running, kicking and catching balls, dancing, tricycle riding, hopping, skipping, jumping, and (safe) climbing are developmentally appropriate forms of exercise for preschool-age children.

School-age Children Older children need daily exercise that focuses on aerobic activity to build large-muscle strength and endurance. As muscles become stronger, children can perform more work for longer periods of time and protect their body against injury from sudden movement. Flexibility also helps to prevent injuries and makes children feel more in control of their bodies. The ideal fitness formula involves a warm-up, a stretching period, and vigorous exercise, followed by a cool-down period of stretching to reduce the danger of muscle strains or spasms. Varying the type of exercise makes the program more interesting, helps prevent injury from overuse of specific muscles, and serves as a better motivator to keep children interested. A 30- to 40-minute period of gross motor activity every day is a minimum fitness goal. Numerous fitness programs are available for school-age children; some are listed at the end of this chapter.

Fresh Air

In fresh, outdoor air, children do not have to re-breathe the germs of the group. If the outdoor air is not polluted, time spent outdoors is time away from the minute quantities of toxic substances commonly found in the indoor setting, such as pesticides and volatile cleaning chemicals. Recirculating ventilation systems concentrate indoor pollutants. Improved insulation and sealing of gaps in buildings to prevent heat loss has decreased ventilation. Opening the windows at least once a day (or during the evening for night programs) to air out the child care area helps counter these problems.

Taking children outdoors daily, even in winter, is a healthy part of the schedule. Daily outdoor play gives children an opportunity for a change of scene, for gross motor activity, and for fresh air. Even children who are sick but active should go outside provided the weather is not severe. Temperatures above 40 and below 80 degrees Fahrenheit are generally suitable for routine outdoor activity. At lower temperatures, children may be outdoors for brief periods, but they must be dressed in warm, light, dry clothing that has lots of air pockets to prevent excess loss of heat. Bare skin, fingertips, and toes need special protection to prevent frostbite. In hot weather, children can go out for brief periods if they are dressed in light, loose clothing, they are given plenty of fluids to drink, and their skin is wiped frequently with cool water to prevent overheating. Playing under a sprinkler is a great activity in hot weather.

Stress management is critical to the health of families, staff, and children.

For Families Life can be hectic for families in which parents work, children attend child care, and household chores are done in whatever time is left. Often, little time is available for relaxation. Child care is an environment where family stress can be recognized and reduced by providing advice and support for common problems and by directing parents to sources of help when they seem overwhelmed.

For Staff Child care is interesting work partly because the day is varied and challenging. But variation and challenge produce stress. Excess stress can raise blood pressure and can cause stomach troubles, heart disease, headaches, backaches, sleep problems, and fatigue during the day. Physical activity relieves stress as long as the exercise is not associated with too much competitive pressure. Prolonged stress is most harmful. Wherever possible, breaks should be used to leave the child care facility, even if only to go for a walk around the outside of the building. Special areas of escape need to be provided within the child care building for caregivers to use when going outside is difficult.

For Children Caregivers can help children pace themselves, using easy transitional activities to move from one part of the day to the next. In general, quiet activities should alternate with more active ones, with each child having the opportunity to opt out of the schedule for some private time when needed. Nurturant caregivers provide hugs, space for privacy, and retreat from bedlam. When children have a nap or rest time, both the caregivers and the children can listen to tapes that give soothing sounds and relaxation instructions. Taking a 15-minute break before launching into naptime cleanup and setup chores can make a big difference.

A special area is necessary to provide temporary escape and stress reduction.

Personal Hygiene, Health Habits, and Cultural Issues

Children cannot see, feel, or smell germs, but they can learn to control germs without being frightened or confused. Using a plant sprayer with water in it while children simulate the sounds of a sneeze or a cough helps children understand how a sneeze or cough spreads germs and how covering the nose or mouth will put germs on their hands. Hand washing makes more sense to them when they view it in concrete terms. Practicing positive health behaviors as routines helps children adopt these behaviors as lifetime patterns. Hand washing should be routine after toileting, before meals, and after any contact with body fluids. Keeping nails short makes effective hand washing easier.

Clean hair and skin help to maintain health, but during the winter in cold climates, excessive bathing can lead to dry skin and eczema. In hot weather, inadequate bathing and removal of perspiration and body oil from the skin can block the openings of pores on the surface of the skin, producing a rash called prickly heat. Adjusting bathing routines to climate and individual needs is an important part of personal hygiene.

Children learn to wipe themselves after toileting by doing it. Toilet paper must be kept within easy reach of the child, with enough adult supervision to ensure that the paper is used properly. Girls need to wipe from front to back to avoid pushing germs from the rectal area into the vaginal and urinary openings. Both girls and boys need to take time to wipe carefully after a bowel movement so that the rectal area does not become sore from the irritation of stool left on the skin.

There is no better way for children to learn to brush their teeth after meals than to have them do it in the early childhood program. Music to brush your

Proper hand-washing routines reduce infectious disease.

Tooth brushing in child care teaches children good dental hygiene.

teeth by, "brush-ins," and demonstrations with giant teeth and toothbrushes to show how tooth brushing removes plaque and food particles set the scene. Posters on which children can note that they brushed their teeth at home are also reinforcers.

People learn about health in family and community life. Cultural practices influence the way parents teach healthy habits to their children; some beliefs are false. Puerto Rican culture teaches that cold fruit juices and cool mist are bad for a cold but that home remedies such as teas, herbs, or cathartics may help. Russian culture teaches that cold milk will cause illness, while Middle Eastern cultures favor feeding children sweetened beverages. Melding respect for traditions with current scientific thinking is more likely to be successful than head-on confrontation, even when these beliefs are inconsistent with the recommendations made by health professionals.

Parental and Staff Attitudes About Health

Influencing Parental Health Behaviors Child care programs can model different types of successful child-rearing strategies for parents, some of whom have had little child care training themselves. Because of the trend toward small families, many adults of child-bearing age have not been involved with child care. Many do not know what to expect from children at different ages, how to differentiate minor from more serious illnesses, or how to manage cuts and scrapes to minimize infection. Many adults undervalue outdoor play and fresh air for children; they often worry about exposure to cold or dampness. When parents become more knowledgeable about their child's health and safety, they tend to become more competent and confident.

Parents and staff can exchange views about health and safety during pre-enrollment interviews and orientation sessions. As part of the enrollment of the child, families should be asked to identify the child's sources of health care. Each child should have a "medical home," that is, a single source of health care where all other health services are coordinated. Both continuity and quality of care improve when a child has ongoing access to an understanding physician or group of physicians who review the child's health status on a regular basis and maintain a record of the child's health care. Without a medical home, children receive duplicated and fragmented health care that is both costly and ineffective.

Whenever possible, families should select a pediatrician as the primary provider of health care, but family practice physicians may fill this role when pediatricians are unavailable in the community. The primary physician needs to be kept informed about any health services and concerns that involve the child. These include self-referral to other physicians, emergency rooms, drop-in clinics, or consultations for second opinions. Good physicians welcome second opinions, but parents who persistently shop for confirmation of the advice they receive from the child's primary pediatrician probably need to change to a new medical home.

In selecting a physician for the child, parents should be encouraged to look for a practice that provides 24-hour coverage for telephone advice and office hours that match the parent's availability to bring the child for care. Pediatric care can be provided by nurse practitioners and physician assistants, but non-physician care should be provided under the supervision of a pediatrician who keeps the health care team up-to-date with current recommendations for child

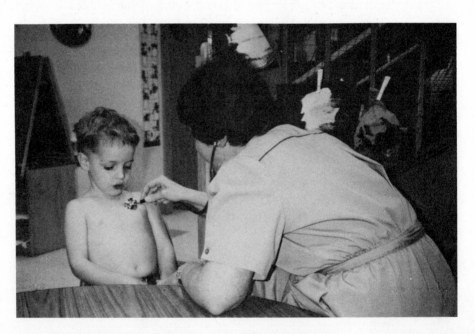

An ongoing relationship with one physician promotes both continuity and quality of care.

health care. Preference should also be given to choosing a pediatrician who will coordinate the child's health care by communicating (with parental consent) with other physicians, agencies, and all those who are involved with providing care for the child.

After the preenrollment and orientation period, parents can be given information about health issues via program newsletters, handbooks and brochures, bulletin boards, and guest speakers at parent meetings. Parents also learn by becoming involved in the development of program policies and by observing how the program operates. Parent education and empowerment promote development of parenting skills and better child care in the family.

Individualized parent education, organized around a child's and family's needs, can be very effective. Hands-on opportunities for parents to work with their own children in the child care setting are most useful. Good early childhood programs support parents and refer them to services needed for their own problems.

Staff Health Behavior The saying "See one, do one, teach one" applies well to caregivers. New caregivers learn about child care from more experienced caregivers and from reading and listening to the advice of experts. After finding the ideas that make sense and work for them in practice, caregivers can share their ideas with parents and other caregivers. In the process of teaching others, the concepts become clarified, streamlined, and reinforced for the caregiver who communicates them. For example, caregivers who teach children and parents about using seat belts are more conscientious about buckling their own belts for every ride. For each aspect of health and safety taught in the curriculum and shared with parents, caregivers are apt to upgrade their own behavior.

Checkup visits provide the opportunity for health professionals to offer advice to parents on how to prevent illness and injury and to identify problems when they are most easily corrected. The minimum schedule recommended by the American Academy of Pediatrics (AAP) for routine health care visits is based on the

ROUTINE HEALTH CARE EVERY CHILD SHOULD RECEIVE

need for specific issues to be discussed at critical points in development and on the likelihood that certain problems will be discoverable at particular ages. Children with special needs need more frequent visits. The schedule, including the recommended content for each of these visits, is documented in manuals available from the AAP and is described briefly in Appendix A.

Routine health supervision should include assessment of the physical and psychological status of the child, the functioning of the family, and the nature of the child's environment. The procedures recommended by the AAP are designed to allow the physician to gather information needed to make this assessment. Parents and caregivers should periodically check that children have received recommended services, since tracking health supervision is usually done only at well child, not sick care, visits to the doctor.

The AAP guidelines for routine health supervision are the current best judgments of pediatric experts. From time to time, these recommendations are reviewed and revised. All child health professionals may not use the guidelines as standards for their own practice behavior. However, the guidelines give parents and child advocates a checklist for seeking quality preventive health care.

DENTAL HEALTH

Good dental health is required for good nutrition, speech, and self-image. Thus, dental health is an intrinsic part of overall health. Fostering good dental habits in child care includes recognizing dental problems and promoting good dental hygiene, dentally sound nutrition, protection against tooth injury, and appropriate dental care.

Tooth Development

The first teeth form during fetal life, with about 20 "baby" or primary teeth and four permanent molars already growing at birth. All 32 permanent teeth have formed by about 14 years of age. During childhood, the health of the teeth is affected for life by the minerals and other nutrients the child eats, the exposure of the teeth to decay-causing foods, and dental hygiene.

Fluoride

If children receive appropriate amounts of fluoride from infancy through puberty, they incorporate fluoride into the tooth structure, permanently hardening the tooth against decay. Children who receive appropriate amounts of

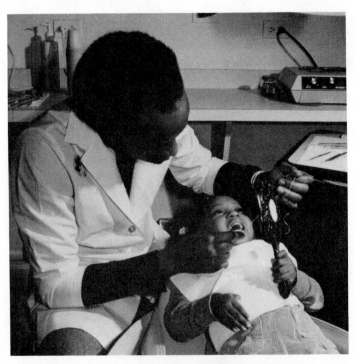

Appropriate dental care is part of overall health care for children.

fluoride throughout childhood will have at least 65 percent fewer cavities for the rest of their lives and save $50 in unused dental care for every $1 of fluoride they take.

Some communities have fluoride in their drinking water, but many do not. Outer surfaces of teeth can acquire fluoride from watery fluoride gels, toothpaste, and fluoride rinses. But only the daily swallowing of proper amounts of fluoride gives optimum protection to the teeth forming inside the jaw during childhood. For infants who do not receive fluoridated water, daily fluoride supplements should be prescribed by a doctor or dentist. Although the use of fluoride toothpaste helps reduce tooth decay, children should not use toothpastes containing fluoride until they are old enough to avoid swallowing it, usually about 3 years of age.

Irregular and excessive doses of fluoride can result from swallowing toothpaste or taking fluoride supplements when fluoride is already in the drinking water. Spots and uneven coloration of children's teeth can result. Regular, controlled amounts of fluoride should be given to children daily for protection and good appearance of their teeth. The additional fluoride applied by the dentist to teeth that have already erupted will harden the tooth surface but will not put the fluoride throughout the structure of the tooth. However, taking daily fluoride in drinking water or as a supplement during the period of tooth development (usually birth to 14 years of age) will incorporate the fluoride within the whole tooth.

Nutrition and Dental Health

Young children learn about the taste of different foods they are fed as new experiences. If they are fed sweetened foods and drinks, they will come to expect and seek sweet-tasting foods. Sugars promote acid production by the bacteria commonly found on the teeth. The acid dissolves the surface enamel of the teeth, making pits (cavities) called caries. Holes in the enamel may extend into the pulp of the tooth, causing pain, infection, and ultimately tooth loss.

By routinely giving children unsweetened food and avoiding giving sugared foods as special treats, adults can help prevent children from developing the craving for sweets known as a sweet tooth. Raw fruit and vegetables provide good nutrients with more than ample sweetness. Sweet, undiluted natural fruit juices are loaded with sugar and should be limited to mealtime feedings. Fruit juices fed to infants should be routinely diluted with water. Prolonged drinking of fluids such as fruit juice, milk, or other sugar-containing beverages should be avoided. Water is a great thirst quencher!

Dental Hygiene

With so many meals and snacks being served daily, dental hygiene is a natural component of health promotion activities in child care. By age 2, children should be having their teeth cleaned by daily brushing. Swishing and rinsing with water after a snack should start as soon as a child can learn the technique. Brushing must be done well enough to remove the spongy, sticky, colorless buildup called plaque. Plaque is secreted by the bacteria that live on the

teeth. Plaque accumulates near the gum line around and between the teeth and in the pits and grooves of the chewing surfaces of the back teeth. Dentists sometimes apply sealants to the hard-to-brush chewing surfaces to help prevent the buildup of plaque in these areas.

Adult supervision and assistance with tooth brushing are required until 5 years of age, when most children have developed enough dexterity to do the job themselves. To remove plaque from tooth surfaces, brush each tooth with a rotary or short back-and-forth motion. Hard scrubbing may injure the gums and allow bacteria to enter the bloodstream. After the teeth are clean, the tongue should be gently brushed also. Then the whole mouth should be rinsed with water.

In addition to practicing daily dental hygiene, children between 2 and 3 years of age should begin to see a dentist regularly, every 6 months. At these visits, the teeth should be cleaned and checked for decay and growth problems, and fluoride should be applied to all erupted tooth surfaces.

Some dental hygiene benefits can result from eating crunchy, low-sugar foods like fresh vegetables and raw fruits. These foods help to remove other, more sugary foods and plaque from the teeth. Since harmful bacteria produce decay-causing acid in the mouth for at least 20 minutes after sweet foods are eaten, following rather than accompanying sugary foods with crunchies is a good idea.

NUTRITION

Nutrition is an integral part of many aspects of health promotion. Nutrition is related to growth, socioemotional development, and the healthy functioning of every system of the body. Because of the central role played by nutrition in health, this topic is addressed separately in Chapter 3.

MENTAL HEALTH

Mental health is the cornerstone of child development services. For children to thrive, their emotional, cognitive, and social development must be nurtured. Unlike physical needs, mental health needs cannot be met by focusing on the child alone. The child is a part of a family and a social structure of which the early childhood program is an integral part.

To assess the child's mental health and need for special care, child care providers must learn about the normal stages of gross motor, fine motor, language, and personal/social behavior development for children. Once mastered, the expected patterns of development can be used to assess a child's progress and define a child's strengths and weaknesses. By using a child's areas of strength to work on improving the areas of weakness, the child's overall development can be encouraged. Thus, a child who is advanced in language development but slow in gross motor development can be encouraged through verbal instruction to practice and attain gross motor skills.

When children are under stress from family dysfunction, life events, or other disruptive forces, they may regress, or at least stop progressing normally. When abnormal developmental patterns or unusual behaviors are noted, closer scrutiny is warranted. With young children, behavioral disturbances are sometimes reflected in sleep problems, difficult-to-control behavior, or regression to a level of function of a younger child. Serious disturbances in mental health can also be manifest by a child's becoming withdrawn, failing to interact with peers and adults in an age-appropriate way. These are signs of depression in a young child. Other symptoms of depression are similar to signs of physical illness: loss of interest in eating, irritability, and failure to progress developmentally.

Some children are more vulnerable than others to stress. For a very vulnerable child, the stress of crossing boundries between home and child care may exceed the child's ability to cope. When a child is showing signs of mental health problems, the child's source of routine health care should be consulted.

Early childhood programs can contribute significantly to mental health for both the child and the family. By providing appropriate expectations for parents to use with their children, a positive parenting relationship can be fostered. Parents can become involved in assessing their child's progress and in planning how the curriculum of the early childhood setting can mesh with experiences at home. When families are not coping well, the child care program can help by identifying the need for outside intervention and suggesting community resources that can be used.

Preventive mental health can be practiced when the curriculum is planned. The essence of planning a curriculum for young children is identification of the skills of the child so that activities can be organized that reinforce recently mastered skills and offer small incremental challenges to reach for the next level of skill in the continuum of development. Many assessment tools have been developed to help caregivers define children's skills and behavioral characteristics. A mental health professional can work with the staff of an early childhood program to select one or more such tools for use.

Mental health professionals include social workers, psychiatrists (physicians), pediatricians who specialize in management of developmental problems, psychologists, and early childhood education consultants. Mental health professionals are often affiliated with hospitals, clinics, and mental health agencies. Some mental health professionals work with adults, some with children. Some can provide training for teachers, work with parents, do assessments of children suspected of having problems, and provide treatment. Not all mental health professionals provide the full range of mental health services, however.

The entire United States has been organized into geographic catchment areas called base service units. If a mental health professional is not already a part of the program's team, a base service unit can identify community resources where help for a child, family, or troubled staff member or general consultation can be obtained. Base service units are generally listed in the phone directory under the special page listings for human services.

TEACHING HEALTHY HABITS TO CHILDREN

From late infancy onward, children learn to avoid injury and prevent disease one day at a time. A skillful caregiver will use "teachable moments"—times when the situation provides an enhanced opportunity for children to learn. Handwashing becomes an expected routine when it is routinely practiced; safe play behaviors are learned by consistently structuring the play environment and positively stating safety rules during play. Children learn best about prevention from caregivers who both model and counsel good hygiene, safety, appropriate nutrition, rest, and exercise.

Prevention of injury and disease can be taught most effectively by integrating the necessary skills and information with other curricular activities. Many classroom routines can be taught with health and safety messages. The number of strokes with a toothbrush can be counted; a trip to the dentist is a way to learn about community helpers. Songs like "Wash, Wash, Wash Your Hands"[1] can accompany hand-washing activities and also can be used during circle time as a song that is fun to sing.

Many other songs can be invented or modified to carry health messages. A verse of "Wheels on the Bus" emphasizes the use of seat restraints: "Buckled in my seat belt makes me safe, makes me safe, makes me safe. . . ."

Circle-time activities provide many opportunities to teach about prevention of disease. Caregivers can ask the children how they feel when they are healthy to help them understand the value of working to stay healthy. Each child can show with facial expressions or body movement how wellness feels. Caregivers can help children learn words to describe wellness, such as "happy, strong, hungry, ready to play, ready to sing, ready to sleep all night long." Conversely, children can talk about and show how they feel when they are sick.

Germ theory is a tough concept for young children (and some adults) to grasp. It's hard to understand that some things are so small we can't see them without looking through a special type of glass. Playing with a magnifying lens helps teach this concept and is also a great science activity.

Once children have learned that some things are too small to be seen easily, they need to know that germs are everywhere. Some help digest food inside our

---

[1] Sung to the tune of "Row, Row, Row Your Boat" (from "Healthy Child Care, Is It Really Magic?" a video by Health Professionals in Child Care):
Wash, wash, wash your hands. (Motion = rub hands together)
Play your handy game. (Motion = show hands)
Rub and scrub and scrub and rub. (Motion = rub hands together)
Germs go down the drain. (Motion = wiggle fingers, lowering arms)

bodies and are good germs; some can make us sick when they get into places in our bodies where they don't belong. When children understand that germs live on the skin, in the nose, in the mouth, and in bowel movements, they can also understand why they should wash their hands after nose blowing, before eating, and after toileting. Washing off cuts and scrapes where dirt has been given an open door into the body makes sense in these terms. Germs aren't all bad, but we don't want too many of the wrong kind to get inside.

Learning Healthy Routines

Sleep, exercise, hygiene, and good nutrition are essential to good health. Teaching children how to avoid and handle sleep problems and how to seek exercise and good nutrition gives them lifetime tools to be healthy. Caregivers can help children understand a variety of ways people keep themselves healthy by discussing different cultural and ethnic customs used to ensure healthy sleep, exercise, hygiene, and nutrition.

Sleep Sleep problems are very common in childhood. Normally, sleep consists of cycling between two different states. One, called rapid eye movement (REM) sleep, is a light level of sleep when children wake easily, may vocalize, and may move around. The other, called non-REM sleep, is a deeper level of sleep when waking occurs with more difficulty. The length and pattern of cycling between these two different kinds of sleep develops from fetal life to adulthood. REM sleep appears around the sixth to eight month of gestation and accounts for about half of the time that a term infant sleeps. Non-REM sleep develops at around the time of birth and gradually occupies 75–80 percent of the total period sleep by adulthood. Infants start sleep with a REM cycle, whereas adults do not usually have REM sleep until one and a half hours after going to sleep. The total amounts of sleep required varies greatly from individual to individual. Adequate amounts of sleep are those that provide for spontaneous waking without fatigue or irritability.

Some parents prefer to have children sleep close to them or to other children. Infants and toddlers who go to sleep while being fed or held tend to need the same routine repeated if they awaken during one of their REM cycles in the night. Parents who put children into bed after they are asleep are more likely to sleep with their children to avoid having to get up to comfort them back to sleep when they wake. Children who are put into bed awake will be more likely to be able to put themselves back to sleep when they wake during the night. In either case, solid periods of sleeping are less important than the accumulation of needed amounts of sleep. By practicing relaxation with music or a soothing story, children can learn how to prepare for sleep and how to return to sleep once awakened.

Curricular activities related to sleep include adequate physical activity earlier in the day, naptime routines, role play, and reading. Naptime sleep routines can reinforce the importance of wind-down time, when activities are slowed by talking about the events of the day. A quiet, soothing story or song helps relax everyone. Sleep-related fears can be played out during role play to diffuse their power.

Night terrors, sleepwalking, and sleep talking are some common sleep disturbances that young children experience. They occur during the transition from non-REM to REM sleep. Night terrors are different from nightmares in that children usually cannot be awakened or comforted during the episode. Children are rarely disturbed about these problems, but working parents find frequent interruption of sleep intolerable. Difficulty falling asleep and night waking occur in 20–30 percent of children age 1 to 3. These problems are often related to separation concerns or a need for a transitional object to cope with the stress of separation. Child care program staff can help parents understand that sleep problems are not deliberate misbehavior and can offer suggestions on how to cope with these problems in the child care program and at home.

Many children need help to be comfortable about falling asleep—leaving the security of loving adults and the excitement of events in the conscious world. Caregivers can help by talking about the sounds that children might hear while falling asleep—outdoor sounds, such as cars, trains, trucks, birds, and sirens, and indoor sounds, such as television, adults talking, blowing shades or blinds, and toilets flushing. Children can be encouraged to identify a toy, blanket, pillow, or other special object that they would like to take to sleep with them. Needing a special object does not mean the child is a baby; it means the child has found a way to help make the bridge between needing adult comfort and being able to sleep alone.

Many good children's books about sleeping are available. Reading these stories to children is a natural way to relax or trigger talk about sleep. Some examples are listed in Appendix B.

Teaching the Value of Exercise Even toddlers can be taught to recognize that their restlessness means they need increased activity. Instead of an admonition to "sit still," children can be given motor activity suitable to the situation to use the restlessness constructively. Jumping jacks can usually be done in place; bending front to back and side to side stretches and exercises muscles without requiring special equipment or a lot of room. Children can learn an exercise vocabulary to express their desire for movement—to stretch, to bend, to jump, to run, to climb, and so forth. Moving with music builds listening and movement skills. March music, dance music, and hopping music—each sounds different and can be represented by different motions. At circle time, children can talk about how they feel when they exercise and play hard. With a little adult guidance, they will agree that they feel stronger, hungrier, and more tired when they exercise.

Staff can highlight each child's progress toward acquisition of motor skills for parents by placing a star under the child's name on a posted chart of developmentally appropriate activities. For example, the chart for infants can list "lifts stomach, head and chest; rolls over; sits, stands, crawls, walks." The chart for toddlers and preschoolers can list "climbs steps, kicks a ball, jumps, hops, skips, runs, climbs, stretches, rolls, dances, pedals a tricycle, throws a ball, catches a ball, walks a line." Enthusiasm for retention and acquisition of new motor skills is a healthy lifetime value.

Teaching about Hygiene Hand washing is critical to prevention of the transmission of infectious diseases. Ideally, the child care facility should be designed so children can easily wash their hands under running water, by themselves, at as early an age as possible. Children should wash their hands when they come to child care (before handling toys and objects that others will handle), after toileting or diaper changes, after contact with nasal or oral body secretions, and before eating or handling food.

Dental hygiene instruction begins with children learning about the importance of their mouths to help them eat, speak, and look attractive. They can then understand why keeping the mouth and teeth healthy is so important to them. Toothbrushing as a part of the child care curriculum follows as naturally as serving food. After eating, removing food and plaque from the teeth keeps them healthy. When sinks are not available, children can brush with a dry toothbrush, followed by a swish and swallow of water from a cup. Toothbrushes should be individually labeled, rinsed, and stored upright (a washed, styrofoam egg carton makes an inexpensive, disposable holder).

Teaching about Nutrition Use a snack game to reinforce healthy food choices. Have the children sort food into healthy and unhealthy choices, using pictures of snack foods cut from magazines. Healthy food choices can be reinforced by applause and cheers; unhealthy foods can be discouraged by facial expressions learned at circle time when the children discuss how they feel when they are sick.

Child care programs have a special opportunity to teach children how to stay healthy at a time when they are most impressionable and when healthy habits can have the maximum benefit. Health can be approached as a fun, interesting, and creative learning experience. If caregivers and parents work together to plan and conduct health education in the child care setting and in the home, the messages are more likely to have lasting impact. Caregivers and parents may also adopt healthier behaviors for themselves.

SUGGESTED ACTIVITIES

1. Have participants do a self-assessment of the status of their own health behaviors, using each of the headings in Chapter 2 as a guide. Rate exposures, activities, and other items on a scale of 1–10 for each, 10 = best. How do they score? What can be changed?

2. Have participants prepare and lead a classroom activity to teach a healthy habit to their peer group.

FOR MORE INFORMATION

Aronson, Susan. The Health Needs of Infants and Children Under 12. In *Better Health for Our Children: A National Strategy. The Report of the Select Panel for the Promotion of Child Health to the U.S. Congress and the Secretary of Health and Human Services*, vol. IV. Washington, DC: U.S. Superintendent of Documents, 1981, pp. 243–283.

Galinsky, Ellen, and Hooks, William H. *The New Extended Family*. Boston: Houghton Mifflin, 1977.

"Healthy Child Care, Is It Really Magic?" a videotape from InSight Productions, 745 Page St., Berkeley, CA 94710.

Recommendations for Preventive Pediatric Health Care. Elk Grove Village, IL: American Academy of Pediatrics, 1988.

Richmond, Julius B., and Janis, Juel. Health Care Services for Children in Day Care Programs. In *Day Care: Scientific and Social Policy Issues.* Ed. Zigler, Edward, and Gordon, Edmund. Boston: Auburn House, 1982.

Fitness Programs for School-Aged Children: "Feeling Good" for children from kindergarten emphasizes noncompetitive games. Family involvement is encouraged. Charles Kuntzleman, Ph.D., Fitness Finders, 133 Teft Rd., Spring Arbor, MI 49283-0507.

The Governor's Golden Sneaker Awards Program is a basic aerobic exercise program with points earned toward awards for units of time spent in exercise. The Utah Governor's Council on Health and Physical Fitness, c/o Primary Children's Medical Center, 320 12th Ave., Salt Lake City, UT 84103.

Nutrition in Child Care

IN THIS CHAPTER:

PLANNING THE NUTRITION COMPONENT
ESTABLISHING A HEALTHY FEEDING RELATIONSHIP
ADULT MODELING OF HEALTHY EATING
FEEDING CHILDREN OF DIFFERENT DEVELOPMENTAL LEVELS
FOOD SERVICE OPERATION AND FEEDING EQUIPMENT
MENU PLANNING FOR MEALS AND SNACKS
INTEGRATING EATING WITH SOCIAL DEVELOPMENT AND WITH
CULTURAL AND ETHNIC PREFERENCES
FOODS PREPARED AT HOME
SPECIAL EVENTS
OVERWEIGHT AND UNDERWEIGHT CHILDREN
VITAMINS AND OTHER SUPPLEMENTS
NUTRITIONAL ASPECTS OF PREVENTING HEART DISEASE
ACCOMMODATING FOOD INTOLERANCES AND SPECIAL DIETS
NUTRITION AS A PART OF THE CURRICULUM
SPECIAL FOOD PROGRAMS
SUGGESTED ACTIVITIES
FOR MORE INFORMATION

Nutrition is a major component of all early childhood programs. Children need to eat good food frequently to stay healthy, grow, and learn. For children from low-income families, food served in an early childhood program may provide the major part of children's nutritional needs. For children from affluent families, the early childhood program can play a significant role in children's health and development of good lifelong eating practices.

Many excellent books have been written about nutrition in early childhood that provide much more detail than space allows in this book. In addition, helpful films, classroom curricula, and guidance materials on nutrition for young children and their families are available from the Head Start program and from the community food programs described at the end of this chapter.

PLANNING THE NUTRITION COMPONENT

The complex and varied role that nutrition plays in early childhood programs requires that every program for young children have input from a qualified nutritionist. If a registered dietician with experience in early childhood programs is unavailable, look for a consultant who has a bachelor's degree in foods, nutrition, or dietetics and two years of nutritional experience in community programs that serve young children. To make best use of a nutrition consultant, a nutrition policy should be drafted. This will help identify gaps and misperceptions in basic nutrition information needed by the staff to effectively implement the program's nutrition policies.

Many aspects of nutrition should be included in the nutrition policies of an early childhood program, as well as in preservice and inservice training for staff:

- establishing a healthy feeding relationship with children
- adult modeling of healthy eating
- developmentally appropriate feeding, meal service practices, and equipment
- menu planning for meals and snacks
- integrating eating with social development with attention to cultural and ethnic preferences
- preparing foods at home and for special events
- assessing the adequacy of nutrition for individual children

- □ sanitation and managing food resources
- □ managing overweight and underweight children
- □ providing vitamins and other supplements
- □ preventing heart and other diseases through nutrition
- □ accommodating food intolerance and special diets
- □ including nutrition in the curriculum
- □ operating community food programs
- □ other topics suggested by the nutrition consultant.

The feeding relationship consists of the way caregivers and parents interact with a child about selecting and eating food. From birth, children indicate their interest in being fed by body movements and sounds. Parents and caregivers must

ESTABLISHING A HEALTHY FEEDING RELATIONSHIP

learn to recognize the child's signals about feeding and respond appropriately. Some children perceive and respond more clearly to hunger than others. The job of the adult is to accept and support the child's internal rhythm and signals of hunger and satiety, helping the child to acquire developmentally appropriate feeding skills.

Many adults have been taught rigid rules and rituals of eating that make them insensitive to the child's feeding cues. As a result, the child does not get enough to eat, eats too much, or eats an unhealthy mix of foods.

Much of our cultural practice is related to food and eating. Think about the role food plays in the celebration of happy events and in comforting during times of sadness or disappointment. Because the association between food and events

Healthy eating habits are fostered when adults enjoy a relaxed meal with children.

is so strong, adults must strive to overcome the negative implications of these ingrained behaviors. Food should not be used for punishment or reward, because such reinforcement of behavioral cues for eating disturbs the healthy use of food as nourishment. Abnormal eating patterns are related to strong associations between food and behavioral cues. For children, healthy eating habits are fostered when the roles of adults and children are clearly defined and separate. The adult is responsible for offering the child nutritious food in a nurturant physical and emotional setting. The child should be responsible for what and how much is eaten of the food offered by the adult.

ADULT MODELING OF HEALTHY EATING

Children study adult behavior. If an adult does not eat with the children and does not seem to think that the food being offered is desirable, the child is unlikely to adopt a positive attitude about the food. Feeding skills and table manners are learned by observation more than by verbal instruction. After infancy, adults should try to eat meals with children, engaging them in pleasant discussions about colors, tastes, textures, and shapes of food as well as other topics. From the newborn period on, mealtime is a social occasion, a time for relaxation and nurturance of mind and body. Rushed, pressured, or isolated eating is inherently nonnutritious. Adults should refrain from bringing or eating food in the child care setting that they would not want children to eat. Some staff may have special reasons for eating different foods at different times from the children. These needs should be respected, but generally even these special needs can be satisfied by eating some of the same food the children eat at the times when the children eat.

FEEDING CHILDREN OF DIFFERENT DEVELOPMENTAL LEVELS

The approach to feeding of children must be adapted from infancy to adulthood based on the oral, neurological, gastrointestinal, and personal/social capabilities of the child.

Infant Feeding

More child care services for infants are being developed because the majority of parents of infants are working. Early childhood educators who want to provide infant care need to become familiar with the close association between an infant's development of physical competence, personal/social, fine motor, gross motor, and language skills and nutrition. Infants begin life with the ability to use only one type of food and a total dependency on adults to put food directly into their mouths. By the end of the first year of life, most children have developed the ability to feed themselves and to eat a diet very like that of adults. This remarkable transition follows the steady development of physiological changes in the functioning of the digestive system and the remarkable acquisition of motor and socioemotional skills during this same short period of time.

Feeding an infant child in child care.

The mechanisms required for intake, absorption, and utilization of nutrients are complex, but their development follows a predictable and observable pattern. These patterns vary from one individual to another. To accommodate individual variations, general recommendations for infant feeding need to be adjusted based on observations of each infant's development.

General Principles of Infant Feeding   Newborns and very young infants should be fed using the infant's rooting, sucking, swallowing, and extrusion reflexes. At this age, an infant will push out food placed in the front of the mouth. By 6 months of age, most children can get food and feeding utensils (spoons, cups, and bottles) more or less accurately to their own mouths and are able to move food put in the front of the mouth to the back to be swallowed.

In infancy, when the primary developmental task is the establishment of trust based on adult response to the infant's needs, children should be fed on demand, whenever they are hungry. Schedules for infant feeding are adult contrivances for making the adult's life more predictable, at the infant's expense. Infants should be fed the amounts they want and can hold without discomfort or large amounts of regurgitation.

Healthy babies are those who grow as expected for their age. Growth patterns are observed by plotting measurements of the infant's height, weight, and head circumference on a graph against growth curves established for large populations of healthy children. The standard growth curves currently in use are those developed by the National Center for Health Statistics. Sample growth charts for length, weight, and head circumference for children under 3 and

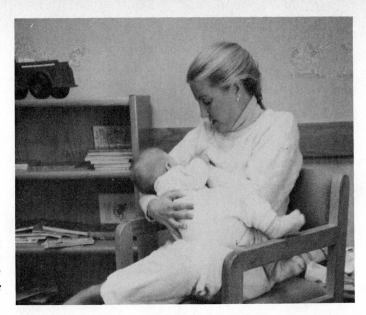

Breast-feeding areas should be available in child care programs for a mother to nurse her baby.

height and weight for children 2–18 years of age are provided in Appendix D. These graphs are readily available from most pediatricians, health departments, and some formula manufacturers.

A fat baby is not a healthy baby; overfeeding in infancy is associated with obesity in childhood and adult life, and weight gain may not be accompanied by the balanced nutrient intake required to maintain health. Many children have strong oral needs for stimulation and attention that caregivers and parents understandably attempt to satisfy by feeding even when other solutions to these demands are more appropriate.

Breast Feeding The best food for infants is breast milk. No equivalent substitute has yet been found for mother's milk. Formula cannot provide the protection from infection and disease without risk of an allergic reaction as effectively. Early childhood programs should be as supportive of breast feeding as possible, even if breast feeding is carried out only on a token basis for one or two feedings a day. A quiet, comfortable, and private place for a breast-feeding mother to nurse her baby before she leaves should be provided. These areas should be available at lunchtime, during breaks, and after work. Frequent nursing maintains the mother's milk supply and a high quality of interaction during the mother-infant reunions. Many breast-feeding mothers think that they have to keep the workday schedule even when they are at home with their babies. In fact, full-time nursing whenever mother and baby are together is the best stimulus for the breast to keep up with the infant's needs. Women who cannot come to the child care setting to nurse during the workday can use a hand or electric pump to express their milk at work and bring the milk to be fed to the infant the next day. Alternatively, a woman may discard her expressed breast milk and have the baby fed formula for bottle feedings. Many patterns work. The important thing is to encourage women to breast feed as much as possible, preferably until the time when weaning to a cup and regular milk can occur.

The alternative to breast feeding is the use of iron-fortified infant formula. Whole milk is not a good substitute for iron-fortified formula for infants because intake of whole milk has been associated with microscopic blood losses from the intestinal tract that can lead to the development of anemia in the first year of life. Furthermore, whole milk contains little iron. When more than three cups of whole milk are consumed per day, children may become iron deficient because they do not eat enough of iron-containing foods. Infants may begin whole milk as early as 6 months of age if they are also eating iron-rich cereal to make up for any microscopic blood loss. The safest approach is to use breast milk or iron-fortified formula throughout the first year of life.

Water Except on very hot days, infants from birth to 4–6 months of age need no food other than breast milk or iron-fortified formula. Water can be offered to formula-fed infants under 6 months of age during warm weather and to all babies by cup as soon as a cup is introduced (around 6 months of age). Plain, unflavored water is an important part of a healthy diet.

Starting Solids Many parents start solids too early, in part because of advice from older relatives or friends who recall that early solid feeding was the standard practice 15 or 20 years ago. Many parents mistakenly believe that early solid feeding helps infants sleep through the night. Research has shown that night sleeping patterns are not related to feeding at all but are developmentally determined by brain maturity. Most infants are able to sleep through the night by 4–5 months of age regardless of how they are fed. Some have trouble sleeping through the night even at 8 months. Understandably, parents will seek any method to achieve uninterrupted sleep as early as possible. However, the introduction of foods other than breast milk or iron-fortified formula should be delayed until the baby can sit relatively well and can push away and reach for food.

The first solid food to be offered (at around 4–6 months for normally developing infants) is iron-fortified infant cereal. This food is followed by the addition of soft-cooked, salt- and sugar-free vegetables and then fresh and soft-cooked fruits. Half-strength vitamin C-rich fruit juices are usually added when fruits are being tried. Juices are diluted because full-strength juice has as many calories per ounce as milk and may displace milk and other foods from the infant's diet if fed in quantity. Furthermore, infants fed more than a few ounces of undiluted fruit juices may develop loose stools.

Introducing New Foods Generally, new foods are not offered more often than every three days so that reactions to the new food can be readily identified. Meats and eggs may be added at around 9 months. Bland foods should be introduced before sweet foods so that children do not learn to expect sweetness in food. Infant cereals mixed with formula may be anywhere from a runny to a thick consistency and should be fed by spoon. Solid foods should not be fed by bottle or by force-feeding devices; readiness for spoon feeding is linked with the development of the ability to swallow solid foods. Many infants can begin solid feedings of vegetables with small helpings of diced soft-cooked table foods which they can eat with their fingers. Bread, dry cereal pieces, and fruits of types that do not pose a choking hazard can be fed this way as well. Although young children require close supervision during feeding, self-feeding should be encouraged, with suitable foods cut into swallowable-size pieces. When older infants pick up food pieces and put them in their mouths, they develop hand-eye coordination and learn to self-regulate their intake. Cup feedings of milk and juice can be offered when solids are begun, but the age when children show interest and skill in drinking from a cup varies over a wide range, from 5–18 months.

Vitamin Supplementation for Infants Supplements are recommended for breast-fed infants because of the variability of the vitamin D content of breast milk from one woman to another, in part related to the amount of sunshine the mother receives on her skin. Numerous cases of rickets have been reported in exclusively breast-fed infants who have not received Vitamin D supplements. Commercially prepared vitamin preparations also contain vitamin A and vitamin C, even though these are less likely to be deficient in breast milk. Commercially prepared infant formulas have vitamins added in the proportions generally found in breast milk of well-fed infants.

When a fully diversified diet has been established (usually by 15–18 months of age), vitamin supplementation can be discontinued because there is an abundant supply of vitamins in a usual mixed diet. Rare exceptions occur when the child has some special problem for which a physician will prescribe vitamin supplementation. After 1 year of age, a varied diet from each of the four major food groups (fruit and vegetable, bread and cereal, meat and other animal proteins, and dairy) is the best way to ensure nutritional adequacy.

Iron Supplements The reason for iron fortification of formula, vitamins, and cereal is to provide the iron needed to help infants meet the demand for production of new blood cells associated with rapid growth in infancy. Infants usually exhaust their maternally supplied iron stores by around 3 months of age, but they are still growing very fast. The little iron that is in breast milk is maximally absorbed, but introduction of formula or other foods interferes with efficient iron absorption from breast milk. Because infants vary in growth rate, initial storage pool, and time of introduction of mixed feeding, iron is included in formula from the beginning and added to the supplements given to breast-fed infants by 4 months of age.

Fluoride Supplements Fluoride supplements that are started early in infancy help to ensure the long-term benefits of intake of the mineral during the entire period of growth of the permanent teeth. Growing teeth incorporate fluoride into the tooth structure, markedly increasing the lifetime resistance of the tooth to decay. Later applications of fluoride to the surface of the tooth can harden the surface, but the only opportunity to incorporate fluoride into the entire tooth structure is when the tooth is still growing inside the gum. Permanent teeth are beginning to form at birth and continue to form until puberty.

Children who receive fluoride in their formulas via fluoridated water mixed with formula concentrate or powder or who receive it by drops or pills have up to 65 percent reduction in lifetime dental decay. All studies of children receiving appropriate doses of fluoride have failed to identify any adverse effects. Fluoride supplementation via drinking water or at a daily dose of 0.25 milligrams per day for children up to age 2 immunizes children against tooth decay. The dose is increased to 0.5 milligrams per day for 2- to 3-year-olds and 1 milligram per day for older children.

Milk Preparation, Storage, and Feeding in the Early Childhood Program

When infant formulas or breast milk are fed in child care, policies must be established and followed for the safe transport and storage of these highly perishable foods. Mothers who bring expressed breast milk must ensure that the milk is collected under sanitary conditions and stored at temperatures below 45 degrees Fahrenheit to prevent bacterial growth until the milk is fed. Breast milk that has been refrigerated (not frozen) for more than 48 hours must be discarded. Frozen breast milk will keep for several months.

Formula should be prepared in the child care setting from factory-sealed containers of ready-to-feed concentrate or powdered formula, following the instructions on the container. Accepting formula mixed at home and transported to the program by the parent is inherently risky. Bacteria introduced during preparation at home may grow to harmful levels during transport and handling until the formula is actually fed. Unlike breast milk, which has its own antibacterial properties, formula and regular milk products are excellent breeding grounds for bacteria.

Once a bottle of breast milk or formula has been warmed and fed, any remaining contents must be discarded. Refeeding a bottle that was only partly consumed even an hour later is not safe because the infant's saliva will have inoculated the milk with bacteria which can grow to hazardous numbers in a short time. If formula is mixed at the child care program by using an approved (e.g., treated municipal) water source, no sterilization is necessary. Some programs will find that bulk purchase of ready-to-feed, room-temperature-stored formula in feeding bottles is worth the extra cost. This practice avoids the problems of formula transport from home and the work of bottle cleaning and formula fixing. If this form of formula is too expensive for the program or the parents to provide, powdered formula is the next best choice. It is the least expensive and easiest to store and prepare, and it leaves less waste than other forms. Water can be heated to feeding temperature at the beginning of the day and stored in a thermos container until a bottle is needed. By mixing the warm water with powdered formula at the time of feeding, the extra step of bottle warming is eliminated.

Room temperature formula is acceptable to most infants. Because liquids heated by microwave may continue to heat for a period after the food is irradiated and may become scalding hot while the container remains cool, microwave heating of infant food should not be permitted. Conventional bottle and food warmers are safer.

Bottles filled with sweet liquids or milk should not be given to infants to carry around or take to bed with them. Prolonged bottle feeding and drinking while lying down are associated with tooth decay, ear infections, and choking.

Many a toddler has suffered tooth injury from falling while wandering around with a bottle. Feeding is a social as well as nutritional activity. Infants need to be attended by an adult during feeding to provide interaction and readiness to respond to choking.

Coordination of feedings between home and the child care setting requires special attention for infants. Patterns of formula and food intake are important indicators of infant health and development. Daily recording of intake by time and amount by parents and caregivers facilitates communication and analysis when problems occur.

Some very young infants may need feedings as often as every hour and a half, while others are content with feedings every four hours. Many infants vary the intervals between feedings. The infant's self-determined feeding pattern is a clue to the child's temperament.

Feeding Solid Foods to Infants in the Early Childhood Program When solid feedings are being introduced, the plan should be consistent for child care program and home trials. Usually, the child's physician will suggest an approach to solid feeding that is based on the child's developmental progress, growth, and need for special supplements. Many parents will benefit from informal discussions with caregivers about the rationale behind recommendations made for salt and sugar restriction and for bottle and solid feedings. Explanations provided at the physician's office may need to be reviewed, since they are necessarily brief and often provided while the parent juggles listening with supervision of the child.

Written records of foods accepted, rejected, and reintroduced help to ensure variety in the child's diet. In addition, logs of improved feeding skills, mealtime interactions, and difficulties related to feeding are helpful in gaining a view of the child's progress in feeding. This information can be recorded on a daily log that includes information about feeding, bowel movements and voiding, medicine, activities, and any other information to be communicated to parents when they come for the child. Even though the caregiver should stop to talk to the parent at pick-up time, all of the details are more likely to be remembered with use of a daily log to keep notes during the day. A sample form for a daily log is provided in Appendix D, page 229.

Health professionals monitor the adequacy of infant nutrition by plotting the child's growth and by obtaining a hemoglobin or hematocrit count between 6 and 9 months of age to detect anemia related to inadequate iron intake. Information on the child's feeding behavior is essential to making a diagnosis when a problem in infant nutrition occurs.

Feeding Toddlers

Special Issues of Toddlerhood For toddlers, the primary developmental task is learning to be independent of constant adult control and identifying reasonable limits. Toddlers need to be offered choices within acceptable boundaries. A toddler may choose among nutritious foods but should not be offered nonnutritious foods as an option. Toddlers need to eat small, frequent meals, but they should not eat continuously.

Children's appetites vary from time to time, depending on growth rate, illness, and catch-up needs. If nutritious foods are made available and unhealthy foods are not offered, children will generally eat what is needed over a period of time. Temporary refusals to eat certain foods are not uncommon, but they can be converted into lifelong rejection if caregivers and parents are overly anxious about such refusals. One of the most common problems with feeding young children is that parents and caregivers who are concerned that the child must eat something will offer anything to encourage the child to eat. A day or two of missed meals is rarely harmful as long as the child's fluid intake is adequate.

In the second and third years of life, growth rates are much slower than in infancy. Appetites are erratic and are sometimes related to intermittent growth spurts. Healthy children differ widely in caloric intake from one day to another and from one child to another. Normal daily food intakes of toddlers range from 700 to as much as 1800 calories; most toddlers will take in an average of 700–1000 calories per day. A toddler's whole day of eating may add up to what a healthy adult might consume in one meal. To caregivers and parents, the intake of a toddler may sometimes seem to be at a starvation level. By frequently plotting growth data against the growth curves of normal children of the same age, the adequacy of a specific child's intake can be checked.

Meal Planning for Toddlers Toddlers eat as they live—willfully. Because their total intake is so low, each food must be considered an important element in the overall balance of diet. Toddler snacks are really minimeals that should exclude "empty-calorie" sugary or fatty foods. With the increased mobility of toddlers and limited attention span, mealtime needs to be planned to provide varied stimuli with different textures, colors, and smells to encourage tasting and experimentation. Two foods can be offered at a time to offer choice, but not become overwhelming. If those are finished, another choice of foods can be offered as a new experience for the same meal. Small portions are more likely to be eaten than larger servings. Four ounces of beverage, fruit, or vegetable, one ounce of meat or cheese, two tablespoons of peanut butter, or a half slice of bread makes a toddler portion.

As in other phases of life, children who eat from the four basic food groups (fruit and vegetable, bread and cereal, meat and meat substitutes, and dairy) will receive an adequate intake of all essential dietary components. Although a child may not eat something from the four basic food groups every day, a balanced intake over one or two days is sufficient. It is not unusual for a toddler to eat only one or two foods at one "meal." Five minimeals should be offered (e.g., breakfast, lunch, dinner, and two snacks).

Toddlers and preschoolers enjoy being involved with all phases of food, from growing it to eating it. Many children will try a food that they have picked themselves during a shopping expedition or one that they helped prepare. Too much variety on the plate may overwhelm a young child. Small portions with a chance for seconds work best.

Foods cut into bite-size pieces can be offered to children beginning in the second half of the first year, with full table food for toddlers. Eating by self-feeding teaches eye-hand coordination and gives toddlers their desired control of their own eating. Arranging for children to sit at a table that is at or just below

Children enjoy in-volvement with all aspects of food, includ-ing shopping expedi-tions.

elbow height for meals and snacks teaches them appropriate mealtime comfort and how to prevent choking by not walking around while eating. Sitting down at a properly sized table also makes it easy for children to learn to feed them-selves and promotes social interaction that is so much a part of good nutrition. Young children should be allowed to eat with their fingers; mannerly use of tableware is a skill to be learned after they learn to eat good foods. The introduc-tion of new foods is a perfect time to discuss food color, taste, texture, aroma, and health value as an interesting experience. Eating should never be forced.

Unsafe Foods and Feeding Practices for Toddlers While variety is important, some foods are not safe for toddlers. Whole pieces of round firm foods can lodge in a toddler's airway, with disastrous consequences. Such foods should be off limits to this age group. Because the danger of choking is increased when the child is eating while doing other activities such as walking or running, children should be required to sit down to eat, preferably at a table. Honey ingestion has been associated with botulism in infants under 6 months of age. Despite the convenience of using canned foods, frozen foods generally have less salt and sugar and are therefore preferable. Young children under 3 or 4 years of age should not be offered the following foods:

- □ honey
- □ nuts
- □ candy
- □ whole grapes
- □ watermelon
- □ raw carrots

- □ popcorn
- □ gum
- □ hot dogs
- □ salted foods or foods canned in salt
- □ sweetened foods.

Attention to beverage intake is also important. Fruit drinks often contain little fruit juice, even though they may be fortified with vitamin C. Many fruit juices are naturally rich in vitamin C, but care must be taken not to overuse juice as a fluid. Juice is also rich in sugar, and if children are fed juice and milk to the exclusion of water, they may learn that all beverages must be flavored and sweet. Water is a good, basic beverage. If adults drink water, children will learn to drink it too.

Bottle feeding usually ends by 18 months of age. Children who walk around with bottles in their mouths risk falling and injuring their front teeth. Bottle drinking, like later cup drinking, is a sit-down, focused activity. Bottles do not belong in beds, nor should drinking be done lying down. Drinking is a part of feeding, a social, not a solitary, activity. Dental decay, increased incidence of ear infections, and the risk of choking are good reasons why children should sit up to drink.

Special Issues in Feeding Toddlers and Preschoolers

Milk Drinking too much milk can also be a problem. More than 16 ounces of milk a day will usually interfere with the child's consumption of foods from other food groups. Children who do not drink any milk at all can meet their calcium needs from numerous other calcium-rich foods such as other dairy products (yogurt, cheese, cottage cheese, or foods cooked with milk) or other foods that contain significant amounts of calcium (collards, sardines, turnip greens, self-rising flour, oysters, rhubarb, mustard greens, spinach, salmon, herring, kale, molasses, and soybeans). Feeding milk with reduced fat content is not generally recommended for children under 2 years of age because the protein/calorie ratio of such milks may be higher than is desirable for body and brain growth.

Salt Adding salt in greater than necessary amounts during cooking or at the table can result in a heightened taste for salt. Salt is included with many recipes because it is a flavor enhancer. Canned foods are less desirable than fresh or frozen ones because they tend to have a high salt content. Salty foods such as salted pretzels or chips are particularly poor food choices. Many crackers have too much salt, but whole-grain, low-salt crackers are available.

Sugary Foods and Sweets The timing of the intake of certain types of foods may also be important. Data on the effects of food on brain function suggest that high-carbohydrate meals decrease alertness and impair concentration while large meals decrease mental efficiency. The most carbohydrate-rich and caloric meal should be fed at lunch (before naptime), with lighter meals before periods when children are working on cognitively stimulating activities (breakfast, mid-morning snack, and midafternoon snack.)

The association of sugar intake with hyperactivity has no basis in fact. In studies in which children who were said to be sugar responders by their parents were given sugar and aspartame or sugar and saccharin, the children were less active with the sugar meal than with the sugar substitute meal. The researchers found that sugar tends to make children sleepy in the short run. If little protein or fat accompanies the sugar, the body rapidly digests the sugar, leaving the child irritably hungry in a relatively short period of time. Sugar calls out the body's insulin in an amount that is sufficient to handle the ratios of sugar to fat and protein found in natural foods. Sweetened foods often do not contain enough other nutrients to make use of the outpouring of insulin that they stimulate. Thus, a rapid fall in blood sugar may follow a rapid peak when a sweet food has been eaten. A rapid fall in blood sugar is often associated with irritability. Thus, cookies, cake, and candy make poor snack foods and are better served as small dessert portions after a full meal.

This information can help caregivers and parents to schedule their alert periods also. Inattentiveness on the part of a staff or parent group may be the result of serving sweet rolls or cookies before the meeting. Donuts are not as good as cereal and milk for breakfast.

Iron Iron is an essential dietary component that has far-reaching effects on behavior and health. Iron is involved in transport of oxygen in the body as a part of the hemoglobin molecule found in red blood cells and as a part of the myoglobin molecule found in muscles. It is also found in enzymes and intracellular components. Although iron is recycled from breakdown of worn-out red blood cells, iron intake is required to produce the expanded volume of blood needed as a result of growth.

Infancy is one of the most rapid periods of growth. If enough iron is not available during this period, the toddler or preschool-age child may develop anemia and poor functioning of iron-dependent body functions. Such children perform less well at developmental tasks, have an increased risk of infection, have decreased absorption of nutrients (including iron), and have a decreased growth rate. Children who have not yet become anemic but are somewhat iron deficient score higher on mental development tests when they are given iron. Good iron sources include red meats and enriched bread and cereal products. Although the total amount of iron required is not great, absorption can be enhanced when acid fruit juices are fed with iron-containing foods.

Nutrition for Dental Health Tooth decay is fostered by consumption of sugary fluids over a prolonged period or frequent drinking of sugary fluids. By encouraging water drinking between meals, prohibiting bottles in bed, and encouraging eating of so-called detergent foods such as celery or apples, some of this tooth decay can be prevented.

Meal Planning for Preschoolers Generally, feeding needs to be relaxed, allowing young children to make choices from a limited range of acceptable alternatives. Breakfast can include one serving from each of the dairy, bread and cereal, and fruit and vegetable food groups. A midmorning snack can consist of a serving from the milk or meat food group, with one serving from the fruit and vegetable or bread and cereal group. Lunch and supper can include one serving of each of the four food groups. Young children should be offered a midafternoon snack if dinner is late or a before-bed snack if dinner is early. The second snack can include two servings from food groups not eaten well at the other meals during the day.

Fostering good nutrition for older preschoolers and young school-age children involves working with children's desire for increasing autonomy and responsiveness to adult guidance that characterizes this period of development. Many opportunities are available to form lasting habits that are significantly related to lifetime health. Older children develop their understanding of the world through intellectual challenge and guided experimentation. New foods and food-related experiences from farm to store to kitchen to table are all part of building the older child's nutrition knowledge and desired behaviors. Children allowed to try new foods without pressure are likely to try more new foods. When adults use pressure, bribery, or games to get children to eat, the control of eating becomes the issue and feeding relationships are distorted.

Nutrition for Older Preschoolers and Young School-age Children

FOOD SERVICE OPERATION AND FEEDING EQUIPMENT

Running a food service program for a group larger than the usual family takes planning, skill, and knowledge that go well beyond home cooking experience. Menu planning, food purchasing, food storage, food preparation, serving of food, food handling, sanitation, and disease control are addressed by courses for food handlers and certified by a food handler's examination. Even food handlers who have worked competently in restaurants and large adult institutions need special training to adapt their skills to feeding young children. Special equipment and serving dishes are needed to provide developmentally appropriate foods and facilitate the child's determination of portion size without contaminating the food that will be served to other children. Portion sizes, food consistency, and types of foods are different for children of different developmental levels. The training and supervision of food service personnel in child care should be the responsibility of the nutrition consultant to the early childhood program. Sanitation in food service is generally supervised at least annually by a licensed sanitarian.

Furniture, dishes, and utensils used for serving and feeding children should be planned to facilitate self-service and self-feeding whenever possible. Children should be held for bottle feeding until they are able to sit comfortably in a seat that provides a platform for their feet. Feeding should be a pleasant, relaxed, social time. Letting children have some finger food and a chance to handle a spoon even if the result is a mess helps to free the caregiver to assist with rather than take over feeding of solid foods. The surfaces in contact with the food must be cleaned and sanitized before the meal so that the expected spills on the table or tray can be safely recovered by the child for another attempt. Food that drops to the floor or any unsanitized surface must be discarded before it is retrieved by the child. Keeping the children a little more than a child's arm reach away from one another will deter mouth-to-mouth sharing of food.

Plates, cups, and tableware should be chosen for the skills of the intended users. Use of deep serving dishes and preportioned food makes it easy for the child to take a small helping to start. Seconds should be available for everyone. For children who need portion control, offer less for the first helping and permit

Child-sized equipment encourages self-feeding.

a small second helping if the child wants one. Using small plates will make a child who has smaller portions feel more satisfied. Plates, cups, and tableware should not be made of styrofoam or easily broken plastic because pieces could become choking hazards. Unless plastic tableware is specifically marked for reuse, it should be considered disposable and not used again.

MENU PLANNING FOR MEALS AND SNACKS

Menu planning guides for child care programs are available from the Child Care Food Program of the U.S. Department of Agriculture (USDA). These guides are written to specify types of foods and portion sizes for children of different ages. Menus should be developed for a month at a time, at least one month in advance so that a variety of foods can be planned, supplies can be ordered, and parents can be informed to help them plan their home feeding around the meals they know their children are receiving at the program. Menus can be cycled on a monthly basis but should be varied by season to use foods when they are plentiful and fresh. Texture, color, taste, ethnic and cultural familiarity, and diversity should be considered in planning the menu. Reviewing menu plans provides another good opportunity for the nutrition consultant to offer helpful input.

Young children generally need something to eat or drink every three to four hours. Empty-calorie foods, those whose principal nutrients are sugar, fat, or salt (e.g., cookies and salted crackers) are nutrition-poor snacks. Because young children often prefer many little meals rather than a few larger feedings, snacks should be viewed as a portion of the child's overall nutrient intake. Snacks should be nutritious meal-type foods in small quantities. Examples of some good snacks are fresh fruit, yogurt, cheese, fresh soft vegetables or crunchy ones that have been briefly cooked to soften them, celery stuffed with cottage cheese or peanut butter, quartered sandwiches or rolled-up bread alternatives filled with meat, fish, egg, or cheese, any nutritious filling rolled in a lettuce leaf, and blender-whipped fruit and milk drinks.

Food should not be used for punishment or reward, since doing so adds a value to eating that undermines healthy eating habits. Many families still believe that children should finish any food they take rather than accept the child's mistake and help the child learn how to judge the amount for the next time.

INTEGRATING EATING WITH SOCIAL DEVELOPMENT AND WITH CULTURAL AND ETHNIC PREFERENCES

Because of the central role that nutrition plays in survival during periods of food shortage, many cultural and ethnic practices have developed that promote inappropriate eating behaviors for children. The "clean plate club" and use of the phrase "If you behave, I'll buy you some candy" are remnants of the way food was used only a few generations ago to foster compliant behavior. In the United States, where food is abundant and where healthy eating behaviors are closely linked to prevention of disease, using food for leverage to achieve desired behavior merely distorts eating behaviors. Even for mentally disabled children, food should not be used as a punishment or reward unless other methods of discipline and training have been tried and failed.

Foods are distinctive symbols of cultural identity. Although foods differ from one culture to another, the types of foods that make up balanced nutrition are the same for all cultures. Thus, children who eat rice, potatoes, tortillas, shortbread, pasta, bagels, or other bread foods are eating distinctive versions of complex carbohydrates. Whether protein comes from milk products, meat, poultry, eggs, or lentils, protein or meat-related foods are essential. Vegetables and fruits may differ, but they must be present in some form in the diet of every culture. These foods may be eaten alone or, most often, in a variety of combinations familiar to children and families who share a common cultural background. Learning to appreciate the similarities while accepting and enjoying the differences is an important life lesson.

FOODS PREPARED AT HOME

When foods are prepared at home and transported to the early childhood program, the program has little or no control over the wholesomeness and sanitation of the food during the preparation and transport process. Brown bag or lunchbox foods can easily spoil while being transported during the summer months. Foods brought from home for special events are risky for the same reasons.

Some foods are safer to transport and serve than others. Cheese and peanut butter transport well, as do most baked foods or foods with an acid base (e.g., those made with tomato, vinegar, or citrus fruits). Perishable meats, foods with eggs in them, and preparations that involve mixing uncooked foods with cooked foods are all dangerous items. Before caregivers accept foods from home to serve in the early childhood program, even if only to the child from whose home the food was sent, clear guidelines should be established and reviewed with the nutrition consultant. The guidelines need to specify the types of foods that will be accepted, how they should be transported to maintain safe food temperatures during the time of transit, who is responsible for transferring perishable foods to a refrigerator, and how the food will be served. Safe food holding temperatures are below 40 degrees Fahrenheit for cold foods and above 140 degrees Fahrenheit for hot foods. In general, foods for large group gatherings should be prepared at the early childhood program or be of a type that is unlikely to be a source of food poisoning (e.g., cheese).

SPECIAL EVENTS

Special events like birthdays and holidays are celebrated by activities, not just with food. Too often the focus of the celebration becomes the food instead of the other activities. By involving parents in making plans for celebrations that focus on games, trips, and communal projects, families can learn to shift their focus from "birthday = ice cream and cake" to "birthday = fun outings and activities with a snack."

Because staff behavior in early childhood programs is almost always observed, staff carry a heavy burden for responsible behavior. Soda bottles, potato chips, and candy bars are inappropriate for public eating in early childhood programs. Staff parties should also make special activities and nutritious foods the focus of the celebration, not the high-sugar, high-fat foods that tend to dominate typical party menus.

Special events like Halloween should be celebrated with activities, not unhealthy foods.

Even with self-feeding of a nutritious diet, some children will overeat. Confirmation of the theory that an increased number of fat cells in adulthood results from excess multiplication of fat cells in overweight toddlers and preschoolers awaits further research. However, fat toddlers and preschoolers have more difficulty with activities, may have skin problems related to skin surfaces being in continuous contact with one another, and may have an increased risk of injury.

OVERWEIGHT AND UNDERWEIGHT CHILDREN

As for infants, by plotting weight and height for preschoolers on a growth chart, the length/height and weight percentiles can be compared with one another and with those for normal healthy children. A child who is more than one percentile line in weight above the percentile line in height needs medical evaluation. Such children may benefit from being offered smaller, predivided servings to gain portion control, increased physical activity, and reduction of intake of foods with high fat and sugar content. Control of excess food intake in children can also be accomplished by modification of the reward system to emphasize pleasurable experiences unrelated to food. Restriction of dietary fat through use of skim milk or substantial restriction of the variety of nutritious foods offered is generally not recommended in early childhood. Children who are overweight must not have their caloric intake severely restricted, because such restriction can interfere with normal growth. Advice given to families by physicians for an individual child may differ from these generalizations, but whenever a child's intake is being modified, a physician should be closely monitoring the child's growth. Because feeding guidelines for early childhood programs are designed to provide a large part of the child's total daily intake while the child is in the program, a child who has a tendency to be overweight will need adult assistance to control portion sizes and coordinate home and program feeding routines. Increasing the child's activity before mealtime often helps to reduce the overeater's appetite.

Some children who are small or thin for their age are following family patterns of growth. However, all children whose weights are more than one percentile curve below their percentile curve for height (more than one standard deviation from the norm) should be evaluated by a health professional to see whether and why they are failing to thrive. This evaluation should include an examination by a pediatrician at a minimum and may include laboratory testing, nutritional diagnostic evaluation, and socioemotional evaluation of the child and the family.

Higher than recommended doses of vitamins can lead to serious toxic effects. Excess vitamin A can cause increased intracranial pressure mimicking a brain tumor. Large doses of vitamin C can inter-

VITAMINS AND OTHER SUPPLEMENTS

fere with vitamin B_{12} absorption and metabolism and, in carefully performed research, have not been shown to have any benefit as a cold preventative or remedy. Excesses of vitamin D and vitamin E are also associated with known disease syndromes. Vitamin deficiency is rare; vitamin supplements for normal children are not needed after infancy.

NUTRITIONAL ASPECTS OF PREVENTING HEART DISEASE

For more than 20 years, medical investigators have been hard at work to find ways to control heart disease. Their research findings show that control of adult heart disease requires adoption of a prudent diet and life style, beginning in childhood and continuing throughout life. Pediatricians now counsel parents about ways to prevent heart disease in their children. For these measures to succeed, all those who care for children must join the effort.

Controlling Blood Cholesterol

Since abnormally high levels of blood cholesterol are clearly associated with heart disease, lowering blood cholesterol levels makes sense. Fat streaks can be seen in the arteries of children as young as 3 years of age. These fat streaks are the earliest evidence of the beginning of the condition that leads to heart disease. The extent of fatty streaks is closely related to the child's blood level of cholesterol.

Blood cholesterol levels for children of greater than 170 milligrams per deciliter are considered to put the child at risk of heart disease. Recent pediatric literature urges pediatricians to check for special risk factors by asking every family about them. Appropriate tests should be conducted when significant risk factors are present.

Child care professionals can play a part in helping to prevent heart disease in several ways:

1. Remind parents that every child should have a checkup visit that includes checking for heart disease risk factors and evaluation of growth. These procedures are part of the routines included in the Recommendations for Preventive Pediatric Health Care published by the American Academy of Pediatrics.

2. Make sure that the meals and snacks provided by the child care program conform to the guidelines for a prudent diet. Juice and cookie snacks are not acceptable. Heavy reliance on hard cheese, plain or iced pastries, ice cream, or coated fried foods will result in excess amounts of saturated fats in the diet. When foods must be prepared with some form of grease or oil, olive oil should be given first preference, since it is high in monosaturated fat and low in saturated fats. Other vegetable oils and margarine made from vegetable oil are better than butter or animal fats.

3. Teach and model good eating habits, exercise, and taking stress breaks.

4. Teach wellness:
- *At circle time, talk about how wellness is related to activity, rest, and good food.*
- *Read books about sleep, good food, and exercise.*
- *Encourage developmentally appropriate exercise routines.*

5. Work with parents to help them recognize modifiable heart disease risk factors and special risks related to the family history.

6. Urge all adults (including those in your family) to seek information about their own blood cholesterol levels. The current recommendation is that universal blood cholesterol screening should begin at 18 years of age and be repeated every 5 years throughout adult life.

The opportunity to change factors that may lead to heart disease is greatest with young children. Excessive restrictions or overzealous implementation of exercise regimens should be avoided. A prudent diet, weight control, healthy exercise routines, and the use of preventive pediatric health care can make a difference.

ACCOMMODATING FOOD INTOLERANCES AND SPECIAL DIETS

Food intolerance is uncommon in early childhood, and true food allergy is rare. Many supposed food intolerances or allergic reactions do not reoccur when the offending food is offered again. Children should generally not have their diets restricted unless a health professional has determined that a child's reaction justifies such a restriction. Generally, this determination requires that the food be eliminated for a period and then reintroduced with careful monitoring of any symptoms.

When a child has a food intolerance or allergy, the program's feeding will need to be adapted to accommodate this special need. For children with significant restrictions that are not easily handled by using the food supplied by the program, this adaptation is most easily accommodated by having the child bring meals from home to be served when meals are served in the program. For many single-food problems, the program can easily plan to meet the child's need. In either case, the child's special food problem must be communicated to the cook, caregivers, and volunteers so that no inadvertent feeding of the restricted food occurs. The cook should be involved in planning alternate food selections whenever the menu includes offending food. The teachers need to discuss how the child will be protected from the food if it is brought in by another child or is encountered on an outing. Caregivers, parents, and volunteers can be reminded about the precaution by posting the child's name and the food allergy in an easily visible area where the children eat.

Many cultural and ethnic dietary modifications can be accommodated by selection of food from the regular menu with input from the nutrition consultant to be sure that the child's nutritional needs are met. When this is not possible, the parent may need to supply food from home. Parents who require vegetarian diets for their child should meet with the nutrition consultant to be sure that the diet provided by the program or sent from home meets the child's growth needs.

NUTRITION AS A PART OF THE CURRICULUM

Children learn about food and eating by experience. They need to learn about where food comes from, how to choose food to purchase or prepare, how to prepare food, and how to choose what and how much prepared food to eat. Good food habits can be reinforced by food and feeding experiences that take place every day of the child's life. Children learn to wash their hands before meals by doing it. Proper hand-washing technique can be reinforced by pictorial posters mounted over the sinks where children and staff wash. Such posters are often available from local health departments.

Mealtime is an opportune time for adults to talk about food among other topics of conversation. Head Start has a Nutrition Education Curriculum that provides lessons on each of the major food education areas. Many more materials, children's cookbooks, and food experience guides for young children are available from the extension services of state universities and the USDA.

SPECIAL FOOD PROGRAMS

The Child Care Food Program

The Child Care Food Program is a federally funded source of money to offset the cost of feeding children who are enrolled in nonprofit licensed or registered child care centers and family day care homes. The program is administered at the national level by the USDA and at the state level by the agency that administers the school lunch program, usually the state Department of Education. Participating programs must meet the feeding guidelines of the funding agency. Reimbursement levels are determined by the income levels of the families that the early childhood program is serving, with higher rates of reimbursement given for lower-income families. For-profit programs may also participate if 25 percent or more of their children are funded by (federal) Title XX social service block grant money. Early childhood programs that participate in the Child Care Food Program automatically receive an application to receive surplus foods supplied by the USDA Food Distribution Program.

Women's, Infants', and Children's Program

Although administrators of early childhood programs are generally familiar with nutrition support available through the Child Care Food Program, some may not realize the special benefits available to families whose infants qualify for the Women's, Infants', and Children's Program (WIC). WIC provides food as a prescription for infant formulas and cereals. Milk, cheese, eggs, peanut butter, juices, dried peas, or beans are also available to eligible children through 4 years of age. Parents may take a prescription or form to the food market or distribution center and receive these foods in appropriate amounts.

Eligibility for WIC is based on receiving medical care for residing in a high-risk (poverty) area, demonstration of economic need, and nutritional risk as determined by a health professional. Many families who are not eligible for other benefits qualify for WIC. Any potential recipient should be referred to the local public health authority or WIC office.

The Food Stamp Program provides coupons for low-income families to exchange for approved foods at stores that accept food stamps. Eligibility is determined by social service offices authorized by the state to issue the coupons.

Food Stamp Program

Special funds are available to states to provide training and technical assistance to staff who are involved with feeding children and teaching children about nutrition. Information on how to tap these funds is usually available from the extension services of state universities or the office of the Child Care Food Program.

Nutrition Education and Training Program

SUGGESTED ACTIVITIES

1. Visit a child care classroom. Weigh and measure all of the children and then plot their growth data on a graph. Which children are more than one percentile curve different in weight from height? Are these children thin, fat, short, or tall when you look at them? Are their parents of similar build? Has a physician evaluated their growth?

2. Plan one week of menus for a program for infants, for toddlers, and for preschoolers. Check the plans against the guidelines of the Child Care Food Program.

FOR MORE INFORMATION

American Academy of Pediatrics. *Health in Day Care: A Manual for Health Professionals*. Elk Grove Village, IL: American Academy of Pediatrics, 1987, pp. 23–26.

American Academy of Pediatrics, Committee on Nutrition. *Pediatric Nutrition Handbook*. Elk Grove Village, IL: American Academy of Pediatrics, 1985.

The Food and Nutrition Information Center, National Agricultural Library, Room 304, Beltsville, MD 20705.

Goodwin, Mary T., and Pollen, Gerry. *Creative Food Experiences for Children*. Washington, DC: Center for Science in the Public Interest, 1974.

Kendrick, A., Kaufmann, R., and Messenger, K., ed. *Healthy Young Children*. Washington, DC: National Association for the Education of Young Children, 1988, pp. 151–186.

Report of the Task Force on the Assessment of the Scientific Evidence Relating Infant-Feeding Practices and Infant Health. *Pediatrics*, vol. 74, supplement, 1984.

Satter, E. *How to Get Your Kid to Eat . . . But Not Too Much*. Palo Alto, CA: Bull, 1987.

4

Adult Health in Child Care

IN THIS CHAPTER:

ADMINISTRATIVE ADULT HEALTH ISSUES IN CHILD CARE
HEALTH EXAMINATIONS FOR ADULTS
OCCUPATIONAL HEALTH CONCERNS OF CAREGIVERS
PREVENTING ILLNESS WITH A WELLNESS PROGRAM
SUGGESTED ACTIVITIES
FOR MORE INFORMATION

The health and well-being of adult workers who care for children is a key element in the quality of care. Because consistency in human relationships is so important in child care, the quality of care is diminished when a caregiver is absent or ill. Many child care programs lack the resources to hire and retain enough staff who are able caregivers, much less maintain a well-trained cadre of familiar substitutes.

When a caregiver is absent or leaves because of illness or a desire for a less stressful position, those who remain often suffer from the increased demand placed on them to keep the program running. When staff or volunteers who are not feeling well remain on the job, their inability to keep up is usually apparent to everyone. Even among workers who do not provide direct care for children, illness and turnover related to the occupational health problems of child care result in gaps in service which are hard to fill.

ADMINISTRATIVE ADULT HEALTH ISSUES IN CHILD CARE

Because of the significant impact of illness on the quality of child care, program administrators have a legitimate interest in the health status of adults who work in the child care setting. Concerns of child care administrators are as follows:

- potential hazards and problems for children and other staff posed by the illness of a worker
- the economic and service implications to the program of a worker's inability to carry out her/his child care role
- possible legal liability for compensation or damages associated with a health problem developed by an adult related to her/his role in child care.

Taken together, these concerns justify the effort required to promote safety and health for adults in the child care work force.

HEALTH EXAMINATIONS FOR ADULTS

Health examinations for all adults working in the child care setting should be required as a prerequisite for service. The results of health appraisals are confidential and may not be given to employers unless the patient gives permission. There is no reason for the physician to give details about the findings of the examination to a child care employer unless a potentially disqualifying abnormality or health problem is discovered. In such a case, information must be provided that allows the employer to decide whether an adjustment of work role or work environment is feasible.

Each program needs a standard requirement for adult examinations which specifies (1) the content of the examination, (2) the intervals between required examinations, (3) which special examinations are required for specific child care roles, (4) who receives the findings of the examinations, (5) where the examinations can be performed, (6) who pays for the examinations, and (7) the health criteria for qualifying or disqualifying adults for child care roles. Health professionals who are asked to perform the adult health assessments need to understand the nature of the role in child care for which clearance is being sought. Some detail about the requirements should be provided with the request for clearance, since few health professionals understand the demanding nature of child care work. For example, the physical fitness requirements of an adult who must keep up with a group of toddlers all day are different from those of a social worker whose job is more sedentary. Similarly, the hearing ability of a caregiver or social worker is more an issue than that of the cook or custodian.

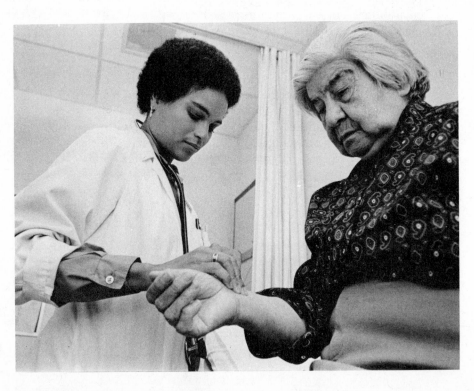

Health examinations for caregivers should be required.

Adults who work in the child care setting need to be evaluated for orthopedic, psychological, neurological, and sensory limitations that might affect their job performance. Health professionals should look for the adult's ability

- □ to move quickly to supervise or assist young children
- □ to lift children, equipment, or supplies
- □ to sit on the floor or child-size furniture
- □ to experience frequent hand washing
- □ to eat the food served to the children
- □ to hear and see at a distance for playground supervision
- □ to drive safely.

In addition, adults should be screened for tuberculosis by having a skin test or, if their skin test is known to be positive, by having an initial chest X-ray and ongoing annual supervision by a physician. The frequency of repeated tuberculosis skin testing should be determined by consultation with the local health department, based on the prevalence of tuberculosis in the community.

The first time that an adult health assessment is necessary is before the job offer is final and before contact with the children in the program begins.

Preemployment Examinations

In practice, this requirement poses several problems. Many adults have no "medical home," or usual source of health care to provide the needed health assessment. For them, a health service resource must be found. Another problem is that appointments with health professionals for complete examinations are rarely available on short notice, but the child care program's need for the job candidate or volunteer may be so acute that delay in starting work may be burdensome. For volunteers, the requirement may serve as a deterrent to participation. Despite the burden and disincentive, the same standard of health clearance should be required for volunteers as for paid staff. Health risks and program liability are unaffected by whether or not the adult is paid.

Unless true preemployment assessments are obtained, it may be very difficult to use information revealed by the examination. The information could indicate the need for termination of an employee or volunteer with whom children and staff have begun to develop a relationship or reveal risks to which other staff and the children have already been exposed.

In the preemployment examination, the issues are:

- □ physical and emotional fitness for the job
- □ conditions that might result in frequent absence from the job
- □ medication or special diet requirements that might affect job performance
- □ need for restricted exposure to situations that are a part of child care work (such as difficulty working without regularly scheduled breaks, poorly controlled hypertension, difficulty being outdoors in cold or

dampness, skin conditions incompatible with frequent hand washing, or allergy to art materials)
- □ conditions that might require emergency management at work
- □ unhealthy habits such as smoking during work hours
- □ immunization status (for measles, mumps, rubella, diphtheria, tetanus, and polio), previous experience with childhood infections such as chicken pox, and need for flu vaccine
- □ freedom from contagious infectious diseases such as tuberculosis
- □ sensory abilities as tested by audiometry, and both near and far visual acuity screening.

The purpose of the assessment is to identify disqualifying conditions, correctable problems, and problems for which compensatory arrangements must be made. Bus drivers or others involved in transportation for the child care program require some special evaluations in addition to the items appropriate for all child care staff. These special tests include visual field, color, and depth perception testing, audiometry to test hearing, urinalysis (including a drug screen if permitted by law), emotional and mental health assessment, and cardiovascular evaluation, including an electrocardiogram where indicated.

Some of the health conditions that might preclude original employment are poorly controlled diabetes, hypertension, or seizures, gross weight deviations, and lack of stamina required by the job. These same conditions may not preclude continued employment when they develop in a person who has been working for some time in the program if adjustments can be made in the program to ensure that the quality of child care is not affected. Such adjustments might include a move to part-time status, a change in role in the program, or temporary disability leave until the health problem is brought under control.

In addition to preemployment exams, there are other key points at which adult health assessment is indicated:

- □ before completion of probationary service when the probationary period has raised questions about the health of the individual
- □ after a severe or prolonged illness, when a health evaluation can help identify significant residual disabilities, need for modification of job role or environment, and expected time required for transition back to a full work role
- □ on return from a job-related injury, when a written release from a physician helps protect the program from liability for placing the adult in the same role that was associated with the injury
- □ on a periodic, age-related basis to identify newly appearing conditions. (Generally, exams should be conducted every four years for people in their forties and every other year for people in their fifties and older.)

Whenever a health condition seems to be affecting job performance, administrators should be able to request a reevaluation. The administrator should also be able to request a second health professional's opinion if the first examination does not yield information needed to make job decisions. However, care must be taken not to try to shift administrative decision-making responsibilities to health professionals. Poor job performance may be related to mental illness which could benefit from treatment, but administrative accountability requires that job performance standards be upheld regardless of cause for the sake of the children and others involved in the program.

A health assessment is also required when a staff member is being considered for promotion or reassignment to another role that could be significantly affected by the individual's health status. If a caregiver begins to drive the program's van for trips or the custodian becomes a substitute caregiver, a health assessment to address the special requirements of these roles is indicated.

Finally, an examination is required whenever there are legal liability issues such as workers who have a history of back injuries, a heart attack, intractable ulcer, mental illness, or other stress-related conditions. The possible consequences to the health of such workers need to be carefully evaluated, and risks need to be properly assigned and accepted before individuals are exposed to aggravating activities such as lifting children, sitting in furniture sized for children, or living with the stress of child care operation.

Who Pays for Examinations?

In the best of worlds, the cost of employment-related examinations would be paid by the employer. In many industrial settings, employee health is considered a cost containment activity for the business. Employment-related exams may be the only health care that adults receive and may provide the only health record available for reference in the event of claims made against the employer for workman's compensation benefits. Medical coverage of child care personnel is especially important because of the increased potential for communicable diseases and stress-related conditions that caregivers may experience. Sick leave is also important to minimize the spread of communicable disease and maintain the health of staff. Lack of benefits is a common reason given for leaving child care as a profession. This contributes to high turnover in staff and reduction in the quality of child care.

In practice, few child care programs can afford the direct cost of adult health assessments even when the cost is viewed as part of the total fringe benefit package available to the employee. It is customary for many types of workers to accept costs related to their jobs, such as costs for maintaining educational qualifications, professional licenses, and uniforms. However, the low status and low pay of employees and volunteers in early childhood programs make assumption of these costs by workers particularly burdensome. It is hard to ignore the fact that staff members in child care are so poorly paid. Their near-poverty status has a perverse affect on the need to evaluate their health status. Individuals from low-income groups are more likely to have health problems that can adversely affect job performance, but they are least able to afford medical advice.

The health problems of adults who work in child care cannot be ignored. As with so many components of child care, conscientious administrators must work toward goals within the limits of program constraints. If adults who work in child care settings are to promote health for children and families, promotion of staff and volunteer health must be part of the overall program.

OCCUPATIONAL HEALTH CONCERNS OF CAREGIVERS

Job-related health problems of caregivers not only cause discomfort and disability, but also strain the ability of the program to provide good care for children. Occupational health concerns for child care workers include:

□ potential discomfort suffered from illnesses to which child care work may contribute
□ limitation of function both on and off the job
□ potential long-lasting effects of illness resulting from child care work.

Three areas of adult health risk are known to be increased in the early childhood education setting:

1. Increased exposure to infectious diseases is associated with toileting, diapering, nose wiping, hugging, and lap sitting. Infectious disease outbreaks among staff and parents have been documented. Many child care professionals believe that new staff have higher rates of illness than those who have been exposed for several years.

2. Stress-related illnesses can be aggravated by the emotional challenges of caregiving.

3. Aches, pains, and fatigue can result from lifting, bending, sitting on child-sized furniture, and long hours of service with few breaks.

When caregivers become pregnant, these health risks become more significant.

Exposure to Infectious Diseases

Because of the necessary intimacy of contact with young children and pooling of organisms across multiple families, the child care setting has an inherently increased risk for transmission of infectious diseases. The many potential pathways of transmission are illustrated in Figure 4.1.

At the least, people whose immune systems are being suppressed by special medications or who have immunodeficiency diseases should be cautioned about the infectious disease risks of working in a child care environment.

F I G U R E 4.1
Potential pathways for spread of infections.

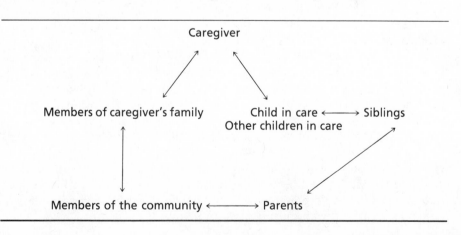

The majority of short-term illnesses experienced by caregivers are respiratory infections, most of which are caused by viruses. Each type of virus has its own typical season, but the seasons overlap and many viruses can cause similar symptoms. Many adults have had some experience with the common respiratory viruses that infect children in child care, but there are so many different types of the same virus that immunity from previous infections usually offers only partial protection. The common cold, for example, is caused by rhinoviruses, parainfluenza viruses, respiratory syncytial virus, adenoviruses, enteroviruses, and influenza viruses, in descending order of frequency. Each of these viruses can cause a single symptom such as sore throat or runny nose or can cause a more serious flulike illness, depending on the individual's resistance. Bacterial illnesses such as strep throat or ear infections are less common in adults than in young children but, as in children, may occur as a secondary complication of a viral illness.

Both personal resistance to infection and hygiene play important roles in protection. The old advice about eating right, sleeping right, and exercising to stay fit applies to child care staff, including administrators. Common cold viruses and gastrointestinal infections are transmitted primarily by direct or indirect hand contact—from the hands or handled objects of an infected person to the hands of another person. People introduce infectious disease agents (viruses, bacteria, and parasites) into their bodies by touching their hands to their eyes, nose, mouth, food, or objects that are used for food. Illness will occur if there are enough virus particles to overwhelm the person's resistance. Thus, both good hygiene and maintenance of a healthy schedule of rest, nutrition, and exercise help to keep adults who work in child care settings well.

Some infections are of special concern for caregivers but not for children. Infections of special concern to adults in child care settings are:

□ Chickenpox   □ Cytomegalovirus (pregnant women)
□ Hepatitis A   □ Parvovirus (pregnant women)

Most short-term illnesses of caregivers are viral respiratory infections that are easily transmitted.

An adult who comes down with chickenpox can become extremely ill. Adults are usually protected by having chickenpox in earlier life. Even among those adults who do not think they had chickenpox, only a quarter are actually at risk. When tested, 75 percent of adults who do not remember having had chickenpox have antibodies in their blood (indicating that they did have the disease). Prevention of chickenpox in susceptible adults will be possible when a chickenpox vaccine becomes available. Adults who have contact with children in early childhood programs and who think they have not had chickenpox should be urged to discuss this problem with their physicians.

Hepatitis A is another viral infection that does not usually cause serious disease in children but may be associated with significant symptoms for an adult. Spread of the disease can be controlled by good hygienic principles and judicious use of gamma globulin soon after exposure to the infection. Rapid diagnosis is needed for anyone who shows signs of yellowing of the skin (jaundice) associated with nausea, fever, and loss of appetite. Prompt consultation with public health authorities is needed to institute measures to limit the spread of Hepatitis A. A vaccine against Hepatitis A is being developed.

Another infectious disease concern that has been raised for caregivers is cytomegalovirus infection (CMV). This virus is common in the normal population and rarely causes serious disease. By childbearing age, many women (30–50 percent) have already had CMV and are not at risk from this infection. The concern is for pregnant caregivers who have never had CMV. Between 10 and 15 percent of fetuses of women who develop their first CMV infection during the early part of pregnancy will develop birth defects such as hearing loss, learning disabilities, or mental retardation. Severe disease occurs in about 5 percent of infants who are infected during the pregnancy. About 1 in 1000 newborns are born with major complications from CMV infection.

CMV infection can be found among 40–80 percent of children in child care centers between 1 and 2 years of age, compared with a rate of 20–30 percent for children in the general population who are infected by 5 years of age. The magnitude of the problem for children in family day care homes is not known. A high rate of early infection for female children in child care is likely to provide protection for them when they reach childbearing age. However, children who are infected with CMV are a source of infection to susceptible pregnant child care staff and to their own susceptible pregnant mothers.

The virus that causes CMV disease is transmitted by contact with children's tears, saliva, and urine, contacts which are to be expected in the course of providing child care. Good hygiene can reduce the transmission of this virus, as shown by studies of susceptible nurses who care for children with CMV and who have no increased rate of CMV infection. However, increased transmission has been found for susceptible mothers of children in child care. These findings suggest that improving hygienic practices may be a reasonable method of prevention.

A vaccine against CMV has been developed, and is being tested in child care programs. Until the results of the vaccine trials are complete and a safe vaccine is available, pregnant women who have contact with children in child care should be advised to discuss this risk with their obstetricians. Many obstetricians can do a blood test like the test done to check rubella immunity to determine whether the woman is protected by already having had CMV. Those who are at risk should be advised to be especially careful about good hygiene or to avoid child care duties during early pregnancy.

Another virus that can damage the fetus is parvovirus B19, which causes a disease in children called erythema infectiosum, fifth disease, or slapped-cheek syndrome. This respiratory illness is very common among young children; it is transmitted easily and often without symptoms. By the time the symptom of a bright pink rash on the cheeks appears in a child who does become ill, the child is no longer contagious.

About half of all women of childbearing age have already had an infection with parvovirus B19 and are immune. The virus grows in the cells of the bone marrow that make new blood cells. Women who contract the illness during early pregnancy may infect their babies. Some of these fetuses will develop a fatal anemia and be miscarried about four to six weeks after they are infected. Infections later in pregnancy may cause anemia in the baby but do not seem to cause serious problems. The risk of having a parvovirus infection that causes a fetal death in the first 20 weeks of pregnancy is estimated to be much less than 1 percent.

Women who have not previously been infected with parvovirus B19 and who work with young children are at increased risk of becoming infected. However, because of widespread inapparent infection, routine exclusion of pregnant women from the child care setting is not recommended. Eventually, blood testing for the antibody of the parvovirus B19 that causes the problem will become available, and women who intend to become pregnant will be able to have their susceptibility determined by their physicians to assess their risk. Meanwhile, transmission of this infection, like most others, can be lessened by routine hygienic practices for control of respiratory secretions, including hand washing and the proper disposal of tissues containing secretions.

Stress

Stress is the vital force that challenges us to perform. Too much stress without relief drains our physical and mental resources below functional levels. Signs of distress include frequent headaches, insomnia, digestive problems, tension or irritability, a constant feeling of fatigue, and depression. Caregivers need planned stress relievers such as private time and changes of pace to regenerate the enthusiasm and energy required by their jobs.

Personal recovery time is hard to find in the active child care day. Caregivers must become quick-rest artists, grasping and using the few slack moments whenever they occur. Good use of a few minutes of recuperative time several times a day can make the difference. A few minutes can be found before the children arrive; another few minutes are usually available when one caregiver conducts a transitional activity while the other caregiver is "off-line." This recovery time can be coupled with a leisurely paced cleanup of the prior activity and setting up the next event. When staffing permits, a real break away from the children is desirable. Well-designed child care facilities include a pleasant place for adults to escape and relax. Naptime is ready-made for extra chores, but some time should be saved for adult "downtime."

Effective use of these moments can be made by engaging in any of the relaxation routines described below.

Exercise Exercising to reduce stress seems almost paradoxical, but expending effort in different types of activities can be soothing. Running, taking brisk walks around the block, or doing quick rounds of stretching exercises can relieve feelings of being cooped up, controlled, and pressured. Even five minutes of exercise is relaxing.

Have a Chat Talk to someone about how the day is going. Sharing a burden makes it lighter. Usually, there is someone else who would also like to discuss the day. The caregiver who takes some time to chat with a colleague and unwind usually interacts better with the children later in the day.

Laugh Find something funny in whatever is happening. Laughter is good medicine. In every occasion, there is a lighter, positive side.

Use Lists Make a list of essential tasks, order them by importance, and check off each task as it is completed. Cross of the least important tasks if the list seems overwhelming or move less critical tasks to the bottom of the list. The practice of crossing off completed chores can be very satisfying.

Daydream Temporary escape from stress by imagining a pleasant scene or allowing the mind to wander can help ease the burdens of the day. "Let's pretend" games can be played with the children to help everyone relax. Imagine a favorite setting—on a beach, in a forest, stretched out in the garden, or walking through a spring meadow. Read a book about such a setting to the children. Tapes and records of background sounds are available to help recall many favorite scenes.

Relaxation Exercise Relaxation means releasing the tension in the muscles. Begin the relaxation exercise by lying down or sitting in a comfortable chair. Only 5–10 minutes are required to be refreshed. With practice, relaxation becomes easier. To help the body relax:

1. Lie or sit in a position that feels very comfortable, with all parts of the body supported. The joints (elbows, wrists, and knees) should be slightly bent.

2. Stretch to relieve tension; some people learn to relax by tensing and relaxing one body part at a time. Yawn if possible or take a deep breath while stretching, blowing out all the air in a deep sigh. At the same time go limp, sagging against the bed or chair.

3. Concentrate on a single thought such as the rhythm of breathing or a favorite scene. Everytime some other thought interrupts, replace it.

4. Breathe slowly and deeply. Be aware of increasing limpness and sagging of all parts of the body.

A relaxation exercise is a quick way for a caregiver to release physical tension and reduce stress.

Caregiving is hard on body parts. Constant hand washing dries out the skin, but good hygiene is a must to prevent transmission of infection to caregivers and children. To help prevent dry, sore

Coping with the Physical Requirements of Caregiving

skin, encourage the use of a dab of hand lotion after washing by keeping lotion in a handy pump dispenser near the sink. Using hand lotion immediately after washing will help replace natural oils that seal the skin against evaporation of moisture.

Musculoskeletal problems are common among caregivers. Children's furnishings are appropriately sized for their needs but are inherently awkward for adults to use. Stepstools that help children use adult-level sinks are obstacles for adults, encouraging them to adopt awkward postures as they lean over to help with hand washing or tooth brushing. Sitting in child-size chairs or on the floor requires flexibility and durability, which become scarce commodities as people grow older. Young children need to be lifted and carried, cradled, and assisted. All of these activities put stress on the musculoskeletal system.

Backaches are common problems among caregivers, especially those who are pregnant. For the vast majority of individuals with low back pain, the underlying problem is mechanical. Poor posture, improperly sized equipment, muscle weakness, and tight, short ligaments combine to produce pain. The solution for most people is a combination of time, changes in posture and equipment, and exercises that will prevent excessive demands on lower back structures.

Bending forward involves forward rotation of the pelvis and an increase in the curvature of the lower spine. During bending, the abdominal muscles stabilize the front of the body and the muscles of the buttocks hold the back in line.

Weakness in these muscles allows an excessive forward curvature of the upper spine and backward curvature of the lower spine to exist at rest so that the muscles, ligaments, and other tissues of the back become shortened and tight. Sudden movement or even normal bending and lifting can cause pain in these shortened structures. Many doctors can provide printed instructions for exercises designed to strengthen back muscles and stretch shortened tissues.

Even those with good posture and flexibility should avoid back strain by following some simple practices:

- Avoid slouching, keep the lower back as flat as possible.
- When standing for a long time, put one foot up on a stool or step.
- Avoid leaning, but when leaning is necessary, bend at the knees.
- Wear low-heeled shoes. High heels force increased lower back curve to compensate for the forward slant of the shoes.
- Sit so the back is flat, not with a forward curve, preferably with the knees slightly higher than the hips. Try to have a chair that is sized properly to allow sitting in this position. Ideal chair height is low enough for knees to be higher than hips with both feet firmly on the floor. Seat backs are best when they are hard, in contact with the back starting no more than 4–6 inches above the seat, providing flat support at least to the bottom of the shoulder blades.
- Sleep on a firm mattress, with the body partly curled to help reduce the curve in the back. Avoid sleeping prone; sleeping on the back is alright if the legs or knees are elevated.
- Lifting is part of a caregiver's job. To lift correctly, bend the knees, tuck in the buttocks, and pull in the abdominal muscles. Hold the child (or object) as close to the body as possible. Avoid twisting when either lifting or lowering a child. If a child is too heavy or is in an awkward position for lifting, change the arrangement. Have the child step up on a stool for a hug; move the child closer before lifting or ask for help to share the lifting task.
- Avoid standing for long periods holding a child on the hip. Doing so both increases the curvature of the back and puts sideways strain on the back muscles.

Other physical problems that beset caregivers are especially troublesome to pregnant workers. Swollen feet and varicose veins are the result of increased pressure in the blood vessels of the lower body. The best remedy for this problem is exercise and frequent changes in position. Putting the feet up at every opportunity and wearing support hose will help.

Hemorrhoids are a problem common to pregnant women and adults over 40 years of age. They are caused by pooling of blood in the blood vessels just inside the anus. The distended blood vessels then fall outside the anal opening. They can hurt and may bleed. Problems with hemorrhoids can be reduced by eating lots of high-fiber foods to keep the stools soft, drinking lots of liquids, and avoiding prolonged standing or sitting in one position. If leg swelling or hemorrhoids are a continuing problem, medical advice should be sought.

Caring for young children is physically and emotionally demanding. In addition to the usual requirements of supervision of children during the workday, caregivers are often asked to work overtime to attend meetings, prepare curricula, and participate in fund-raising or other special projects. If sustained high expectations of the job are coupled with inadequate physical fitness, illness, or a small increase in personal or family needs, a caregiver can easily become overwhelmed. Some of these problems can be prevented; some can be kept from becoming major problems if they are handled promptly and appropriately. Without support to address occupational health problems, caregivers can easily lose their enthusiasm, become exhausted or ill, and leave.

In addition to the mental health, exercise, and hazard reduction efforts needed on the job, caregivers will benefit from a general wellness program. Many employers have found that promoting and rewarding wellness activities results in improved worker satisfaction and productivity. Smoking cessation, exercise, weight control, and stress management programs all pay off. Child care programs can foster participation of staff in such programs by sharing the cost of enrollment in the fitness program between the staff and the program, fostering competition among the staff, giving special awards for achievement of health goals, making the child care facility available after hours for the conduct of fitness programs, and recognizing physical fitness as a part of routine staff evaluation.

How Administrators Can Help Keep Staff Well

In addition to setting up a wellness program for staff, administrators can help promote staff health with appropriate policies, caregiver education, furnishings, and supplies. Adults with significant symptoms need to be able to stay home during the initial phases of illness to rest and shorten the total time they are below par. Adult-size tables and chairs should be provided for staff to use when doing curriculum work and for staff meetings. Space for private adult time and scheduling of genuine breaks are essential. Provide trained substitutes, parents, or volunteers to relieve caregivers on a staggered basis so that committed caregivers need not feel guilty when they take breaks or necessary time away from their classrooms. Watch for times of stress in the personal and classroom lives of caregivers and provide extra support for those times.

Emergency contact information must be available for staff so that next of kin can be contacted in the event of a sudden medical problem or injury. Medical information about any special health problems that might affect medical management in an emergency should be recorded in staff health records. Confidentiality must be maintained for all medical information, but access to key facts must be provided in a situation in which the staff person is unconscious or is otherwise unable to give necessary information.

For child care administrators, addressing the needs of caregivers is an integral part of assuring the quality of care for children in the program. Unless the staff are well nurtured, they cannot nurture the children. Caring is contagious; a caring administrator spreads an attitude of concern for the needs of others among staff, who will in turn tend to express this attitude toward co-workers, children, and parents. The level of caring in a program shows in touches of concern for the personal needs of caregivers as well as in the efforts that are directly focused on the children.

SUGGESTED ACTIVITIES

1. Have students check their immunization records for measles, mumps, and rubella to verify that all those born after 1957 had vaccine against these diseases. For measles vaccine, two doses should have been given after 12 months of age. Ask them to check when they had their last booster to diphtheria and tetanus—due every 10 years throughout adult life.

2. Ask students when they last had a health maintenance examination, not just a visit to the doctor for a specific problem. Was it within the past five years?

3. Ask students to check whether their health insurance covers preventive health care and visits to the doctor's office for minor illness.

4. Ask students to practice a stress reduction exercise in class and then practice the exercise daily for a week. Have them report the results after a week of practice.

5. Ask the students to observe for one hour in a child care center and identify worker behaviors that could lead to illness or injury. Make a list of these behaviors as a composite of the reports of all those who observed.

FOR MORE INFORMATION

Almy, Millie. Day Care and Early Childhood Education. In *Day Care: Scientific and Social Policy Issues.* Ed. Ziegler, E., and Gordon, E. Boston: Auburn House, 1982.

American Academy of Pediatrics. *School Health: A Guide for Health Professionals.* Elk Grove Village, IL: American Academy of Pediatrics, 1987.

American Academy of Pediatrics. *Report of the Committee on Infectious Diseases.* Elk Grove Village, IL: American Academy of Pediatrics, 1988, p. 170.

American Academy of Pediatrics. *Health in Day Care: A Manual for Professionals.* Elk Grove Village, IL: American Academy of Pediatrics, 1987.

American Academy of Pediatrics/American Public Health Association. *National Reference Standards for Health and Safety in Child Day Care.* Washington, DC: American Public Health Association (to be published in July 1991).

Child Care Employee Project, P.O. Box 5603, Berkeley, CA 94705.

Kendrick, A., Kaufmann, R., and Messenger, K., eds. *Healthy Young Children, a Manual for Programs.* Washington, DC: National Association for the Education of Young Children, 1988.

The Child Care Facility

IN THIS CHAPTER:

CHOOSING THE CHILD CARE SITE
PLANNING AND EVALUATING THE STRUCTURAL DESIGN OF THE FACILITY
SUGGESTED ACTIVITIES
FOR MORE INFORMATION

The design and maintenance of the areas for children and adults to use together require careful thought about how the space is to be used and how it will influence the behavior and feelings of the users. Open spaces invite gross motor activity, while object-filled spaces focus attention on the objects to be seen, touched, or used in some way. Odors, sounds, sights, textures, temperatures, and tastes all play a role in the experiences an environment provides.

Many child care facilities are located in buildings never designed for young children. Churches, stores, warehouses, and office space are being pressed into service as the need for child care exceeds the supply and as inexpensive facilities are sought to keep the cost of child care down. Sometimes, buildings are constructed specifically for child care. Even then, compromises must be made between cost, design constraints, and desired features of a child care facility.

Sometimes child care facilities are designed and constructed in new office buildings.

Factors such as proximity to the population to be served, zoning, and cost play key roles in site selection for child care. However, issues related to health and safety should also be considered. Areas with high levels of air pollution, loud noises, or heavy traffic should be avoided. Safe pedestrian routes that allow caregivers and children to go exploring in the neighborhood are important, as are safe pick-up and drop-off points for vehicle travel.

The size of the site will determine the size of the facility that can be constructed or used for child care, and the square footage of the indoor facility is usually the primary constraint that governs the maximum number of children who can be in care in the child care facility at any one time.

Indoor Space

Child Care Centers At least 35 square feet of clear floor space per child is needed for children of any age, exclusive of kitchen, toilet, and sick areas, special areas for care of ill children, offices, staff rooms, hallways, stairways, and storage, laundry, and mechanical equipment areas. Usually, 50 square feet per child measured wall to wall provides space for movement and avoids the increased risk of infectious disease associated with crowding.

Family Day Care Homes and Group Homes The same floor space per child is required as in a center, but because of the nature of the home setting, the eat-in kitchen and open passages may sometimes be counted as usable child care space. The areas of the home used for child care should be easily monitored by the caregiver from any place in the home where she may be.

In planning for use of a residential facility, the areas used by children for sleeping and play should be on the same floor where the caregiver expects to spend most of her time so that she is available to evacuate the children in the event of fire or other emergency. Stairways in homes may quickly fill with smoke in the event of fire, precluding access from one floor to the floors above. Areas used for child care must have two exits to the outside (e.g., a door and a window) in case fire or smoke makes the usual route impassable. Smoke and fire breaks in institutional buildings protect against this problem.

Infants When the same room is used for sleep and for play, a minimum of 25 square feet of space for play and 25 square feet of space for sleeping per child are required. At least 36 inches of corridor space between cribs must be provided for ventilation to prevent airborne transfer of infection and for easy access to infants in an emergency. If separate sleeping rooms are used, 30 square feet per child in the sleeping room is needed.

Toddlers and Preschoolers If cots or mats are stacked or hung when out of use, a minimum of 35 square feet of clear floor space per child is required. If cots or beds are left in place in a room that is used both for sleeping and playing, a minimum of 55 square feet of space is needed to provide sufficient play area and permit placement of beds with 3-foot separations between them. Separate sleep rooms for toddlers and preschoolers should be planned with a minimum of 30 square feet of space per child.

School-age Children A quiet space for uninterrupted work on school projects or hobbies should be provided where younger children will not have access to small parts or art materials that could pose a choking or toxic hazard.

Outdoor Space

The size of the site should also provide enough adjacent outdoor space to maintain amply spaced play centers separated by natural or other barriers that allow children to enter the necessary safety zones around equipment in ways that avoid injury. Generally, a minimum of 75 square feet per child for the number of children using the outdoor play area at any one time will suffice. The soil in and around the outdoor play area should be checked for the presence of lead and any toxic chemicals or materials that the previous or nearby use of the land suggests might be present. The presence of stray or unleashed animals should be considered as well.

Infants Only 33 square feet of outdoor space per child is needed.

Toddlers Only 50 square feet of outdoor space per child is needed.

School-age Children Safe access to community resources such as libraries, school activity centers, and bike routes is an important consideration.

Space for safe drop-off and pick-up zones and for parking of cars, vans, and delivery trucks is also needed.

PLANNING AND EVALUATING THE STRUCTURAL DESIGN OF THE FACILITY

Facilities used for child care usually have to meet many local and state requirements for building and fire safety, sanitation, and zoning. Some of these requirements were written to apply to buildings used for purposes other than child care. Unfortunately, public authorities may not appreciate that child care in a home setting differs significantly from care of an adult in a boarding home and that child care centers are unlike hospitals or schools. More communities are beginning to use regulations written specifically for child care facilities. While variances from the requirements can sometimes be obtained, the rationale for any requirement from which a waiver is being sought must be thoroughly understood to be sure an alternative approach achieves the intended safeguard.

Climate

A good facility is one where the structure serves the program well in the location. For example, consideration must be given to climate in choosing the placement of windows where sun will warm and brighten rooms at different times of the day during different seasons. In some locations, buildings

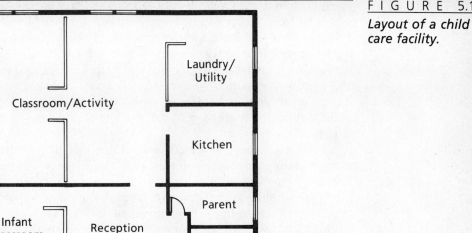

FIGURE 5.1
*Layout of a child
care facility.*

that are partially below grade may provide protection from severe temperature fluctuations, but below-grade installations require special attention to fire escape routes and control of high levels of humidity, which tends to foster the growth of mold.

Plumbing

One of the most important and often most costly features of the facility is the placement of sinks, toilets, and water outlets. Drinking water should always be available to children and adults, especially outdoors on warm days. Having a water outlet outdoors provides an easy way to cool off on hot days and clean up before bringing outdoor messes inside. If an outdoor fountain and hose outlet cannot be provided, an alternative approach is to bring drinking water outside in a thermos container with cups and to bring a bucket of water outside for washing up.

Frequent hand washing in child care is essential to preventing the spread of infectious disease. Hand-washing facilities must be readily accessible, preferably in every child care room, but at least in an easily accessible location that is not separated from the child care area by doors or other barriers. These facilities must not require that the adult leave the other children to supervise a child who is using the sink or to wash her own hands. Every diaper-changing area must have an associated, adjacent hand-washing sink. Sinks used to clean the facility and objects or children contaminated by body fluids must be separated from those used to prepare food or to wash up for eating. If separate sinks are not available, the sink must be sanitized between uses, an extraordinary burden in a busy child care day.

A faucetless sink has been developed that may help prevent the problem of accummulating germs on faucet handles. The water is activated when a person standing in front of the sink reflects a light beam produced by a source on the wall over the sink or under the tap. Because the user does not have to turn the tap on or off, this source of contamination of clean hands is eliminated. Single-lever faucets work well if they are turned off with the wrist rather than the hand that will later touch food and other surfaces. If a faucet that requires handling is used, a paper towel can be used to turn off the faucet and avoid soiling clean hands.

Unless the hot water supply has been adjusted to deliver hot water at or below 110–120 degrees Fahrenheit, all hand-washing sinks should be installed on lines that include a thermoregulatory valve that limits the maximum hot water temperature to this level. If adults cannot tolerate the temperature of the water when they keep their hands under the running stream of hot water, the water is over 120 degrees Fahrenheit and too hot for children.

Sinks need to be supplied with towel holders and liquid soap dispensers located at levels where the intended users can easily reach them. When children must reach for towels or soap, they will either forget to use them or drip water everywhere while reaching for them. Water on the floor around sink areas makes slippery spots where injuries can occur.

Toilet facilities will be needed often by young children, not just at prescribed times in the curriculum when trips to the toilet are planned. For very young children, toilets must be close at hand to all activities, including outdoor play.

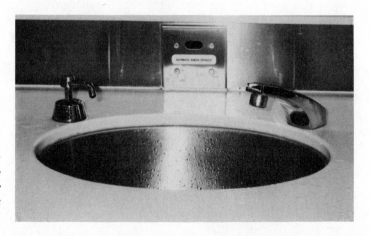

Sinks with faucets that are operated by an electric eye reduce the spread of germs from dirty hands.

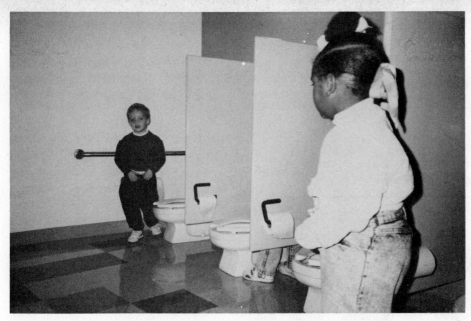

Toilet facilities should be child-sized and easily visible to care-givers at all times.

Location of toilets in child care deserves careful attention and planning. To limit the circumstances under which sexual abuse has occurred in child care and to ensure that young children are adequately supervised while around toilets, privacy in toilet areas where children require assistance should be limited. Doors to toilet rooms used by toddlers and young preschoolers who may need assistance with toileting should be removed. Close supervision of toilet areas accessible to toddlers is also important because toddlers have drowned in toilet bowls. Out-of-sight, back corners are not good locations for toilets.

Some separation of toilet and diaper-changing areas from areas where food is prepared or eaten is essential because the concentration of germs is usually greater in toilet and diapering areas than anywhere else. Toilet paper should be easily accessible to children so they do not have to climb off the toilet to reach the paper.

The minimum number of toilets needed is usually specified in state regulations. Ratios of 1 toilet to 10 users are commonly cited, but no objective data are available to determine the optimum number. One toilet to every five users is much more comfortable and easier to maintain than the 1 : 10 minimum ratio included in many state regulations. Portable toilets, potty chairs, and training chairs pose such a great sanitation hazard that they should not be used in child care. If they are used, each use must be followed by cleaning, sanitization with a bleach-water solution, and air drying. The alternative is cleaning and sanitization in a commercial bedpan-cleaning device. Because of the extra staff time and trouble that use of training chairs requires, child care programs are better off using child-size flushing toilets or stepstools with regular flushing toilets. Toilet paper holders must be installed within the reach of the intended users to avoid having children get off the toilet with a dripping bottom to get to the paper.

Bathing Facilities

Having a laundry tub or bathing area where a child can easily be cleaned is handy when diapers or underpants overflow or when a child is covered with paint, mud, or vomit. Bathing facilities should be located away from food preparation and eating areas. A hot water control device should be put on the hot water line supplying any tub used for bathing so that the hot water temperature cannot exceed 110–120 degrees Fahrenheit.

Food Preparation and Eating Areas

When meals or snacks will be prepared in the child care facility, a separate kitchen is required that is not used for play or as a passageway while food is being prepared. Because good advance planning can avoid many problems, a sanitarian and nutritionist should be consulted about how to set up this area. Food preparation area surfaces will be sanitized repeatedly during the day. Cracks, crevices, and porous surfaces that can harbor food and grow germs must be eliminated. Storage areas with off-the-floor shelves to permit easy cleaning and viewing of any evidence of vermin are required. Special provision is needed for fire safety around cooking equipment.

When food is brought from home, adequate space should be provided for refrigeration of perishable items, with access to the refrigerators for parents to put these items away as soon as they arrive.

Infants The sanitation requirements of formula, food preparation, and storage of foods require special provisions. Refrigerators and food warmers need to be close to the feeding locations so that caregivers can prepare food when an infant seems hungry. Microwave heating of infant food is not recommended because of the potential for the foods to be overheated or to continue to heat while the food containers feel cool.

Family Day Care Homes The usual household kitchen may need modification to meet current sanitation guidelines. Wood chopping blocks and cooking tools are notorious places for germs to lurk. Although mechanical dishwashers are best, dishwashing by hand can suffice if air drying of all dishes is used. Dish towels are germ spreaders and should not be used.

Laundry and Dishwashing

Many facilities will find laundry equipment useful for washing and drying soiled toys, articles of clothing, throws, pillows, and other desirable soft elements in the child care setting. However, the laundry must be located where soiled clothing will not contaminate food preparation areas. Similarly, the availability of a dishwasher to wash mouthed toys as well as tableware that is not disposable, and infant bottles, is a great timesaver. Dishwashers should have booster heaters that raise the temperature of the water used to sanitize the dishes to at least 170 degrees Fahrenheit.

Windows and Vision Panels

Windows and vision panels are needed to provide access to daylight and ventilation. They also provide the psychological and curricular benefits of viewing the activities and weather outdoors; windows that can be opened also allow children to smell seasonal changes in odors. Rooms used for play, work, and sleep should have a total window area of at least 10 percent of the floor area. At least some of these windows should be operable for ventilation, but all windows that can be opened will require safeguards to keep them from being opened wide enough to allow a child to fall out (an opening of less than 6 inches) and screens to prevent insects and rodents from entering the building.

Toilet rooms and kitchens need not have as much window area as other parts of the facility, but ventilation must be provided in these areas by operable windows or exhaust fans. If operable windows cannot be provided, mechanical ventilation that circulates the air volume of the room every hour is necessary. In some areas, the poor quality of outdoor air makes mechanical ventilation and air cleaning preferable.

Heating, Ventilation, and Humidity

Most people think of heat, humidity, and ventilation as it relates to comfort, but these features of the environment have a significant impact on health as well. Excessive heat results in increased fluid losses as the body uses evaporation of perspiration to keep the body temperature normal. Inadequate heat requires use of energy to keep the body warm, taking energy that would be used otherwise. The temperature of a child care facility should be measured at the level where the children play and work, often within 2 or 3 feet from the floor. A comfortable temperature range lies between 68–75 degrees Fahrenheit. To safely achieve this comfort zone where children play and sleep, heat and air conditioning sources must be carefully located to prevent children from coming into contact with hot surfaces and excessive flow of air. Thermometers to measure the temperature in child care areas should be located on interior walls at child height, usually with protective plastic covers to prevent children from playing with them.

Wood stoves, kerosene heaters, and fuel-burning space heaters are unhealthy. Fuel-burning space heaters use oxygen from the room in which they are located and release some products of combustion into the air around them. Although this happens with the air around a furnace in a mechanical room, the air involved is not immediately shared with the people being warmed.

Adequate ventilation reduces the concentration of germs in the air, thus diminishing the challenge to the immune systems of those breathing in the area. With operable windows, caregivers can bring fresh air into the room at least once a day. Operable windows make it possible to use fresh air to dilute undesirable odors and to ventilate when mechanical systems break down. Mechanical systems that have zoned thermostats and positive pressure air flow are ideal. These systems provide maximum comfort and, by circulating air from each child care room to the outside, keep germs such as the chickenpox virus from migrating from room to room with the air flow. The recommended ventilation for children's classrooms is three complete air exchanges per hour.

Humidity also plays an important role in comfort and resistance to infection. When cold, dry outdoor air is heated, it has an increased ability to hold moisture. The heated, dry air acts like a sponge, drawing water from all sources of moisture in the environment. Mucous membranes that line the nose, mouth, and throat require maintenance of a moist surface to keep their protective mechanisms operating. When these membranes come in contact with heated, dry air, infection occurs more easily. On the other hand, when the humidity rises above 70 percent on a hot day, the body has trouble evaporating perspiration off the skin fast enough to keep the body cool, resulting in overheating and heat-related illness. Maintenance of comfortable levels of humidity, generally 40–60 percent, is important to health.

Doors, Landings, and Door Swing Space

Doors opening into or out of areas where small children are in care should be fitted with vision panels that allow view of children who might be right against the door on either side. Sometimes doors are designed to open into rooms rather than into corridors or onto landing areas at the top of stairs. This design prevents disruption of the flow of traffic in the hallway or pushing someone down the stairs by opening the door. In the best design, all doors have sufficient swing space outside the door to open

FIGURE 5.2

Door with child and adult level vision panels and finger pinch protection.

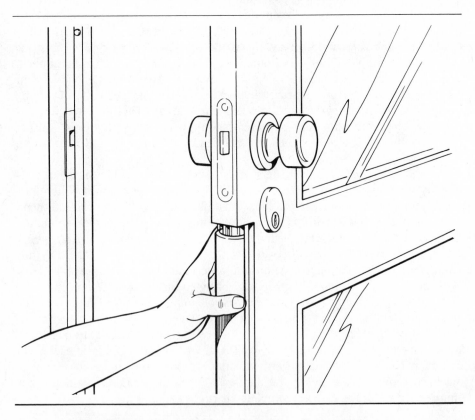

outward, in the direction of exit. Whenever possible, have doors open outward into recessed areas off the corridor, or onto wide landing spaces at the top of stairs, to provide a safe emergency exit from the room.

By installing closing devices on doors that limit the speed at which the door closes, fewer instances of smashed fingers will occur. These are the type of closing devices commonly found on screen doors in homes and routinely installed in many institutional settings. Another way to prevent fingers from being pinched in doors is to cut 1 to 2 inches from the door edge from the floor to about two-thirds of the way up the door from the floor (excluding the location of the hinge), filling this space with a rubber gasket. If the door latch is mounted above the level of the cutout, very young children cannot open the door and leave the supervised area unnoticed. Another approach to guarding the door hinge surface of the door is to mount a strip of indoor-outdoor carpeting on the door and on the adjacent door jamb with a strip of molding on each side. The carpeting should lay flush when the door is closed. When the door is open, the carpeting will buckle but prevent finger access to the space.

Doors in toilet rooms and closets must be openable by children from the inside and by adults from the outside to prevent entrapment of children in these spaces. Closet doors and doors that open into any area unsafe for unsupervised entry by children should be fitted with safety devices to keep a child from using the doors. Simple devices will suffice. For example, many hardware stores sell

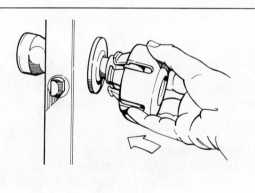

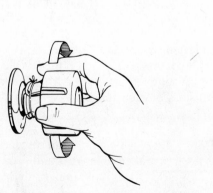

FIGURE 5.3
A safety door-knob cover.

plastic knobs which, when placed over a standard round door knob, will slip as a young child tries to palm the door knob open but can be easily grasped and opened by an adult grip across the knob.

Exit Doors

Some child care facilities are located in areas where security is a problem. Even in the nicest neighborhood, unmonitored entrance of a stranger into the facility can result in tragic consequences. Hardware installed on the exit doors should limit access from the outside to a single monitored entrance while maintaining readiness for emergency exit from the inside at all times. Except in family day care homes, panic hardware should be installed on all doors.

Glass

Any glass in windows, mirrors, or doors within kicking distance of the floor (approximately 32 inches) should be made of a shatter-resistant plastic material or a safety-grade glass and be protected by mesh or other means to reduce breakage and injury. Decals placed on large glass panels will help alert people to the presence of the glass and prevent the smashed noses and broken glass that can occur just after these panels are freshly cleaned.

Stairs, Porches, Platforms, and Balconies

Elevated surfaces in a child care facility are areas where injury can be expected to occur. Any surface elevated a distance equal to or higher than the waist of the user requires a guardrail. This rule of thumb has been applied in industrial settings for adult safety and is equally applicable to facilities for children. Falls to hard surfaces are a common source of injury for children in child care. The majority of these falls are preventable.

Protective railings and handrails must be placed at a height easily grasped by the users; sometimes more than one handrail may be required on a stairway. The handrails must be constructed in conjunction with the other elements of the stairwell so that the rails do not serve as climbing bars to launch a child out of the stairway. The space between the slats or spindles on open stairways should not be greater than $3\frac{1}{2}$ inches to prevent entrapment of a child's head.

Because most people are right-handed, at least one handrail on stairs and steps should be located on the right, descending side. Right-handed adults often carry packages and children balanced on the left hip, leaving the right hand free to steady themselves, open doors, and so forth. Preferably, a handrail should be installed on both sides of each stairway.

Surfaces and Finishes

Because child care facilities are exposed to considerable wear and tear, the finishes used should be durable and easily cleaned. If carpeting is used, hypoallergenic, short-pile, tightly woven, stain-resistant, easily cleaned synthetic types are best. Painted surfaces will hold up better to the repeated washing required in child care if epoxy or enamel paints are used. Wallpapers made of scrubbable substances are sensible. Most walls will need cleaning at some time, even if only to remove the residue of the adhesives almost always used to hang up children's work, notices, and other objects. Toilet room floors and walls need daily cleaning and periodic sanitization with a diluted bleach solution. The materials used for these surfaces must be able to stand up to such vigorous hygiene. Floors throughout the facility should be easily cleaned. New materials are available that are sound absorbing, nonporous, and cushioning, thus making excellent flooring for the entire child care facility. All materials and surfaces, including insulation, must be of nontoxic substances.

Noise Control

Noise pollution is one of the greatest sources of stress in the child care setting. Some degree of control can be achieved with acoustical ceiling tiles, sound sponges mounted on walls or partitions, carpeting on floors and walls, and other sound-absorbing wall, floor, ceiling, and window coverings. Good sound absorbers are often porous. These must be easily cleaned so that they do not hold dust and soil.

Sound transmission also affects ambient noise. Sound transmission is reduced by sealing cracks between partitions and closing gaps between partitions and the ceiling. Ventilation ducts may act as conduits of noise but can be insulated and designed to reduce this problem.

High ceilings and large rooms tend to aggravate noise problems; heating and cooling may be more difficult in tall spaces as well. However, very low ceilings may make ventilation and storage a problem and may limit variation in the use of space. A ceiling height of around 10 feet is a good compromise.

Lighting

Lighting must be tailored to the activity. Bright fluorescent lighting is not conducive to relaxation and rest at naptime. Dimly lit rooms make close inspection of pictures, reading of fine print, and working with small items difficult. Meters that measure illumination in footcandles are often available from photographers and architects. Lighting fixtures are sold with information about the amount of light they are expected to provide. The usually recommended amounts of light by type of activity are listed in Table 5.1. Emergency lighting must always be available. In institutional settings, special fixtures mounted on

For reading, drawing, and close work—About 50 footcandles at the work surface
For play—About 30 footcandles
For stairs, halls, driveways, and entrances—About 20 footcandles on the surface
For sleeping areas—5 footcandles or less during use

T A B L E   5.1
RECOMMENDED ILLUMINATION BY TYPE OF ACTIVITY

recharging battery boxes are usually required by building codes. In other settings, readily available flashlights need to be kept on hand.

Electrical Outlets and Fixtures

Child care facilities can be constructed with child-resistant electrical outlets and switches that are mounted above the reach of toddlers. Hardware stores sell several devices to cover accessible outlets so as to protect young children against shock. Use of extension cords should be avoided, since young children have been known to chew on cords and thereby receive severely damaging burns to the mouth. Placement of extension cords under carpeting or behind objects can cause a fire if wires overheat.

Communication Systems

Telephone contact has become commonplace. Not only does readily accessible phone service provide for improved communication with parents, it also serves as a safety line to obtain help in an emergency. With new portable telephones and two-way radios becoming affordable, these devices will increasingly become standard equipment to be taken along when the caregiver takes children away from the usual telephone system used by the child care program.

Swimming and Wading

When children bathe or swim, many pass urine or bowel gas, bringing germs into the water. Children also swallow or at least mouth the water in which they play. As a result, swimming activities pass germs from one child to another. To reduce this risk, pools are chemically treated and tested frequently. Portable wading pools and water that is not tested and treated to maintain sanitary standards must be limited to use by one child, emptied and refilled for another child to use.

Drowning is a major cause of death in children ages 1–4. Between 5–20 percent of children who are hospitalized for near drowning suffer severe brain damage. Drowning can occur in only minutes. Because pools are associated with many episodes of drowning, several safety measures are required if pools are present on the premises:

- The pool should be surrounded by a 5-foot or higher fence on all four sides of the pool, with a secure, alarmed, self-closing gate that has a latch out of the reach of a small child. The fence should not restrict a clear view of the pool.
- No floating objects should be left in the pool to attract young children.
- No flotation devices should be used for children who cannot swim without maintaining one-to-one supervision.
- Child-resistant pool covers with alarms to alert adults of unsupervised pool entry should be in place when the pool is not in use.
- A nonskid surface must surround the pool.

□ Every adult in the facility must have current certification in infant-child cardiopulmonary resuscitation (CPR).

Adequate pool supervision by caregivers qualified in water safety and rescue techniques requires high staff/child ratios, 1 : 1 for infants, 1 : 2 for toddlers, 1 : 4 for preschoolers, and 1 : 6 for school-age children. Because of sanitation and supervision problems, many child care programs will wisely choose sprinkler play to cool off and have fun with water during hot weather.

Garbage and Solid Waste

Child care programs generate a lot of trash. Disposable diapers from infant care, disposable food service items, art project debris, and many other items are discarded daily. Some of this material attracts insects, rodents, and other pests. To minimize the hazard posed by the handling of waste, child care programs should use garbage and rubbish receptacles made of metal or other materials that do not leak, absorb liquids, or permit entry by animals or insects. Odor-tight containers, such as plastic bags, placed inside the main container will help, but some method of cleaning and sanitizing refuse containers is needed. Having a hose bib nearby to wash down the containers and the area is helpful. Easy access for refuse pick-up services must be planned to avoid areas where children might be at play. Garbage storage should be as far as possible from areas where children will play.

SUGGESTED ACTIVITIES

1. Conduct a site survey of an operating child care program to see how well the facility meets the recommended guidelines in this chapter. Where there are differences, discuss how modifications could be made within reasonable limits of cost and effort. What options are there? What compromises could be made?

FOR MORE INFORMATION

American Academy of Pediatrics/American Public Health Association. *Health and Safety Standards for Child Day Care Programs.* Washington, DC: American Public Health Association, 1990.

Greenman, Jim. *Caring Spaces, Learning Places:* *Children's Environments That Work.* Redmond, WA: Exchange Press, 1988.

Kendrick, A., Kaufmann, R., and Messenger, K., eds. *Healthy Young Children, A Manual for Programs.* Washington, DC: National Association for the Education of Young Children, 1988.

6

Riding, Walking, and Playground Safety

Injury, not disease, is the leading cause of death for children after the first year of life. The causes of injury vary by the developmental level of the children involved, as shown in Table 6.1.

Injury control is best accomplished by measures that require no active thinking or conscious choices. For example, designing driveways that do not cross pedestrian walkways is a more effective means of preventing children from being struck by cars than teaching children to scan for cars before crossing driveways. When no passive means of control of risk is possible, the people to be protected not only must learn about safe behaviors but must practice these safe behaviors until they become routines. Breaks in safe behaviors are more likely to occur when the rationale for the desired behavior is not well understood and when the desired behavior is not reinforced on a regular basis.

Infants (children from birth until they walk)
    Car related, as passengers
    Burns and house fires
    Falls
    Choking with suffocation or strangulation
Toddlers (children who are walking but have not yet achieved toilet training), and
Preschoolers (children who are toilet trained but have not yet reached the age of mandatory schooling)
    Car related, as passengers and pedestrians
    Burns and house fires
    Drowning
    Choking
    Falls
    Poisoning
Young school-age children (5–9 years of age)
    Car related, as passengers and pedestrians
    Burns and house fires
    Drowning
    Bicycles
    Falls

T A B L E   6.1
PRIMARY CAUSES OF INJURY BY DEVELOPMENTAL LEVEL

Times of stress are known to be associated with increased risk of injury. Hunger, fatigue, new situations, illness, excessive demands for attention, and lack of attention to known risks for the child's developmental age all contribute to the likelihood of injury. Some children are more injury prone. Boys are known to be injured more frequently than girls, even when activity level is taken into account. Surprisingly, increased activity level by itself does not seem to increase the risk of injury, and more timid children are injured more often than those who are more confident. Toddlers experience higher rates of injury than children at other developmental levels.

Living safely does not mean living without risk taking. The challenge of risk taking is a force that promotes learning for children; all child care environments are places where children learn. Whether the setting is a family day care home, child care center, nursery school, before-school program, after-school program, or summer program, children are receiving cognitive and behavioral education about life. One of the most important lessons children can learn is how to manage risk so that they can enjoy productive, creative experiences while avoiding exposure to the risk of serious injury. For example, children need safe surfaces under climbing equipment and lessons on how to climb safely. Safety does not need to be ensured by keeping children from climbing.

Several studies have examined whether children experience more or fewer injuries per unit of time in child care than they do when they are not in child care. Most of these studies have found that children experience medically treatable injuries in child care programs at the same rate or less frequently than in other settings. Although the majority of injuries that children experience in child care are minor, the ones that are serious enough to require medical attention most often occur in gross motor play areas, on playground equipment.

For children in child care, injuries occur more frequently in late morning than at any other time of day. This finding makes sense, since late morning is the most common time for gross motor play in the usual child care curriculum. Injury rates are also affected by the season of the year, with fall being the most common time when injuries occur. This finding is also logical, since fall is the season for vigorous outdoor play and a time when many child care programs have new staff and new children entering the program. New children and staff may be less likely to adhere to safety routines than those who have been in the program a long time.

For children in child care, the most common injuries requiring medical treatment are falls to hard surfaces, followed by a variety of injuries on playground equipment, injuries from interactions between children with hand toys and blocks, and injuries related to doors, indoor floor surfaces, and motor vehicles. The most common types of wounds children in child care receive are scrapes and bruises, most often to the head, face, forehead, and upper extremities. Although many of these wounds require no more than first aid, some are serious enough to require emergency room care and hospitalization. Some body injury is a part of experimenting and failing, but serious injury is not a good teaching method.

As many as three-fourths of all injuries occurring in child care are easily preventable. Lack of adequate supervision plays a secondary, but important, role to removal or modification of obvious hazards. When child care centers and

The most common cause of injury in child care is falls to the playground surface from equipment.

family day care homes are surveyed by self-inspection or by outside inspectors, well-recognized hazards are commonly found. Some examples of findings from recent surveys include: tap water available to children above scalding temperature, exposed space heaters, unsafe playground surfaces, unguarded stairs, lack of information for handling emergencies, and accessible poisons. Accidents don't just happen; safety requires constant vigilance and surveillance.

Comfort, challenge, learning, and warmth must be preserved while risks are controlled. The goal of safety activity is to eliminate the risk of serious injury and minimize the risk of minor injury to the extent consistent with the overall goals of the program. Fortunately, the choices are not of the ''either-or'' nature. Instead, creative planning can preserve the opportunities for fun and learning while reducing or limiting risk.

MOTOR VEHICLE INJURIES

More children are killed in car accidents than in any other way. Each year, more than 3000 children under the age of 15 die as a result of motor vehicle accidents, while less than half as many in this age group die from cancer, the next leading cause of death. In about half of the deaths involving motor

The cargo space of a station wagon is a very dangerous place to ride.

vehicles, the children are passengers in the vehicles; in the other half, the children are injured as pedestrians. Over 50,000 children are injured as passengers in motor vehicles; 80 percent of these injuries involve the head or face. The leading cause of epilepsy, brain damage, spinal cord injuries, and mental retardation is car crashes.

A Safe Ride

The majority of motor vehicle passenger injuries are preventable through the use of age-appropriate seat restraints and close attention to driver training and to drop-off and pick-up routines. No child care program wants to make news with a vehicle-related death.

The motor vehicle fatality rate for children as passengers is closely related to whether safety restraints (car seats or seat belts) are used correctly when children are transported. Decreases in fatality rates in recent years are largely attributed to the increased use of seat restraints for children during this period. All 50 states and the District of Columbia have child restraint laws.

Whether children are being transported by their parents or by child care program staff, they are vulnerable to severe injury from sudden stops, crashes, and ejection from vehicles. Few realize the magnitude of the forces involved. At only 30 miles per hour, a 30-pound 3-year-old child is catapulted from his seat with 900 pounds of force in a sudden stop or crash. There is no way an adult or child can lift 900 pounds, much less resist such enormous forces by using a hand or a foot, even if prepared for the event. No portion of the human body can sustain so much force without significant damage. Think of how a 900-pound weight would crush a 3-year-old child.

Every car crash is followed a split second later by a human collision. Vehicle occupants, adults and children alike, continue their forward motion until their bodies meet a fixed object. Without seat restraints to spread the forces as safely as possible, injury occurs as unprotected heads and bodies strike windshields, dashboards, and road surfaces at highway speeds. Data collected by the National Highway Traffic Safety Administration show that correctly used child restraint devices for young children reduce fatalities by 71 percent and serious injuries by 67 percent. The use of seat belts for older children and adults lowers fatalities and severe injuries by between 40 and 55 percent.

The laws that mandate use of child safety seats vary from one state to another, covering children of different ages, affecting some or all drivers, and requiring different types of restraints in different seating positions. In some states, regulations or laws specifically require that child care programs use child safety seats or seat belts when such devices are available in the vehicle.

All child passenger safety restraint devices manufactured after 1981 have met national crash test standards and are labeled for use as car seats. No other type of device should be used. Studies of the use of seat restraints consistently find that over 70 percent of cars with young children have the devices, but nearly three-fourths of them are used incorrectly. The most common forms of misuse are having a car seat but not buckling the child into it properly or at all, not having infants rearward facing, and improper routing of the safety belt that holds the car seat in the car.

Child care programs have three roles to play in reducing the toll from motor vehicle passenger injuries: (1) advocate safe transport of children by parents and others, (2) transport children safely, and (3) educate young children about how to be safe riders. Each of these roles provides an opportunity for integration of child passenger safety with other activities in the child care program.

Advocating Safe Transport of Children Child care programs are almost always involved in some way in transporting children. At the very least, parents bring children to and from the program daily. This provides an ideal opportunity to observe whether parents are using child safety seats or seat belts and using them correctly.

Part of the orientation procedure for new families should include a review of transportation arrangements, including a checklist provided by the program to the parents giving safe ride pointers. On the first day the child attends the program, a staff member should be available to check whether the child arrives and leaves the program safely restrained. Some parents may require demonstrations and instruction on how to correct unsafe practices. The child care program should also routinely schedule staff to assist parents with unbuckling and buckling children into their safety restraints. During arrival and departure times, extra hands may be needed to take children out of their seat restraints, safely secure them, or escort them to and from vehicles. Staff support is especially important for parents who are tempted by rushed morning and evening routines to make unwise choices about buckling up the children.

For Infants Under 20 Pounds An infant or convertible car seat should be used for infants under 20 pounds. The safety seat should be placed with the infant facing the rear of the vehicle (back toward the dashboard). This position allows the forces that occur on stopping to be distributed over the largest area of the infant's body. The harness straps must be adjusted and fastened over the child's shoulders and pelvic area, with as little clothing between the child's body and the restraint as practical. Bulky snowsuits and blankets may prevent the straps from holding the child's body as intended. When needed, blankets and buntings should be put around the child after the harness is adjusted. The infant car safety seat must be properly installed in the vehicle with a snugly fastened lap belt.

Passive restraints and some inertia-activated seat belts (belts that retract only in an emergency) will not work. If there is no regular seat belt with which to secure the car safety seat, a regular seat belt may need to be installed or a locking clip may be required to convert an inertia-activated belt into a stable mounting for a child safety seat.

Toddlers and Preschool-age Children over 20 Pounds There are many alternative child safety devices available for these children. Ideally, a federally approved child safety seat restraint should be used by all children under 40 pounds or less than 4 years of age. Convertible seats are popular because they serve children from infancy through 4 years of age. These seats are bulkier and heavier than seats made just for infants but involve less cost than buying a seat for

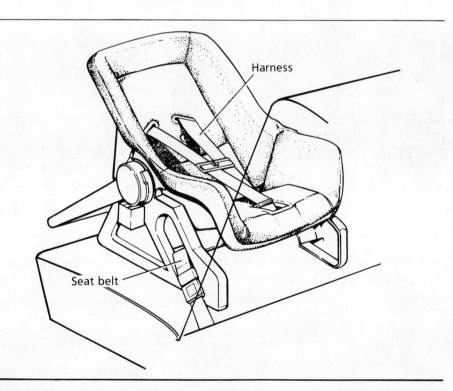

Harness

Seat belt

F I G U R E 6.1

Infant seat in rear-facing position.

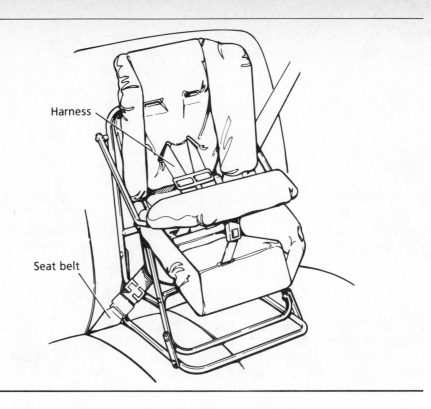

infants then another seat when the child reaches 20 pounds. They are a best buy for parents of newborns.

Some of the least costly and most convenient seats for toddlers and pre-schoolers are booster seats and shields. The shields require only the conventional lap belt and need the least amount of time per child to use. Some booster seats require the use of a vehicle lap belt combined with a harness that must be tethered with a toggle bolt into the vehicle; other seats must be used with an adult type lap-shoulder belt combination. The booster seats are among the most likely devices to be misused. The problem is that unless the booster seat is used with an upper-body restraint as well as the vehicle lap belt, the booster may increase the amount of head excursion in an accident.

Booster seats and shields are popular with child care programs because they are inexpensive, lightweight, adaptable to the widest range of child sizes (usually 20 to 55 or 60 pounds), and take up the least amount of room in the vehicle. Most booster and toddler seats increase the child's ability to see out the vehicle windows and are designed for use until the child grows big enough to see out without the device. This feature has been found to improve significantly children's behavior while they ride and is a good selling point for use of car seats both to parents and to caregivers.

School-age Children and Adults For anyone over 4 years of age or weighing more than 40 pounds, a regular seat belt can be used. There is no evidence

FIGURE 6.3
*Booster car seat
for older pre-
schoolers.*

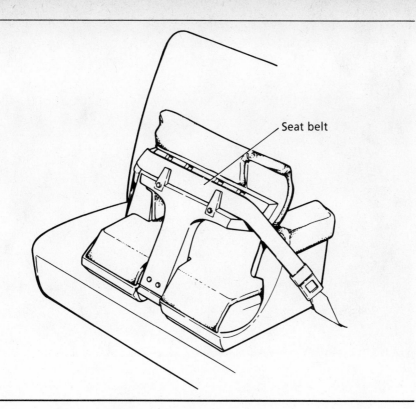

Seat belt

that using an adult shoulder harness-type belt for a child results in increased injury. As long as the strap does not cross the child's face and can be adjusted for comfort over the neck, the shoulder position of a belt should always be used.

Everyone should buckle up; seat belts keep occupants from hitting each other, and they keep the driver in place and in control of the vehicle. Of the people killed in car crashes, 95 percent were not wearing a seat belt. Unbuckled occupants are five times as likely to die and three times as likely to be injured as a buckled person in the same crash. Even when airbags are present, the seat belt provides added protection against side impact and keeps the passenger in front of the airbag.

The safest place for anyone to ride is in the rear seat, but seat belts or car safety seats should be used in all seating positions. For infants, a rear-facing device in the front seat is acceptable so that the infant can be observed by an adult during the trip. Some states permit the use of lap belts for very young children. Child advocates must emphasize to parents that it is always better to ride restrained than loose. However, permitting the use of seat belts for very young children is a compromise to be used only when a properly designed, correctly installed child safety seat is unavailable. Children must never ride unrestrained, whether in the cargo compartment of station wagons or vans or in any other position in a vehicle.

State laws or regulations may provide additional incentive for compliance with transportation safety procedures. Check to see what is required. Even if

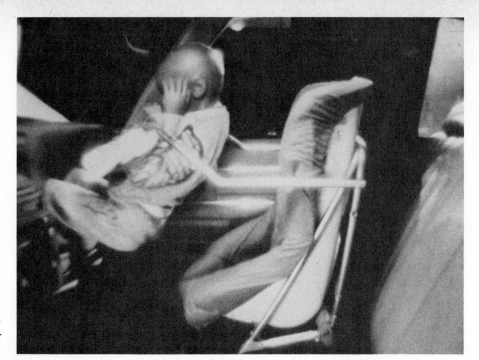

Unrestrained pre-schooler in a car crash.

A safe drop-off area offers curbside access to the facility.

your state law does not cover all drivers or if child care regulations are not specific about safety seats, remind drivers that failure to buckle up children poses an unacceptable risk and could expose the driver to being successfully sued if a child is hurt.

The child care program is responsible for making sure that the drop-off and pick-up points are large enough and sufficiently sheltered from street traffic to protect parents as they buckle and unbuckle their children and carry or walk them from the car and to the program building. Child care programs should provide space for storage of car seats for parents who have only one seat and who use a different car to drop off and pick up the child.

Programs in which parents use car pools to move children between home and child care have special concerns. All drivers must be known to be responsible and willing to ensure that both the children and they themselves regularly buckle up. Whether the parents or the child care program staff make the arrangements, policies should be drafted to cover the following issues:

- rules for car capacity, discipline, and safety restraint use
- policies for driver substitution
- procedures used for drop-off and pick-up
- adequate liability insurance coverage
- responsibility for regular auto maintenance checks on tires, brakes, and steering systems
- driving routes that minimize backing up (to avoid backing over children who run behind the car) and avoid hazardous turns and dangerous intersections
- driving routes that keep travel time down to the tolerance of the riders (no child should have to be in the vehicle more than an hour)
- time schedules that avoid the pressure of loading, unloading, or driving when late
- emergency plans for breakdowns, a problem with a child, a problem with the driver, or bad weather

Some of the rules that make trips go well are listed in Table 6.2.

Transporting Children Safely in Child Care When the child care program is providing the transport, all of the considerations for safe transport by parents apply. In addition, there may be issues related to program liability insurance, training and certification of drivers, availability of first aid supplies and emergency equipment, ready access to emergency contact and medical information in the event of an accident, proper equipment and labeling of vehicles, and permission slips for whatever purpose transportation is being provided. If the child care program provides vehicles, consideration should be given to installing two-way radios so that help can be obtained easily from the vehicle.

School buses are specifically designed for use by school-age children. The seat back heights are intended to compartmentalize children between the seats in the event of a sudden stop if the children are seated properly. Conflicting studies have been reported about the best method to keep children from being injured as passengers in school buses. Although the number of deaths and

1. Pick up and discharge children only at the curb.

2. Have parents put their own children with the car safety seat into the car and buckle them up; reverse the procedure on the return to home.

3. Place all hard objects, such as lunchboxes or things for show-and-tell, on the floor.

4. Close and lock all car doors after checking that all fingers and feet are clear. Inexpensive safety locks are available from auto stores to keep little hands from opening doors, but pose no barrier to an adult.

5. Open passenger windows only a few inches. Turn off power window controls except at the driver's location.

6. Remind the children about the rules of behavior before starting to drive.

7. Make the ride a positive experience. Point out interesting things the children can see while riding. Praise the children often for appropriate behavior and include them in pleasant conversation. Bored children may try to get out of their safety seats or make trouble for the other children. Plan simple games or songs for the trip such as "Who can find a stop sign? a red light? a green light? a truck? a blue car?" The song "The Wheels of the Bus Go Round" is an old favorite.

8. If any child in the group gets out of hand, find a safe place to pull over before you try to discipline anyone. Be firm, state the rules clearly, and praise good behavior. If any child consistently is a problem, exclude the child from group transport.

9. Children can never be left alone in a vehicle. If something happens and the driver needs help, the driver stays with the vehicle until a passerby or police officer can summon assistance.

injuries inside school buses is small relative to the number of miles they travel, use of seat restraints inside school buses improves child behavior, reduces injuries, and carries a lesson for the children.

New York was the first state to mandate installation of seat belts on new school buses. Some local school districts in other states are providing them. Manufacturers and bus drivers often oppose seat belts because they add to the cost of the bus (about $10–$15, an amount equal to the cost of a textbook) and because of unfounded claims about problems with seat belts on buses.

Seat belts should be used on school buses for three reasons. First, they keep children restrained in a rollover or collision, preventing children from being thrown around the interior of the bus. Second, children are being taught to use passenger restraints in family cars. This message and habit are reinforced when the children ride in seat belts in school and child care vehicles. Third, seat belts improve the behavior of children on buses, reducing distractions for the driver and the need for disciplinary action.

The adequacy of school bus safety features for preschool and younger children has not been studied. Buses made after 1977 can be equipped with seat belts for safe transport of young children. The cost for this type of retrofitting is between $10 and $30 per installed belt. Vans often come equipped with lap belts which make it possible to use child safety seats. No vehicles should be used to transport more children than can be safely buckled up.

Children with Medical Problems Children who are unable to sit unsupported, have poor head control, or do not fit in conventional safety seats require special arrangements. Some of the modifications include using a blanket roll on both sides of a small infant, rebuilding a part of the restraint system in a way that does not compromise crash-worthiness, installing a vest restraint with one seat belt through the vest and another around a casted leg, and providing special vehicle mountings for children strapped into wheelchairs. These devices are commercially available. Information about them is available from the American Academy of Pediatrics, Elk Grove Village, IL 60009.

Teaching Children to Be Safe Riders Learning passenger safety is one of the most important lessons for a young child. Children need to learn to ride only with drivers they know and to ride only when buckled up. Children can learn how to buckle themselves into safety seats very early and learn to insist that not only they but everyone else in the vehicle buckle up. Children should be taught how to ask for help politely but with determination to be sure that they are buckled up for every ride.

School-age children may enjoy forming and joining a ''Buckle-Up Bug Club'' whose members are entitled to bug anyone who is not buckled up.

Safe, polite riding can be taught with games, flannel boards, songs, story reading, and all of the other modalities so familiar to early childhood educators. A good example of suitable preschool literature is ''When I Ride in a Car,'' by Dorothy Chlad (Children's Press, 1224 West Van Buren St., Chicago, IL 60607). To make safety props for classroom play, visit a junkyard with a sturdy pair of scissors to obtain several seat belts to mount on classroom chairs for safe ''pretend'' rides. To obtain car safety seats for the classroom, seek donations from families whose children have outgrown their seats.

Other Ideas Some child care programs have developed car seat loaner programs for parents. This undertaking requires considerable effort but, given the benefits, is an excellent parent involvement activity. Several of the car seat manufacturers and many local child passenger safety organizations will provide free kits on how to start up and run a car seat loaner program.

The child passenger safety movement is a coalition of all who care about children: government officials, small groups, volunteers, child-oriented organizations and programs of all types, professionals, and parents all seeking to stop needless child passenger injury. All share a common understanding that transporting children without protective seat restraints is dangerous, irresponsible, and unacceptable.

Playgrounds are the most common location of injuries of child care facilities. Safe, exciting, fun playground play occurs when a developmentally

SAFE, FUN PLAYGROUNDS

appropriate outdoor environment is combined with appropriate supervision to support child-initiated learning. Using their own creativity, children can use a well-designed environment for thousands of safe activities. Color, texture, size, and placement and design of structures and backgrounds all affect how safe and effective a playground can be as a learning environment.

Between one-half and two-thirds of all significant injuries in child care programs occur on the playground. The most frequent and most severe injuries are associated with falls onto hard surfaces. As a result of this association, safety-minded organizations have focused their attention on improving playground equipment and playing surfaces.

Determining the Skills and Appropriate Challenges for the Users

The first step is to determine the developmental tasks that the child users can be expected to practice on the playground. Learning is incremental, building one skill on another. Skill building requires some risk taking, but the cost of failure should be kept small.

Interactive behavior becomes more important as children progress from infancy to school age. Infants use each other as environmental objects; young children are more likely to play alone most of the time. By age 5, formal games with increasingly complicated rules are the norm. By school age, solitary play is limited.

Infants Infants sense the world through visual, tactile, auditory, and mouthing experiences. They enjoy varied surfaces, sights, and sounds and can be expected to try to put everything into their mouths. Most infants can persist at one activity for only 15 minutes or so. With the need for frequent changes of scene in mind, a variety of outdoor sensory experiences can be planned for them.

Toddlers As infants become toddlers, they experiment with different kinds of movement and location of their bodies in space. They practice stepping, running, and using stairs and small objects for climbing. Most toddlers are not ready for independent access to standard slides, swings, or climbers. They like to be in charge, but they need their options limited to acceptable alternatives by adults.

Preschoolers Preschoolers build motor skills through experimentation with ever more challenging situations. When they demonstrate proficiency in stair climbing, jumping from low heights (12 inches), and ability to use the "lock grip" (fingers and thumb wrapped around the handhold part of the equipment), they can be allowed access to more challenging playground equipment.

Preschoolers focus much of their play on socialization skills, impulse control, and defining roles. They characteristically mimic activities they see older children and adults doing, sometimes when they lack the necessary skills and safeguards. Their play is based on scenarios drawn from family life and television viewing. (One 3-year-old jumped out of a second-story window. His first word upon waking 24 hours later was "Batman.") Playgrounds for preschoolers should incorporate opportunities to practice motor and socialization skills under the watchful eyes of adults.

School-age Children School-age children are learning about social relationships and the utility of rules. As children grow more mature, organized games and team play become a more important part of outdoor play. Motor skill development, eye-hand-body coordination, and decision-making skills are practiced by school-age children. Some progress more rapidly than others, but the skill levels of all must be accommodated. Older children can learn about growing and tending outdoor plants and become more independent in their responsibility for gardening. Opportunities for small group play as well as more structured larger team activities are important. Time for quiet enjoyment of the sounds, sights, odors, and feel of the outdoors is desirable.

Opportunities for large-muscle and small-muscle activities, social play, quiet and rowdy play, and creative experiences should be provided outdoors

Playgrounds as Outdoor Classrooms

as in the classroom. A rich, safe, varied environment is based on:

- □ careful site selection
- □ preparation and safe installation of a variety of developmentally appropriate equipment and materials to provide safe challenges
- □ adequate supervision.

Site Selection Child care program outdoor play areas should be easily accessible, near sources of drinking water and emergency assistance, and physically separated from vehicular and pedestrian traffic. Often, natural features of the play area can be used to enhance the quality of activities that go on there. Although toxic plants and materials must be removed, safe trees, shrubs, and floral plantings can be used to add visual appeal, separate certain activities, and provide shade for hot days. Small rises in the ground can be used to create safe

Playground equipment should be close to the ground or, if elevated, have safe landing spots.

climbing and hiding opportunities. Attention must be given to drainage and maintenance requirements under all usual weather conditions. Anticipate and control use of the playground during off hours by neighborhood residents (for play, pet exercise, or litter dumping).

Fixed Equipment Because falls are the leading source of injury on playgrounds, fall distances from climbers should be minimized. This is accomplished by using equipment that is close to the ground or elevated equipment with intermediate safe landing spots. (Usually half the child's height is a safe drop limit.) Surfaces under equipment that can be climbed should be covered with an impact-absorbing material such as compounded materials made from shredded tires or an 8- to 10-inch depth of wood chips, loose (not packed) sand, or other particulate material. Blacktop, concrete, grass, and earth are not safe surfaces.

The height to be used to choose the impact-absorbing material is the sum of the height of the tallest child user and the height to the top of the equipment above the playing surface. The impact-absorbing material should be rated for this height. The ratings are generally calculated by using a maximum height at which 200 g (200 times the force of gravity) is experienced by a head mold dropped from the stated height. The force of 200 g was chosen as the standard from experiments that determined the force usually required to damage the skull. Brain damage can occur at lower levels of force. The material that has the lowest g force from the drop height expected to be experienced is best.

The landing area or fall zone around the equipment must be large enough to protect the most adventuresome child. Before installing a loose fill material, the area must be prepared by excavating it to a 1-foot depth or by placing retaining barriers around the outside perimeter of the fall zone to prevent the loose fill material from scattering and to provide adequate drainage. A bottom layer of coarse gravel will help prevent water retention.

All loose fill materials have some inherent disadvantages. They hide litter and require periodic raking to redistribute the material evenly. The material must be replenished from time to time. Sand attracts cat excrement and insects; it compacts in all seasons and becomes hard as a rock in the winter. Over a period of one to three years, bark and wood fiber decompose, compact, and cease to absorb impact as they did at first. Organic materials tend to stay damp for a long period after a rain.

Shredded fabric-reenforced rubber tires are now commercially available in particle sizes varying from tiny (2 millimeters by 5 millimeters) to chunks (1/2 to 2 inches). Although this material absorbs impact well, the fabric in the rubber serves as a wick to ignite the rubber if a lighted match is dropped on it. Several companies have taken the shredded tire material, extracted the fiber, and recompounded the material into an impact-absorbing mat with air cells. This type of matting is much more expensive than the loose fill materials but has several advantages over other materials: slow decomposition, easy cleaning by rinsing with a hose, and quick drying so the surface is ready for use immediately after a rain. Concern about retained road lead on material made from shredded tires is unfounded. Since rubber is generally chemically stable and not likely to cause problems with contact or small ingestions, the material is nontoxic.

The American Society for Testing Materials (ASTM) is responsible for a standard for playground surfacing materials and playground equipment. The F-08 Committee on Play Surfacing Under and Around Play Equipment has addressed the shock attenuation and resiliency issue. ASTM is also responsible for specifications based on requirements for toxicity, flammability, durability, maintenance, and other factors. New installations of playground surfacing material should be checked against this standard.

Elimination of Known Playground Hazards The U.S. Consumer Product Safety Commission has studied the types of hazards associated with playground injuries. Obvious sources of injury include:

- protruding objects or obstructions in the fall zones under and around equipment
- sharp edges, pinch points on moving parts, exposed bolts, open hooks, or exposed chain links or other holes sized so that they can catch a child's finger
- heavy or sharp swing seats
- steps made of round tubing or steps spaced more than a child's knee height apart
- loosely mounted equipment or exposed mountings and supports
- hard surfaces in fall zones around equipment
- maximum fall height from the head of the child on the highest part of the equipment to the surface exceeds the rating for the surface under the equipment
- spaces between bars of horizontal climbing equipment exceed the easy reach of the users (14 inches for school-age children, less for preschoolers)
- rails and bars on equipment for preschoolers are more than 1 inch in diameter, preventing secure grasp by a child-size hand
- swinging exercise rings (do not belong on young children's playgrounds)
- any spaces hidden or inaccessible to an adult
- any toxic, irritating, or injurious materials and vegetation
- metal equipment that can overheat when exposed to the sun
- equipment located so that moving parts cross paths children might use to go from one activity to another
- broken equipment
- litter
- inadequate supervision
- inadequate source of drinking water
- inadequate shade to protect children from excess exposure to the sun, with resultant sunburn or heat-related illness
- insect nests, fruiting plants, garbage cans, and other objects that attract stinging insects
- lack of barriers to prevent intrusion by animals and to keep children from wandering beyond the limits where caregivers can easily supervise them.

Appropriate Types of Equipment The types of equipment suitable for play areas are listed in numerous articles, videotapes, and manuals on playground design. Types commonly mentioned are listed in Table 6.3.

Materials and Toys for Playground Use Portable materials and toys that are easily stored or are disposable can augment fixed equipment to enrich outdoor play. Examples are listed in Table 6.4.

Safe Playground Activities In addition to the thousands of ways children will use materials and equipment if allowed to play freely, adults can organize special activities and events. Examples of activities that adults can organize on playgrounds are listed in Table 6.5.

Injury Control on the Playground

Children are inquisitive, imaginative, and daring. Risk taking within safe bounds is an inherent part of the learning process. For very young children, the boundaries of safe risk taking must be set by adults. As children reach school age and beyond, they should be increasingly able to define the boundaries of safe risk taking for themselves.

T A B L E   6.3

TYPES OF EQUIPMENT COMMONLY FOUND ON PLAYGROUNDS

Culverts	Slides laid at ground level on small hills and mounds
Smooth-surface dugout canoes and boats	Broad jump pit filled with an impact-absorbing surface
Horizontal tree trunks	Hopscotch patterns
Playhouses	Four-square courses
Securely anchored tents	Painted patterns
Platforms	Ball targets on walls and ground surfaces
Low balance beams and parallel bars	Low basketball backboards
Stepping stones, logs, and tree stumps	Ramps
Water sprinklers	Mazes
Boxes	Trails, paths, and tracks for walking, running, or riding wheeled vehicles
Fences	Coverable sand boxes
Boulders and field stones	Pits
Low walls suitable for dividing activities and outdoor painting	Water play areas
Steps	Hand pumps
Cargo nets	Nonpoisonous plants, shrubs, and bushes; vegetable or flower garden
Low horizontal ladders, climbers, and suspension bridges, mounted over impact-absorbing surfaces	Benches
Earth mounds	Birdbaths and feeders
Tiles	
Tires	

Tricycles and other pedal vehicles	Ropes (closely supervised to prevent hanging)
Outdoor blocks	Balls and frisbees
Reading books	Tops
Music-making toys	Kites
Paints	Butterfly nets
Hammers, nails, and boards (with safety goggles)	Chalk
Child-size outdoor furniture (chairs, benches, and tables)	Hoops
Mounted steering wheels	Clay
Puppets, dolls, and doll carriages	Wheelbarrows, rakes, shovels, hoes, and watering cans
Kitchen stuff (unbreakable, dull-edged pots, pans, eggbeaters, measuring cups, funnels, strainers, tableware, jugs, and bottles; aprons)	Toy vehicles
	Flags, sheets, canvas, and parachutes
	Rubber cones (traffic markers)
	Animal toys
	Pulleys, gears, and ladders

Passive Measures Injury prevention measures are most effective when they require little or no conscious decision making because they are designed into the products and environments. In designing playgrounds, maximum use of passive safety measures should be made. During active outdoor play, children are less likely to make safe choices than they might in a more physically restricted environment. For example, ornamental trees may provide shade, but when their branches are low enough to tempt children to climb them, they are a hazard. Low, climbable branches of such trees should be removed as soon as higher foliage is sufficient to support the growth of the tree. Until the tree reaches that size, some type of fencing around the tree must be used to prevent children from attempting to climb on it.

Playgrounds need to be routinely inspected by staff to identify maintenance problems and previously overlooked safety hazards. Numerous checklists are available for this purpose (see the end of the chapter for sources). Since different people will see different hazards when using the same checklist, the inspection duty should be rotated among the staff, parents, and older children. No less than monthly inspections of playgrounds should be done. In urban settings, the frequency may have to be daily.

Rules of Safe Playground Play Next best to passive injury prevention measures are those that require only limited and easily routinized behavioral choices. If

Relay races	Paint-in	Litter collection
Red light, green light	Plant-in	Singing
Capture the flag	Concerts	Target games
Kick the can	Scavenger hunts	Dancing
Pass the potato		

there are too many rules, the rules are too complex, or the rules are inconsistently enforced, children will not adhere to them. Wherever possible, try to state the rules simply, in positive terms.

Children need repeated practice and adult reinforcement to learn and to abide by the rules of safe play. To define the rules, look closely at the area to see what rules are needed. What rules are required to separate quiet from more active play? In each area, what rules are needed to prevent collisions and falls? What rules are needed to safely play on the available equipment?

Wherever possible, the emphasis should be on the "do's" rather than the "don't's." Positive language can be posted near equipment to help staff consistently reinforce playground rules. Adult behavior on the playground must model the behaviors desired from the children. When staff or older children display unsafe behaviors, injuries to young children who copy what they see are predictable.

Adults should avoid wearing jewelry that can catch on equipment and should watch out for such adornments on children. Children should be told that they need to dress for fun by leaving loose scarves, jewelry, and other hazardous clothing at home or in their cubbies while they play.

For swings, say "Sit in the center of the swing; hold on with both hands; stop the swing before getting off; walk way around the swing; children should swing themselves; only one person may be in one swing at one time; swings should swing only when people are sitting in them; swing chains should always be straight, not twisted."

For slides, say "Hold on with both hands; take one step at a time on the slide ladder; the ladder is the only safe way up; keep at least one arm's length between children; slide down feet first; be sure the front of the slide is clear before sliding down; be patient and wait for a turn; leave the bottom of the slide as soon as possible; check a metal slide that has been sitting in the sun to see if it is too hot to use."

For climbing equipment, say "Use the correct grip with both hands; be careful climbing down; watch for anyone who might be climbing up; only x number of people can use the apparatus at one time; all climbers should start at the same end of the apparatus and move in the same direction; stay well behind the person in front and watch out for swinging feet; make sure to use the climber only when it is dry and not slippery; go slowly, covering a safe distance in each move; drop from the bars with knees slightly bent and land on both feet."

For seesaws, say "Sit upright, facing each other; keep a firm hold with both hands; only sitting is allowed on the board; keep feet out from underneath the board as it descends."

For tricycles and bikes, say "Trikes and bikes ride only on the path."

Teaching Children to Be Safe Many child care programs overlook opportunities to involve children in learning how to play safely and how to manage their own injuries. Preschool and school-age children can help "discover" the rules by talking with an adult about how misuse could result in injury. Indoor discussion about safe play can be reinforced by art projects, flannel board activities, and solo practice on the playground equipment.

The curriculum for teaching safety to children is based on familiar concepts:

- We care enough about ourselves and others to prevent avoidable injury.
- Adults can help children learn how to play safely so children can take better care of themselves (and of their own children when they grow up).
- Adults cannot play safely for children or force children to play safely.
- Learning to play safely and to use first aid when injury occurs is interesting and important to everyone.
- Each safety and first aid rule has a reason.
- Injuries do not just happen, as the term "accident" suggests. Most are preventable by identifying hazards and choosing safe alternatives.
- Children use play to discover and integrate information about how to be safe.
- Gross motor play provides opportunities for constructive modeling and guidance toward appropriate behavior, helping children to identify their own capabilities and current limitations.
- Learning playground safety and first aid skills can have a long-lasting impact on children's general safety consciousness and ability to take care of themselves.

Playground Supervision High-risk equipment like climbers, slides, and swings need to have planned, close supervision. Because adults tend to gravitate toward places to sit or lean while supervising, adult-size benches near high-risk equipment (e.g., climbers and moving equipment) encourage staff to stay within catching distance. Supervision should be planned by establishing a written schedule, assigning more staff to areas of high risk (e.g., climbers, slides, and swings). Gross motor play time is not break time. It is an important part of the curriculum, with very significant learning opportunities and the highest risk of injury.

Not all injuries in gross motor play areas can be prevented, but monitoring of injury reports on a regular basis should give clues about possible corrective measures. Everyone on the playground needs first aid training so that when an injury occurs, it will be handled properly. As the seasons change, staff should participate in a review of first aid measures linked to weather conditions. For warm weather, review the prevention and management of sunburn, heat-related illness, cuts, scrapes, minor wounds to exposed skin, bites, and insect stings. For cold weather, review the prevention and management of hypothermia and cold injury to tissue.

Reworking an Existing Playground

Ask the staff who use the playground to participate in evaluating and redesigning it for more creative, fun, and safe play. Discussion can be focused by the following questions:

1. What, if any, are recurring problems?
2. What rules do you find yourself constantly repeating?
3. Are there areas where aimless activity occurs?

4. Are there areas that never or rarely get used?

5. Are there areas or equipment that are overcrowded?

6. Are there areas that are restricted because they cannot be supervised or are unsafe in other ways?

7. Are there areas where children's play gets interrupted?

8. Are there clear pathways for movement so that children do not interfere with each other's play?

9. Are children's activities inappropriately restricted by lack of equipment, lack of access to water, or lack of manipulable materials?

10. Are there areas that need more maintenance?

11. Do you have adequate storage for movable equipment and materials?

12. Are there areas where injuries most commonly occur?

A Last Reminder About Playgrounds

Outdoor play areas are highly visible to parents and the community. Insurance claims studies show they are the source of the most frequent and most severe injuries to children in child care programs. But the quality of the playground does not depend on putting a lot of money into it. Instead, it depends on careful planning based on the developmental skills of the children for whom the area is designed. Providing a safe, interesting, and challenging growing environment in the outdoors is an intrinsic part of the early childhood professional's job.

WATER SAFETY

Children love the water, but drowning is among the leading causes of death of young children. Regardless of whether children will be involved in swimming or wading activities while in the child care program, they can be taught the basic water safety rules listed in Table 6.6 from toddlerhood on.

Because drowning results from blocking of the airway by water, adults and older children should learn how to clear the airway and perform rescue breathing. Clearing the airway may be as simple as rolling the victim on his side and pulling the jaw forward to move the tongue away from the back of the throat. With this procedure, the victim may begin to cough and breathe spontaneously.

T A B L E   6.6

BASIC WATER SAFETY RULES FOR CHILDREN

1. Swim or play in the water only when an adult is watching.
2. Running, pushing, or dunking in or around swimming areas gets people hurt.
3. Glass and bottles are dangerous near swimming or wading areas.
4. Swimming (and running) with something in the mouth can cause choking or mouth injury.
5. Yell for help only when help is really needed. (Remember the story of the boy who called "Wolf!" and wasn't believed when the wolf really came.)

Vomiting may occur, but if the victim has been rolled to the side so the vomitus can run out, the victim is likely to begin breathing without assistance. If the person has vomited and no suction device is available, roll the victim to the side even if you will not be able to keep the neck perfectly still. There will be no need to worry about spinal injury if breathing is not restored.

PEDESTRIAN SAFETY

Walking trips are special opportunities to teach children pedestrian safety. Vehicle-related pedestrian injuries account for about as many deaths as passenger fatalities. Together, pedestrian and passenger fatalities are the most common cause of death in childhood after the newborn period. Starting with toddlers, caregivers can teach children to scan for oncoming vehicles at driveways and when crossing the street. The concept of scanning in all directions, not just looking to the left and right, will help teach children that cars sometimes come from behind or in front, making turns across the path of a pedestrian. More toddlers are injured because of cars backing up over them in driveways than from darting out into the street.

All children learn to jaywalk from adults—most adults do it. Crossing only with the light, crossing at the corner, not the middle of the block, and walking instead of running across the street are sensible for everyone, yet many people take chances. Self-discipline in modeling for children must become an obsession.

School-age Children

School-age children should be reminded about staying on the sidewalks, walking against traffic where there are no sidewalks, and wearing light colored, reflective clothing. Playing in the street is safe only when the street is blocked by barricades.

SUGGESTED ACTIVITIES

1. Conduct a survey of car seat and seat belt use at a local shopping center. What proportion of the adults are using their seat belts? What proportion of the children are safely restrained? Can you tell if a car seat is present and whether it is being used correctly?

2. Check on family members. How many always ride buckled up? What are the excuses given for not buckling up?

3. Observe arrivals and departures at a child care program. Are the children buckled up? Are the drop-off and pick-up sites and routines safe? Do the staff help with these routines? Write a transportation safety policy for a child care center and for a family day care home.

4. Conduct an inspection of a public playground or a playground at a child care center. Inspect the outdoor play area of a family day care home. What hazards do you find? How could these hazards be removed or corrected?

5. Contact the licensing agency in your area. Arrange to accompany a licensing inspector, a building or fire inspector, and a sanitarian to a child care site. See how this inspection is conducted. Are any hazards overlooked? What is done when a problem is identified? How do the child care staff view the inspector?

6. Discuss how to fund safety programs in child care. Discuss the roles of staff, of parents, of public authorities, and of children.

7. Discuss how routine surveillance for safety hazards can be maintained. Who should inspect? How often should inspections be conducted? How can follow-up on problems be assured?
8. Ask the students to pick a safety topic and use one or more of the addresses in Appendix C to send for curricular materials on safety for parent and child education. With the information in the book and the supplemental materials obtained from the contacts made, have the student plan and present a safety education activity. Encourage students to plan corresponding activities for children and parents.

FOR MORE INFORMATION

American Academy of Pediatrics, 141 Northwest Point Blvd., Elk Grove Village, IL 60009 1-800-433-9016

American Red Cross. *First Aid in Child Care Settings*. Washington, DC: American Red Cross, 1990.

Esbensen, Steen B. *The Early Childhood Playground, an Outdoor Classroom*. Ypsilanti, MI: High/Scope Press, 1987.

Franks, Martha Ross. *The American Medical Association's Handbook of First Aid and Emergency Care*. New York: Random House, 1980.

Greenman, Jim. *Caring Spaces, Learning Places: Children's Environments That Work*. Redmond, WA: Exchange Press, 1988.

Moore, Robin C., Goltsman, Susan M., and Iacofano, Daniel S. *Play for All Guidelines*. Berkeley, CA: MIG Communications, 1987.

Playground Surfacing and Equipment Standards. American Society for Testing Materials Committee F-08, 1916 Race St., Philadelphia, PA 19103, 1989.

U.S. Consumer Product Safety Commission. *A Handbook for Public Playground Safety*, vol. I and II. Washington, DC: U.S. Government Printing Office, 1981.

U.S. Consumer Product Safety Commission. *Play Happy, Play Safely, a Child Centered Playground Safety Curriculum Approach*. Washington, DC: U.S. Government Printing Office, 1978.

7

Indoor Safety and Preparation for Emergencies in Child Care Settings

IN THIS CHAPTER:

SAFE, FUN INDOOR LEARNING ENVIRONMENTS
TEACHING CHILDREN TO BE SAFE
PREPARATION FOR EMERGENCIES
SAFETY SURVEILLANCE AND REPORTING OF INJURY
SUGGESTED ACTIVITIES
FOR MORE INFORMATION

When child care centers and family day care homes are surveyed by self-inspection or by outside inspectors, well-recognized hazards are commonly found inside the facility. Recent surveys in several states found that many programs had tripping hazards, tap water above scald temperature, exposed wiring and outlets, exposed space heaters, unguarded stairs, toxic chemicals and medications accessible to children, and lack of information for handling emergencies. Many of these hazards cannot be permanently corrected by a single action. Safety requires constant vigilance and surveillance.

SAFE, FUN INDOOR LEARNING ENVIRONMENTS

As in the outdoors, safe, challenging, fun play and learning occur indoors when a developmentally appropriate environment is combined with appropriate supervision to support child-initiated learning. Using their own creativity, children can use a well-designed environment for thousands of safe activities. Color, texture, size, placement, and design of structures and backgrounds all determine the safety and effectiveness of a learning environment.

Safety Related to the Skills and Appropriate Challenges for Children in Care

The first step is to determine the developmental tasks that the children are expected to accomplish. Children learn best by meeting challenges scaled to their abilities.

Infants Infants sense the world through visual, tactile, auditory, and mouthing experiences. They enjoy varied surfaces, sights, and sounds. Developmental change in infants occurs at an astonishing pace, with new skills revealed moment to moment. Newborns are capable of wriggling off a bed with pillows placed around them; by 2–4 months, some can flip over and off a diaper-changing table in a flash. A busy caregiver can easily be distracted by the need of another child, by a telephone call, or by the need to reach for a change of clothing that was not known to be needed when diapering began. If these situations occur, caregivers must take the baby along. Infants can rock and move themselves in infant seats and carriers. Many falls occur when adults have placed a child in such a device on a counter or table, thinking the infant is safe. Because falls are such a common cause of injury to infants, adults must adopt a strict rule: *Never leave an infant on any surface from which a fall is possible, even for an instant.*

When infants begin to crawl, stairways require gates at the bottom and at the top to prevent falls. Infant walkers are so commonly associated with injuries that banning them from the marketplace has been seriously considered. Caregivers and parents find walkers a wonderful way to help an older infant take command of the upright position and gain access to a wider range of opportunities. However, these devices give children access to stairwells and tend to tip over when the child moves from one surface to another. Children in walkers need close supervision and should be limited by barriers to smooth, even surfaces when the walker is used.

Infants can be expected to try to put everything in their mouths. They literally try to sense their world with their mouths. Because of this known behavior, all objects must be large enough so that they cannot be entirely fitted into the child's mouth. A choke-tube tester can be easily constructed by making a cardboard cylinder with a diameter of 1½ inches. Anything that can drop through the inside of the cylinder is too small to be given to an infant or toddler as a toy.

Nothing tastes or smells too bad for a child to drink or eat it. Amazingly, a crawling infant will drink bleach and eat roach and mouse bait if it can be reached. They will eat their own feces or animal droppings. The more mobile the child becomes, the greater the risk that the child will find and eat potentially harmful substances in the environment. Medications and poisons should be kept out of the child care area for all age groups. The poison control emergency numbers should be posted; in the event of a poisoning, syrup of ipecac (a medication that induces vomiting) should be available if the poison control center or emergency department of a hospital advises its use.

With increasing mobility, infants become able to explore wall sockets and teethe on wire cords. These hazards are best removed entirely by installing protective covers over outlets and fastening electric cords securely against the wall. Dangling cords can be used to pull heavy objects down onto an infant—a double danger if the cord is connected to an object like an iron that is hot or an appliance like a coffeepot or slow cooker that contains a hot liquid. Even a cup of hot beverage knocked out of hand or off the table onto an infant can cause a severe burn over a large part of the child's body.

Although sudden infant death syndrome (SIDS) is named for its unknown causes, near-miss SIDS has become a recognized phenomenon. Near-miss SIDS occurs when an infant is found not breathing but not yet dead and is able to be resuscitated. To have this important opportunity to avert SIDS, infants must be observed at all times, even when they are asleep. A casual glance at a sleeping infant every few minutes while other duties are attended will do. Infants should not be unattended in separate sleeping rooms in child care even if they are monitored by a sensitive intercom.

Bottle propping is a significant hazard for infants. During feeding, many babies spit up or cough while trying to swallow and can inhale some of the fluid. If lying down, they may not be able to clear the food from the airway. Weaning can be more difficult for a child who has learned to fall asleep only when drinking from a bottle. Bottles also do not belong in bed because ear infections and dental decay are increased in children who take their bottles into bed. Babies who cannot sit up and feed themselves should be held for these reasons and for the social interaction that should occur during feeding.

Infants are also at risk for suffocation from objects around them. Very young infants are able to turn their heads from side to side, but they cannot lift themselves out of a bunched-up pile of fabric or plastic or untangle a cord from around their necks. Avoid covers, pillows, cords, strings (including those that may be used to keep a pacifier with its owner or to tie toys to encourage reaching), and articles of clothing that might pose this type of hazard. Older infants who have begun to crawl may explore the inside of a plastic bag and suffocate, or they may drown in a toilet bowl or bucket of water. Vigilance is required to prevent these hazards from entering the infant's environment.

Smoking is a major cause of fires that kill or injure children. Of course, the health problems that result from having children passively exposed to smoke are more than sufficient reason to ban smoking from child care settings. In addition, cigarettes ignite furniture or bedding, leading to release of toxic fumes which render adults unable to help children escape. Most deaths from fires are due to carbon monoxide poisoning, not from burns.

Scald burns from hot liquids are the most frequent cause of nonfatal burn injuries in young children: 75 percent of scald injuries occur in children between 6 months and 3 years of age. Many of the scald injuries occur in the kitchen when children tip over pans on the stove or knock over coffee cups or other containers of hot liquids on themselves. Other scald injuries result from bathroom exposure to excessively hot water. Since only 7–10 seconds of exposure to water at 130 degrees Fahrenheit is required to produce a second-degree burn in a child, child care facilities should have thermoregulatory devices installed in the hot water lines leading to sinks that limit the hot water temperature to no more than 110–120 degrees Fahrenheit.

A new burn hazard for infants has been introduced by the widespread use of microwave ovens to heat infant food. If the oven is used to warm a bottle of formula or baby food, the liquid can become dangerously hot while the container feels cool. Heating continues to occur for several minutes after food is removed from the microwave oven. Mouth burns can result if the food is not allowed to sit long enough to dissipate the microwave energy and is not tested for warmth before being fed. An inexpensive microwave thermometer can be used to check that the temperature of the milk or food does not exceed 90–100 degrees Fahrenheit, a safe feeding temperature.

Toddlers As infants become toddlers, they experiment with different kinds of movement and location of their bodies in space. They practice stepping, running, and using stairs and small objects for climbing. Protection from hazardous objects can no longer be ensured by putting the objects up high or behind a cupboard door. Some parents call their toddlers ''monkeys'' in recognition of their skillful, fast climbing and undaunted curiosity.

Toddlers require maximum supervision. With increased mobility and lack of experience to judge danger, they are not ready to be in charge; they need their options limited by adults to acceptable alternatives. All of the hazards of infancy remain problems during toddlerhood; the toddler can just get into trouble faster. Because verbal commands may go unheeded, they must be reinforced with physical removal from danger. Taking care of toddlers is a physically demanding job.

Doors must be secured so that toddlers cannot go exploring unnoticed. Simple devices are available in hardware stores that make use of door knobs difficult for the small hand of the child but no barrier to the adult. Gates to prevent access to stairways (top and bottom) are needed to prevent falls; windows must be secured so that children cannot fall out. Insect screens are not reliable barriers.

For toddlers, heating equipment poses a great danger. Auxiliary heaters have hot surfaces that can easily cause serious burns. Heaters can also start fires by being too close to flammable objects. Fuel-burning space heaters also release toxic fumes, making their use in child care highly undesirable.

Preschoolers Preschoolers are more susceptible to adult verbal control and will accept reasonable safety rules. They are working on socialization skills, impulse control, and definition of roles. Injuries are likely to occur when too many children are using a piece of equipment, and when children are first learning to use tools like hammers, screwdrivers, knives, can openers, and other kitchen equipment.

School-age Children School-age children are at risk of injury from tools and equipment involved in hobbies and projects. They must be supervised to be sure that they use safety goggles whenever small parts might be involved. Supervision in the kitchen is a must, since so many burn and sharp-edge hazards are encountered there.

Safety in the Classroom

Certain architectural features of child care facilities such as doors and indoor floor surfaces can be modified to reduce risk of injury. Doors can have slow-closing devices and beveled edges to reduce their finger-pinching potential. Vision panels that expose the presence of young children near the door are helpful. Open floor areas can be broken up into smaller units by furniture placement to limit running where it is unsafe. Floors can be coated with nonskid surfaces.

Safe Toys and Equipment Although the majority of injuries occur on playgrounds, gross motor areas indoors are as likely to be a site of injury as similar areas outdoors. When a climber is mounted over a cement floor covered with a layer of carpeting, the effect is the same as when a climber is mounted over cement or blacktop outdoors. When broken parts of furnishings stick out, the consequence can be as harmful as when a piece of playground equipment has a protruding part. As with the playground, routine surveillance for hazards in the indoor environment is a must. In addition to gross motor play areas, special attention must be given to hallways, toilets and bathrooms, the kitchen, and chemical hazards throughout the facility.

Because falls are the leading source of injury from gross motor equipment, fall distances should be minimized. This is accomplished by using equipment that is close to the floor or elevated equipment with intermediate safe landing spots. (Usually, half the child's height is a safe drop limit.) As in outdoor play areas, surfaces under equipment that can be climbed should be covered with an impact-absorbing material such as compounded materials made from shredded tires. Carpeting does not absorb sufficient impact to prevent injury from falls. The material should be rated for the maximum drop height (top of child's head when on the highest part of the equipment). The landing area or fall zone around the equipment must be large enough to protect the most adventuresome child.

Elimination of Known Hazards Routine use of a checklist to look for common hazards should involve everyone. One person will see a hazard overlooked by another. Safety awareness is increased by the repeated ritual of searching for hazards. Special attention in the classroom should be paid to the following items:

1. Remove protruding objects or obstructions; eliminate sharp edges, pinch points on moving parts, exposed bolts, open hooks, or holes of a size to catch a child's finger or entrap a child's head.

2. Remove toys that might choke, suffocate, or poison the children in care. *Infants and toddlers* tend to put their toys in their mouths. For this reason, toys that have surfaces that might be painted with lead-based or other toxic paints should not be given to them. Any toy that can fit entirely into a child's mouth could block the airway. Plastic bags must not be accessible.

3. Remove or stabilize unstable furniture and equipment. Bolt top-heavy furniture, such as cubbies, to the wall or floor. Be sure that toy boxes have no lids or have lightweight lids that cannot trap fingers or heads. Keep heavy items on lower shelves. Be sure that high chairs have a wide base and that safety straps are used.

4. Provide secure steps and stepstools. Step width should be flat and wide enough for at least three-fourths of the length of the user's foot, with risers no higher than the knee height of the users.

5. Keep an eye out for and remove tripping hazards such as toys on the floor, loose flooring or rugs, and spilled water.

6. As when climbing equipment is used outdoors, cover surfaces in fall zones around climbing equipment with impact-absorbing material rated for the maximum fall height from the head of the child on the highest part of the equipment to the surface.

7. Partition the play area to promote constructive, child-initiated play, limit running, and permit easy supervision of all areas by caregivers at all times. *School-age children* may be allowed to be indirectly supervised if they are studying at the library or are playing or riding their bikes within the vicinity of the child care facility. The limits of this freedom should be determined by the responsibility of the child, the parent's views about the child's need for supervision, and the ease with which the caregiver could be alerted if the child needed assistance.

8. Make sure there is enough space around equipment to accommodate the movement of children and adults around them.

9. Choose only materials that are nontoxic and nonirritating to skin, eyes, and other sensitive areas.

10. Remove or repair broken equipment immediately.

11. Remove any injurious or poisonous plants.

12. Limit artwork to no more than 20% of the wall surface area and mount it with gaps between so that a ring of fire could not encircle the room before the occupants could easily escape.

13. Maintain surveillance for potential supervision problems.

14. Review each injury to identify preventive strategies. Review a cumulative log of injuries in the facility every one to two months to see whether a pattern of injuries can be identified that suggests a need for preventive action.

Rules of Safe Play The principles discussed for outdoor activities also apply to rule making and enforcement in the indoor setting. If the rules are too numerous, too complex or inconsistently enforced, children will not adhere to them. Wherever possible, try to state the rules simply, in positive terms. The rules should be "do's," not "don't's." For example, say "Close the door carefully, so your fingers do not get pinched" and "Blocks are for building, not for throwing."

Caregiver supervising indoor gross motor play.

Children need repeated practice and adult reinforcement to learn and to abide by the rules of safe play. To define the rules, look closely at the area to see what rules are needed.

Supervision Use of high-risk equipment such as gross motor equipment, toys small enough to fit in body openings, blocks, and cooking appliances requires planned, close supervision. Adults who supervise the equipment can help to reinforce the rules by stating them consistently in a simple, positive way. As on the playground, consistency is easier to achieve if the rules are posted in large lettered signs near the equipment.

Remodeling the Child Care Area for Safety Ask the following questions:

1. What, if any, are recurring problems?
2. What rules are constantly being repeated?
3. Are there areas where aimless activity occurs?
4. Are there areas that never or rarely get used?
5. Are there areas or equipment that are overcrowded?
6. Are there areas that are restricted because they cannot be supervised or are in other ways unsafe?
7. Are there areas where children's play gets interrupted?
8. Are there clear pathways for movement so that children do not interfere with other children's play?
9. Are activities restricted as a result of lack of equipment or limited accessibility of materials?
10. Are there areas that need more maintenance?
11. Is there adequate storage for movable equipment and materials?
12. Are there areas where injuries most commonly occur?

Safety in Hallways and on Stairs

Assuming that the facility is designed with safety in mind, the users must preserve the unobstructed passageway. The temptation to leave recently delivered boxes of supplies in the hall or put something on the stairs to carry up on the next trip is understandable. These are the hazards that cause falls. Security problems with outside doors sometimes lead child care programs to bolt or chain panic hardware so that it does not function as intended. Alternative solutions such as door alarms or stronger closing devices must be used to keep security measures from causing a disaster.

Inadequate lighting in hallways and stairs is another potential source of danger. Turning on lights to obtain full illumination in stairways and halls must be routine. For most stairways, two switches are required, one at the top and one at the bottom.

Handrails provide support, assistance, and safeguards to prevent falls in stairways. These benefits cannot be obtained if the user does not have a hand free to grip the railing. Since the greatest risk is falling while coming down the stairs, the ability to grasp the railing with the strongest hand makes a right-hand descending railing safer for the majority of adults and children over 3 years of age. Railings on both sides of the stairway provide best protection.

Safe Bathroom and Toilet Areas

Young children often need stepstools to reach sinks and toilets. These must be stable and easily sanitized. Electrical equipment such as hair dryers should not be left plugged in near any source of water because a child could easily stop up a sink or tub or open a toilet and drop the plugged-in appliance into the water, risking an electrical shock.

Bathrooms are poor places to store medication and cleaning supplies. Rarely is there a way to make such substances truly inaccessible to children, and the tendency to have these rooms warm and moist makes storage of chemicals of any kind better elsewhere. Look for a dry, cool place that can be locked or otherwise made inaccessible to children. Even medications that must be refrigerated can be kept in a locked box (of the check safe variety) in the refrigerator. This precaution prevents accidental spillage into food and tasting by a child who can open the refrigerator door.

Infants and Toddlers Toilet bowls are attractive places to investigate, but can lead to drowning if the child loses his balance. Lids should be kept closed, and young children should not be allowed unsupervised access to the toilet room.

Safety in the Kitchen

Cleansers, sanitizing agents, pesticides, and other toxic chemicals are often found in the kitchen. Extreme care must be taken to ensure that these substances do not contaminate food and that they are inaccessible to young children. Chemical hazards are discussed below in more detail.

Kitchens are also hazardous because they usually contain sharp and hot cooking utensils. Kitchens are the most common site for the start of house fires, often during meal preparation. Careful storage and use of kitchen equipment and readiness to use a fire extinguisher are keys to kitchen safety. Because of the great number of kitchen hazards, infants and toddlers should not be allowed there when any type of food preparation is under way.

Chemical Hazards

Chemical hazards may be more difficult to recognize than other sources of injury. They exist in many forms: gases, dusts, powders, aerosols, caustics, solvents, pesticides, and even radiation (radon gas in the ground around and under the child care facility). The quantity and variety of potentially poisonous substances is vast.

Children are uniquely susceptible to toxic substances. Rates of absorption of chemicals through the skin are higher in children than adults, and adverse effects may last longer. Because growth requires cell division, poisons that can damage the way genetic information is transmitted during cell division are potentially more harmful to children (who are growing) than to adults. Toxins that are retained by the body have a longer period in which to damage tissues in children than in adults. Even one-time damage to neurologic tissue may result in greater secondary losses for a child. Chemically damaged brain tissue may limit the child's ability to develop normal cognitive and motor skills. Chemically damaged adults who lose the ability to develop new skills may retain skills acquired earlier in life. Children do not have as large a reservoir of previously developed skills.

Children have a larger surface area relative to body mass and smaller size overall than do adults. Smaller doses of inhaled, ingested, and surface-absorbed toxins produce more injurious effects in children than in adults. Furthermore, some of the detoxification systems in the kidney and liver are not as well developed in infants as in older children and adults. Immature immune systems may make children more vulnerable to toxins that attack the disease-fighting tissues of the body.

Children's behavior tends to increase their exposure to toxic materials. They mouth objects that may be contaminated by toxins and play close to the ground, where some toxic materials tend to concentrate. Children will drink noxious materials like bleach and turpentine that adults would consider offensive. Children can be expected to have skin, eye, mouth, hair, scalp, and clothing contact with any material accessible to them. Their curiosity is unbounded, and they do not read or heed warnings on containers.

On the other hand, children have some compensatory advantages over adults. Because they heal faster, their body systems are more resilient when poisoned than an adult's. Children are less likely to deliberately seek out and distribute poisons than adults. Usually, children are exposed to toxic substances as a result of the actions of adults.

The variety of toxic materials likely to make their way into the child care facility and playground areas is impressive. Some of them are listed in Table 7.1.

The immediate illnesses that can result from exposure to poisonous substances include nausea, vomiting, diarrhea, lightheadedness and peculiar sensations, blistering, peeling or reddening of the skin, watering of the eyes, and

T A B L E 7.1 *TOXIC MATERIALS LIKELY TO BE FOUND IN A CHILD CARE FACILITY*	1. Pesticides (e.g., insect and rodent poisons, weed and fungus killers) 2. Art materials (e.g., glues, paints, clay powders) 3. Cleaning agents (e.g., pine oil, phenol, oily polishes, all organic solvents, sanitizers) 4. Fuel by-products (e.g., carbon monoxide from gas cooking equipment, kerosene heaters, wood stoves, improperly vented heating systems) 5. Cigarette smoke 6. Building materials (e.g., asbestos, formaldehyde-releasing insulation, fiberboard, lead-based paint) 7. Improperly fired ceramics 8. Ground soil that gives off radon gas to rooms that are below grade level and on the first floor, a greater problem when ventilation is poor

trouble breathing. Long-term conditions from exposure to toxic chemicals result from damage to one or more organ systems such as the kidney, liver, lungs, bone marrow, gastrointestinal system, reproductive system, and nervous system. Significant problems attributed to toxic effects on the body include learning difficulties, behavioral disturbances, emphysema, and increased susceptibility to infection and cancer.

The American Society for Testing and Materials (ASTM) has developed standards for many products, including substances intended for use in arts and crafts. ASTM D4236 is the "Standard Practice for Labeling Art Materials for Chronic Health Hazards." Art materials labeled in accordance with this voluntary standard have been assessed for their toxicity to adults. However, products labeled "nontoxic," even with the designation that the product complies with ASTM D4236, cannot be considered safe for use with children.

Some products that contain toxic substances may be recognized by labels such as "harmful if swallowed," "use with adequate ventilation," "avoid inhalation," or "avoid skin contact." None of these products should be used by young children or be used where young children could gain access to them. Unfortunately, no standard for toxicity of products to children exists.

Art Materials The California Department of Health Services has prepared a "Program Advisory with Guidelines for Safe Use of Art and Craft Materials" which addresses special concerns for choosing materials for programs for young children. The guide advises avoidance of the substances and suggests the acceptable alternatives listed in Table 7.2.

The California Department of Health Services also maintains a list of commercially available art and craft materials considered to be nontoxic for children in kindergarten through sixth grade by type of material, manufacturer, and product name.

TABLE 7.2

ALTERNATIVES TO TOXIC ART MATERIALS

Avoid	Substitute
Clay in dry form (silica or asbestos inhalation hazard)	Clay in wet form
Prints, glazes, or finishes with lead or other metal pigments	Water-based products
Organic solvents and materials with fumes	Water-based paints and glues
Commercial dyes	Vegetable dyes
Permanent markers	Water-based markers
Instant papier-mâché or color print newspapers or magazines with water (lead and other metals)	Papier-mâché made from black-and-white newspaper
Aerosol sprays	Water-based materials
Powdered tempera paints (toxic dust)	Liquid paints
Chalk that creates dust	Crayons
Epoxy instant glues or solvent-based glues	Water-based glues

Asbestos Exposure to asbestos in childhood may put children at risk for cancer and lung disease later in life. Between 1920 and the early 1970s, asbestos was commonly sprayed on ceilings, pipes, and other surfaces of buildings. Many of these buildings now house child care facilities. Over time, the asbestos becomes friable and flakes off as a fine dust that is readily suspended in the air. Airborne asbestos levels may be measured and compared with standards for safe amounts, but this procedure is costly. Asbestos hazards usually are identified by reviewing building records and conducting a building inspection to locate any friable material. If friable asbestos is discovered, control techniques include removal, enclosure by construction of new walls and ceilings, encapsulation by spraying friable asbestos surfaces with sealants, and periodic inspections for changes that require corrective measures. Removal of asbestos by unqualified workers can be hazardous to the workers and increase the hazard to the users of the building after the job is done.

The Environmental Protection Agency (EPA) began a mandatory school asbestos program in 1982. In 1984 and again in 1986, Congress passed legislation to provide federal funding for cleanup activities. Child care programs in operational schools will be covered by this program, but child care programs in potentially hazardous buildings not currently being used as schools should ask for technical assistance and information from the EPA. Each of the 10 federal regions has an EPA regional asbestos coordinator who can help.

Pesticides Insects, rodents, weeds, and molds are common targets for chemical poisons. Unfortunately, the potential hazards of the poisons used to eliminate these pests may be more of a problem than the pests themselves. Even with powerful poisons directed at them, the pests are winning. Insects are developing resistance to the chemicals in insecticides; mice and rats can be found wherever there is food for them and in the smallest unprotected opening; the only weed-free turf is a synthetic carpet; that black stuff in the cracks between the tiles in your bathroom and the source of the dank odor in basements is mold.

Pest problems in child care programs can be addressed safely and reasonably. The first step is to define the extent of the hazard from the pest and the level of reduction of the pest population required to ensure the health and safety of the adults and children in the facility. Only some pests are harmful; others are just unwanted. The pest reduction program should be designed to balance the

FIGURE 7.1

Pest problems must be handled safely.

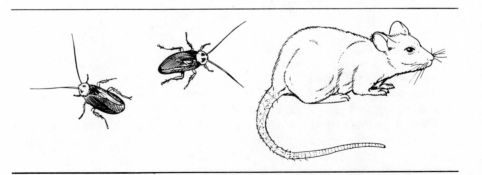

health risk of the pest against the health risk of the measures required to control the pest.

Commercial exterminator companies are often oblivious to the human side of the risk equation. Their goal is to eliminate the pest and keep the payments coming. Finding evidence of pest infestation is not a crisis. The tactics should be carefully chosen to find the least toxic, most permanent, most effective measures. Often these measures include improved sanitation and maintenance routines as well as installation of structural barriers to prevent the entry and breeding of pests.

Sanitation can be improved by using pest-resistant containers for storage and disposal of trash and garbage, reduction of clutter to improve cleanability and reduce nesting and hiding places, and diligent cleaning to remove spilled food and beverages. Facility maintenance strategies that work include:

- repairing water leaks
- cleaning gutters and runoff channels
- repairing holes in walls, windows, and screens
- installing thresholds at the bottoms of doors and vapor barriers under buildings
- caulking cracks and crevices
- removing vegetation from contact with buildings and plantings that attract pests into areas where children play

Cockroaches and rodents can carry disease, but they do not usually have direct contact with humans if they can avoid it. Food supplies can be kept safe from these vermin by using tightly sealed, rigid plastic and metal containers. Stinging insects are attracted by sweet substances like juices, soft drinks, fruit (especially rotting fallen fruit on the ground), and flowering plants. These lures can be removed. Stinging insects are more of a problem in the fall. Special attention to avoiding the known lures for these pests is needed during this season.

Dandelions are considered an edible delicacy by some. Poison ivy, ragweed, and other noxious weeds can be driven out by other, more benign plantings and by general mechanical cleanup of outdoor areas. Weed killers can cause rashes and allergic reactions that are more of a problem than the weeds they are meant to kill.

Between 2 and 3 million pounds of pesticide are used every year. According to a study reported in 1982 by the EPA, 84 percent of these pesticides have not been adequately tested for their capacity to cause cancer, 90–93 percent have not been tested for their ability to cause genetic damage, and 60–70 percent have not been tested for their ability to cause birth defects. The trend has been to ban pesticides when their side effects are studied. Diazinon has been banned from use on golf courses and sod farms. Dursban, a chemical frequently used to spray cracks and crevices in child care programs, is known to cause nausea, blurred vision, and decreased coordination.

Preventive use of chemical pesticides is rarely necessary. It usually results in too much use of chemicals and increases the risk of toxic effects and pest resistance. Many states license pest control companies and require that their owners pass a test to operate the business. However, the operators hired by the business may not be required to have any training or to have demonstrated any under-standing of the poisons they apply. Child care program staff should always find out what poison the exterminator plans to use. Contact a certified Poison Control Center to find out where and how the chemical can be safely used. Then accompany the exterminator every time the chemical is applied in the child care facility to see and control where poison is applied.

Integrated Pest Management A sensible approach to pest control includes using natural predators and other biologic controls, facility sanitation, and maintenance, with only spot use of chemicals as needed to keep the pest population at tolerable levels. Integrated pest management can be illustrated by a program to control cockroaches.

First, one roach is not necessarily an infestation. It may have stowed away in a grocery bag or been brought in as a hitchhiker on someone's clothing. Cockroaches are hardy insects. They can eat nearly anything organic, need little water, like temperatures over 45 degrees Fahrenheit, hide by day, and come looking for food when it is still and dark. They have phenomenal reproductive capacity: one cockroach can lay up to 300 eggs at a time. Some can lay eggs three times a year. Four types cause most of the problem: German, Oriental, brown-banded, and American. They look different, but the approach to controlling all of them is the same.

By strategically planting roach traps around the facility, you can determine how many roaches there are and where they seem to be most concentrated. Entries around water pipes, wires, and other openings into the building should be caulked or otherwise sealed. Food supplies should be kept in roach-resistant containers, off the floor, on racks that make cleaning under and around the containers easy.

The safest and most effective chemical approach to control of roaches is the use of a 99% concentration of boric acid powder. It is dusted in the cracks and crevices only, since if ingested by children it is moderately toxic to them too. The roaches walk across the boric acid dust, get it on their bodies, and then ingest it when they groom themselves. It takes 8–12 days to kill roaches with this approach, but it is said to be 90 percent effective and to remain effective for up to a year or more.

How to Achieve Control of Toxic Substances The following steps are modified from the recommendations for pesticide control published by the National Coalition Against Misuse of Pesticides (NCAMP):

1. Find out the name of the product proposed for use.

2. Contact the EPA to determine the status of the product. The EPA provides technical assistance and information through its regional offices and its central information office in Washington.

3. Consult reliable sources of information on toxicology. The NCAMP suggests looking up information in a university library and consulting an independent toxicologist. However, a more practical approach for child care professionals is to contact a certified Regional Poison Control Center. Certi-

fied Regional Poison Control Centers have been inspected and certified by the American Association of Poison Control to provide a full spectrum of poison control services. They also provide poison prevention education materials for children and parents.

4. Consult with others who have had similar experiences. Child care programs in the same community should share solutions to pest problems and share names of exterminator companies that have been willing to use the integrated pest management approach.

5. Research alternative methods of control.

6. Join with others to form a local committee to support corrective action if chemical hazards are being improperly handled in the community.

Why Worry About Chemical Hazards? Concerned child care professionals want to protect children against chemical hazards. But chemical hazards affect adults too. Chemicals can cause injury to the person who has direct contact with the source of the chemical or to family members and others who come in contact with the chemical carried on clothes or other possessions. Prevention of inappropriate use of toxic chemicals is not hard if experts are asked for advice.

Guns

Child Care Center Guns are among the leading causes of death for school-age children. They are also responsible for deaths of preschoolers. Children have found guns that had been put away by adults, loaded them, and shot themselves and others before being discovered by an adult. No justification can be accepted for keeping a gun in a child care center.

Family Day Care Home Any guns kept for recreational, occupational, or security reasons must be secured by keeping the gun locked up and unloaded, storing ammunition in a locked enclosure in a separate location, securing the gun with a trigger lock, locking the key or wrench used for the locking device in a separate location, and removing the firing pin from souvenir guns.

TEACHING CHILDREN TO BE SAFE

From late infancy onward, children learn to avoid injury and prevent disease in the same way that they develop other skills, day by day. A skillful caregiver will use "teachable moments"—when the situation provides an enhanced opportunity for children to learn. Safe play behaviors are learned by consistently structuring the play environment and positively stating safety rules during play. Children learn best about prevention from caregivers who both model and counsel safety.

Preventing injury can be taught most effectively by integrating the necessary skills and information with other curricular activities. Classroom routines, math, science, language arts, creative drama, social studies, art, and music can all be taught with safety messages.

PREPARATION FOR EMERGENCIES

The first task in an emergency is to stay calm and think clearly and systematically. If the emergency procedures have been clearly defined and regularly practiced, the routine will help meet the stress of the real thing. Emergencies include both individual injuries and situations that can lead to injury such as fire, a dangerous maintenance problem in the child care facility, or a natural disaster such as flood, earthquake, tornado, or hurricane. By far the more common occurrence is an injury to a child that calls for first aid.

First Aid

The most common types of wounds that children in child care receive are scrapes and bruises, most often to the head, face, and forehead, next most commonly to the upper extremities. Although many of these wounds require no more than first aid, some are serious enough to require emergency room care and hospitalization.

First aid is immediate care to help an injured person until medical professional help can take over. First aid includes the "first" things done to assess the situation and to keep the situation from getting worse. First aid does not include treatment or diagnosis.

Giving first aid in child care.

A good basic course on first aid in the child care setting is available from the American Red Cross. This course teaches four steps in a first aid action plan: (1) help the child, (2) call the parent, (3) talk with and care for the other children, and (4) complete the injury report and injury log.

To help the child, four "emergency action principles" must be followed:

1. **Survey the scene.**
2. **Do a primary survey for life-threatening conditions.**
3. **Phone the Emergency Medical System (if the injury is significant).**
4. **Do a secondary survey for specific injuries and give first aid.**

The first emergency action principle, "survey the scene," means to quickly look around to see what has happened. Look to see how many are hurt, if there is still danger, and whether there are others who can help or need help.

The second principle, "do a primary survey for life-threatening conditions," means checking the traditional ABCs (airway, breathing, circulation). See if the injured person is breathing normally; if not, establish an airway and check for problems with circulation, heart beat, and bleeding.

With respect to the third principle, the only help needed may be someone to care for the other children while the injured child is comforted. If the injury is serious, the Emergency Medical System must be called so that competent medical professionals can take charge of the situation as soon as possible. The parents of the injured child must also be notified as soon as possible. If medical care is needed, the parents will be required to authorize any care other than life-saving measures. Even if a caregiver thinks that no medical care is required, the parents have the right to be notified so they can make the decision about whether further evaluation is necessary. The parents should be notified as soon as is practical.

Every caregiver must have a way to get help at all times. At least two kinds of help may be required: help with the other children and emergency medical help. A backup adult who can be counted on must be available for centers that have only one adult in the building during early and late hours and for family day care homes at all times. Plans must include a way to get help if the caregiver is hurt too. Usually the telephone can be used to get help, but alternatives should be planned in case the telephone is out of order. Nearby neighbors, pay phones, and alarm boxes should be scouted out. Emergency telephone numbers should be posted by each phone, and phones should be located close to any area where an adult will be caring for a child. Whenever the children are taken on a trip (to a park, a museum, etc.), the location of the telephones must be known beforehand.

Since Emergency Medical System resources differ greatly from one community to another, walking through the steps of an emergency to see what could happen will help to prepare everyone. Personnel in emergency facilities are usually willing to discuss how they would handle a call from a child care program and are more likely to respond appropriately if informed in advance about how the child care program will call on them.

The fourth and last emergency action principle is to do a secondary survey to look for specific injuries. The secondary survey includes talking to the injured person and performing a head-to-toe check to find all conditions that might require care. The type of care rendered is simple and requires little in the way of supplies or skills. Many excellent charts and reference materials are available that give the basic instructions for first aid.

The second step in the first aid action plan for child care is to notify the parents. In an emergency situation, the caregiver may need to delegate this task to someone else. However, when time permits, most parents would prefer hearing about what happened from the caregiver who was with the child. With a serious injury, the caregiver or someone familiar to the child should accompany the child to the emergency medical facility and can plan to meet the parent there.

The third step in the first aid action plan in child care is to talk with and care for the other children. In the child care setting, there are usually other children present who must be protected from injury and who are likely to become upset by the tension that is usually generated in an emergency situation.

The final step in the plan is to complete an injury report and injury log. The injury report is a form for recording the details of the incident that may become difficult to recall later on. This information must be communicated accurately to parents, to administrative staff, and sometimes to lawyers and insurance companies. Sample forms are available in the manuals listed at the end of this chapter. The injury log is a cumulative listing of the injuries that occur over a period of time in a given facility. The log can consist of copies of the injury report form that are kept in a single folder where they are easily retrieved on a scheduled basis. Prevention, preparation, and practice are the essential ingredients of a successful emergency plan. Written procedures that assign staff, parents, and other adult roles should be posted and practiced. The chain of command and specification of duties should clearly define who is responsible for verifying that everyone is safe, who will notify emergency services, who will contact parents, and how the security of the building will be handled. Having the emergency plans reviewed and evaluated during an actual drill by local fire personnel is a good idea too.

Emergency Evacuation Routines

Emergency evacuation routines need to be practiced at least monthly. By holding drills at different times of the day, including naptime, and during all weather conditions, staff, parents, and children are more likely to approach a real emergency calmly and safely. Naptime drills can be held at the end of the nap period so that caregivers will not be left with cranky children for the rest of the day. Unannounced drills are best, but young children may be upset by them unless there is significant preparation and practice beforehand.

In planning staff/child ratios, enough adults must be accessible to the children at all times to handle an emergency and to evacuate children safely in an emergency. For infants, a practical limit on staff/child ratios is imposed by the number of pounds of child that one caregiver can remove from the building in a single trip. Enough staff must always be available to handle children who are unable to help themselves, including during staff break and naptimes. Staff/child ratios for emergency evacuation are usually coincident with the higher ratios recommended for quality care.

Infants and Toddlers Several infants can be evacuated by putting them in a blanket to carry them out, or they can be rolled out in a crib if no stairs are involved. Toddlers can be moved in a wagon. Having the children link hands to form a chain may help with an orderly exit. Older children and adults who are frightened can be encouraged to move by using your knees to press on the back of their knees as you move forward. Another way is to hold the person's hand with your arm over their shoulder as you move forward.

An alternative shelter should be arranged in advance and listed among the information given to parents at orientation so that they will know where to find their children. Daily attendance records and emergency contact information for parents must be kept easily accessible and portable to be taken with the children to the emergency shelter during an evacuation.

Routine, periodic inspections by parents, staff, and older children can identify hazards before they cause injury. A checklist (such as the one included in the health manual published by the

SAFETY SURVEILLANCE AND REPORTING OF INJURY

National Association for the Education of Young Children) will remind the inspectors to look at potential trouble spots. By rotating the responsibility for safety surveys to a different person each month, different hazards will be found that were overlooked by other inspectors. The result will be a heightened awareness of safety for everyone involved.

A systematic study of injury in each day care program can identify other high-risk areas so that additional preventive strategies can be developed. Individual day care programs can control hazards by collecting and routinely reviewing reports of "near misses" and minor injuries in the program. Merely filing a report in the child's record will not prevent a recurrence of the incident.

SUGGESTED ACTIVITIES

1. Conduct an inspection of a child care center or family day care home. If more than one student is available, divide the facility up into different areas to be inspected, and have two or more students inspect the same area at different times. Compare observations. What hazards do you find? How do the observations of different people differ? When the differences are noted, do the observers agree? How could these hazards be removed or corrected? How can parents, staff, and children be involved to make surveillance most effective?

2. Contact the licensing agency in the area. Arrange to accompany a licensing inspector, a building/fire inspector, and a sanitarian to a child care site. See how this inspection is conducted. Are any hazards overlooked? What is done when a problem is identified? How do the child care staff view the inspector?

3. Discuss how to correct safety problems in child care when expense is involved. Discuss the role of staff, of parents, of public authorities, and of children.

4. Discuss how routine surveillance for safety hazards can be maintained. Who should inspect? How often should inspections be conducted? How can follow-up on problems be ensured?

5. Ask a member of the class to describe an emergency situation from a real experience or provide a scenario from the newspaper. Discuss how each of the emergency action principles would be implemented in that situation.

FOR MORE INFORMATION

American Academy of Pediatrics. *First Aid Chart.* Elk Grove Village, IL: American Academy of Pediatrics, 1989.

American Academy of Pediatrics. *Health in Day Care: A Manual for Health Professionals.* Elk Grove Village, IL: American Academy of Pediatrics, 1987.

American Red Cross. *First Aid in the Child Care Setting.* Washington, DC: American Red Cross, 1990.

Comer, Diana E. *Developing Safety Skills with Young Children.* Albany, NY: Delmar Publishers, 1987.

Committee on Accident and Poison Prevention. *Injury Control for Children and Youth.* Elk Grove Village, IL: American Academy of Pediatrics, 1987.

Greenman, Jim. *Caring Spaces, Learning Places: Children's Environments That Work.* Redmond, WA: Exchange Press, 1988.

Harmon, Murl. *A New Vaccine for Child Safety.* Jenkintown, PA: Safety Now, 1976.

Kendrick, A., Kaufmann, R., and Messenger, K., eds. *Healthy Young Children, a Manual for Programs.* Washington, DC: National Association for the Education of Young Children, 1988.

Swartz, Edward M. *Toys That Kill.* New York: Vintage Books, 1986.

A Program Advisory with an extensive list of safe products for arts and crafts is available from the California Department of Health Services, 2151 Berkeley Way, Berkeley, CA 94704.

To obtain the name and contact information for the nearest certified Regional Poison Control Center, send a note with a self-addressed, stamped envelope to: Dr. Theodore Tong, Secretary for the American Association of Poison Control, Arizona Poison Control Center, Health Sciences Center, Room 3204 K, University of Arizona, Tucson, AZ 85724.

To find out whom to contact at the Environmental Protection Agency on a specific issue, call the federal regional office. More information is also available from EPA, Office of Pesticides and Toxic Substances, Washington, DC 20460.

For more information about the National Coalition Against Misuse of Pesticides, write: NCAMP, 530 7th Street, S.E., Washington, DC 20003.

The Problem of Infectious Diseases in Child Care

IN THIS CHAPTER:

SPECIAL RISKS THAT CHILDREN BRING TO CHILD CARE
SPREAD OF INFECTIOUS DISEASES BY CAREGIVERS
ENVIRONMENTAL AND ECONOMIC FACTORS
PRESSURES TO BRING SICK CHILDREN TO CHILD CARE
TYPES OF INFECTIOUS DISEASES IN CHILD CARE
THE RIGHT TO CHILD CARE AND PRIVACY FOR CHILDREN WITH CHRONIC INFECTIONS
SUGGESTED ACTIVITIES
FOR MORE INFORMATION

The risk of transmission of infectious diseases in child care is a major concern for medical professionals. Reports of outbreaks of illness foster the perception that child care centers are places where germs are routinely passed from child to child, making everyone sick. When the public media pick up these reports, parents become anxious and guilty about exposing their children to a possible increased risk of infection.

Outbreaks of infectious diseases are not unique to child care. The risk of transmission of infectious diseases is increased when children or adults are gathered into groups for any reason. Infections have been known to spread through camps, schools, and residential institutions.

SPECIAL RISKS THAT CHILDREN BRING TO CHILD CARE

Some of the factors that contribute to the risk of catching and spreading infectious diseases in child care are related to the age and developmental features of the children in care, to the caregivers, and to the environmental and economic problems of child care programs. Each of these factors contributes to an overall increased risk of infectious diseases when compared with care for children only in their own homes, especially for children who have no siblings. By examining these features, measures to control infectious diseases that allow good child care programs to nurture healthy children can be planned and implemented.

Some increase in infectious disease risk is inherent in the group setting. However, child care provides social and cognitive benefits for the child and support for families. To reap these benefits while limiting the risks, a balance must be struck between the need to control germs and the primary function of child care as a child development and family support program. Good sanitation and hygiene can be practiced without becoming obsessively clean. On the other hand, being casual about germs is not synonymous with love.

Being young means being vulnerable in many ways. Some of the vulnerability of youth can be offset by adult interventions; some will inevitably result in problems that must be overcome.

Immature Immune Systems

Young children lack immunity to many of the common infectious diseases that they encounter in the course of daily life. During intrauterine life, maternal antibodies are transferred by the placenta to the infant and protect the infant for varying portions of the first year of life, depending on the disease. For the first three months of life, the child is mostly dependent on maternal immunity. Although infants of this age are able to mount a response to an infection, the response is neither as swift nor as strong as that of older children and adults. The possibility of an overwhelming, life-threatening infection occurring in an infant under 3 months old is the reason that physicians institute rigorous medical treatments for relatively minor symptoms in this age group.

Children build immunity each time a germ enters their bodies. Most germs do not enter the body but are halted by the primary defense barriers of the skin and mucous membranes. But when there are too many germs, or when these body barriers are overcome by injury, infection can occur. Until a child's immune system learns to recognize the germs and to swiftly fight them off, each infection can cause enough symptoms to be recognized as illness.

Numerous body defenses prevent the entrance of germs at body surfaces. On the mucous membranes that line the nose, mouth, throat, and gastrointestinal and urinary structures, the moist mucous layer contains both chemical and cellular defenses against the entry of germs. With inadequate body fluid intake, exposure to dry air, or exposure to irritants, the protective functions of the mucous membranes may become impaired. The skin is the other major barrier to the entry of infection into the body. Like the mucous membranes, the skin has both chemical and cellular defenses against invasion by germs. When the skin is damaged, germs can enter the tissues that lie below.

The Course of an Infectious Illness

The usual course of a viral or bacterial infectious illness includes an incubation period, a period of immune response, and a period of cleanup of damaged tissue (Fig. 8.1). The incubation period begins when the infecting germ enters the body and starts to grow in the tissues or cells. During this period, few symptoms are recognizable. The incubation period is followed by a period of increasing response by the child's immune system, a triumph of the immune system over the disease, and a cleanup phase when damaged tissue is shed and removed from the system. Complications may occur during the cleanup phase, when new germs may grow in dead tissue and body secretions.

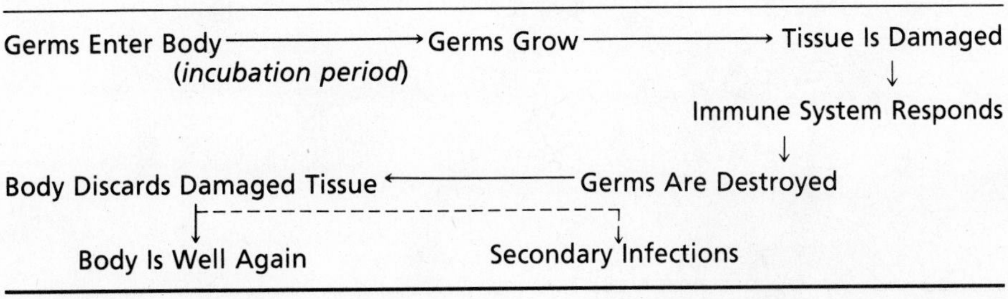

FIGURE 8.1

The Usual Course of an Infectious Illness.

Germs Enter Body ———————→ Germs Grow ———————————→ Tissue Is Damaged
       (*incubation period*)   ↓

                                               Immune System Responds

                                                     ↓

Body Discards Damaged Tissue ←————————— Germs Are Destroyed
     ↓
Body Is Well Again   Secondary Infections

Differences in Body Size and Structure

Young children lack experience with the many different types of germs in the environment. Their bodies are also smaller than those of adults. The distances are small between body locations where infectious disease agents normally reside innocuously and areas where these same agents can cause disease. The spaces and tubes in their bodies are smaller and more easily blocked.

For example, the middle ear space (Fig. 8.2) is easily infected by bacteria from the nose and throat because the drainage and aerating tube (eustachian tube) connecting the middle ear to the back of the nose and throat is very small and short. If there is a swelling of the lining of the tube, or some mucus blocks it, the middle ear becomes a warm, moist, closed space for germs to grow. Also, the eustachian tube is more horizontal in young children than later in life. In adults, the downward slope of the eustachian tube helps to ensure drainage and air flow to the middle ear in the upright position.

The size and position of the eustachian tube are thought to account for the higher incidence of middle ear infections among children who are allowed to drink from bottles lying flat on their backs, especially those who are allowed to take bottles to bed with them. In addition to increasing the risk of tooth decay, choking, and the lack of appropriate social stimulation during feeding, an increased risk of ear infection is one more reason why children should not be allowed to have their bottles in bed.

FIGURE 8.2

Blocked eustachian tubes lead to middle ear disease.

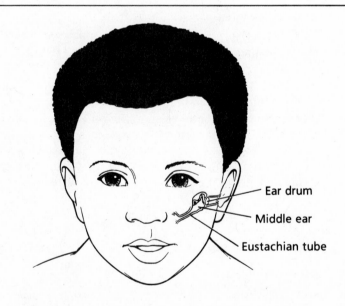

Ear drum

Middle ear

Eustachian tube

Children frequently mouth unclean objects, rarely wash their hands before putting them in their mouths, and enjoy playing in dirt, sand, and other

Lack of Good Hygiene

sites where animals defecate and deposit parasite eggs and where insects propagate. Children are careless about where they put their nasal secretions, urine, and feces and think nothing about handling objects recently contaminated by the secretions and body fluids of others. When a child is hurt, help in washing away the dirt before the germs start to grow must be provided along with comfort and reassurance.

Many infectious diseases are contagious a day or two before any symptoms appear. Germs are spread during the phase of an infection when no symptoms are present. Early in infection, germs

Controlling Exposure to Infectious Diseases

are multiplying in body tissues and cells but have not yet stimulated enough of an immune response to control the disease and have not caused enough damage to produce symptoms. The runny nose and cough of the cold result from increased production of fluid by irritated and damaged tissues. The cough becomes looser and more productive as damaged tissue is cast off by the body, and it raises and helps the body get rid of the debris.

Parents and caregivers often want to have children given commercial cold medications to suppress the symptoms of a cold. Some medications may help relieve the early symptoms of tissue swelling and watery secretions, but using medications (decongestants) that reduce the blood supply to the tissues is not a good idea. The blood is bringing reinforcements for the battle against the germs. Using decongestants later in the illness, when secretions are no longer watery, may lead to complications. Thickened secretions tend to back up and be trapped in the middle ear, sinuses, and large airways in the chest.

Many of the cold medications also contain antihistamines, drugs that block the allergic response mediated by a chemical in the body called histamine. Blocking the histamine response does not help in an infectious process like the common cold, but antihistamines have sedative properties. These medications make children drowsy and, in some cases, more irritable than they would be otherwise.

Children may be brought to child care apparently well on a day when symptoms develop because symptoms often become evident in the late afternoon and early evening. As a result, children may be brought to child care without symptoms and unwittingly share their germs with everyone before they seem sick.

Although caregivers rarely consciously spread germs, they often do so inadvertently. Germs are invisible and difficult to keep in mind with all of the other matters that compete for caregiver attention.

SPREAD OF INFECTIOUS DISEASES BY CAREGIVERS

Inadequate Training in Personal and Environmental Hygiene

Practicing and preaching good hygiene went out of fashion several decades ago. With improved control of infectious diseases through immunization and better handling of sewage, the public became more casual about germs. Today, few people wash their hands before eating a meal in a restaurant, even though they have handled many germ-laden surfaces between the time they last washed their hands and the time they use their hands to put food (and germs) in their mouths. Observing hand-washing behavior in a public restroom is an eye-opening experience. Many people do not wash their hands after using the toilet. Those who do wash often barely do so and then turn off the faucet with their "clean" hands, gathering the germs left on the handle by all who came to wash before them. Even those who wash and avoid using their bare hands to turn off the tap are likely to go to the door and open it by placing their hand on the handle where all those who never washed at all left their germs. Figure 8.3 shows how infectious diseases are spread.

Germ theory has not been routinely taught to young children in schools since the 1940s. Some of what was taught is still thought true today; some is not. Hand contact has been shown to be the most important way that most common infections are spread. Standing in drafts and getting wet do not pass germs from one person to another; hand-to-hand and hand-to-surface-to-hand transmission does the job. The social convention of covering the mouth during a sneeze or cough enhances the spread of germs unless hand washing is done before touching anything or anyone. Turning away to cough or sneeze or coughing into the shoulder is both more polite and more sanitary.

Surfaces in contact with germ-laden fluids can be expected to harbor some types of germs for a long time after the contact. Many germs die when exposed to air drying, but some are so hardy that they can still infect someone days after they were deposited on a surface. In general, all germs need is warmth, moisture, and some body fluid or tissue to grow. The number of germs on a surface is important, because the body's ability to resist infection depends on the number of germs introduced. For some infections, the infecting dose is small; for others, a large amount is required to overcome the body defenses.

The number of germs can be reduced by washing and rinsing them away. Killing germs with chemicals is effective only after the organisms have been removed by washing and rinsing the surface first. Chemicals that break cell walls or otherwise damage germs are good sanitizing agents. The most common, inexpensive agent used in child care is household bleach. The Centers for Disease Control recommend using a 1 : 84 dilution of household bleach (1 tablespoon of bleach to a quart of water, or 1/4 cup of bleach to a gallon of water) both for routine sanitizing (Fig. 8.4) and for blood spills or heavy contamination. All visible soil must be removed before the surface is sanitized.

Breaks in Sanitary Routines Caused by Stressful Demands

Child care is a physically demanding role. A well-designed curriculum helps to minimize chaos, but the unexpected happens despite the best planning. When a child is about to be hurt, a caregiver may not be able to take the time to wash away the germs from wiping a nose or

Most important

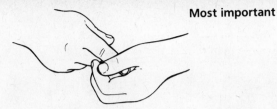

Hand to hand to mouth or nose

Hand to surface to mouth or nose

Also factors

Nose/sneeze

Cough

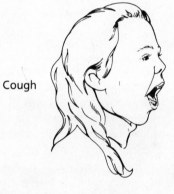

Not related

Drafty windows

Out in the rain

SPREAD OF INFECTIOUS DISEASES BY CAREGIVERS **131**

FIGURE 8.4

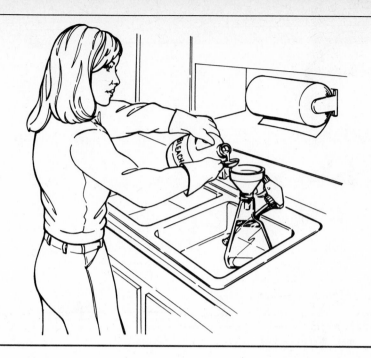

Diluted bleach water makes a good sanitizing solution for routine use.

changing a diaper before moving to prevent the injury. All that can be asked is that the caregiver do the best possible job under the circumstances.

Advance planning helps. During periods when a caregiver can be expected to be involved in diapering or helping children with toileting, the other children should be involved with other activities, preferably under the supervision of another caregiver. When food preparation is under way, simultaneous child care responsibilities should be minimized. At the least, conscientious hand washing must be practiced after activities with potential for contact with body fluids (nose drippings, stool, urine, vomitus, or blood) and before food preparation or eating.

Family Day Care Staggering nap and diapering schedules may help. Diaper-changing routines must be separated from food preparation by careful hand washing. Keeping child care areas close to hand-washing sinks will help make frequent hand washing feasible. When noses must be wiped, a trip to the sink must follow and can be used as a health education lesson for the children.

Child Care Centers Having enough caregivers and assigning the chores that require handling germs to staff other than those who will be handling food will help. The curriculum for children should be planned to provide a transitional activity under the supervision of one caregiver while another caregiver handles food preparation and hand washing. Many child care programs find it easiest to have one caregiver involve a few children in setting up the meal or snack and then call the rest of the children from the transitional activity to wash their hands, a few at a time.

When a caregiver moves from one group to another or cares for children from more than one group, the opportunity for sharing of germs is increased.

Cross-coverage of Groups

In child care programs in which only a few children need care at the earliest and latest hours that the child care program is open, cross-coverage is a common practice. To minimize the risk involved, diapering and feeding should be limited as much as possible in the mixed groups. Staffing plans should include separation of groups as early in the day and for as long in the day as possible. During the day, staffing patterns should be planned to avoid unnecessary shifting of caregivers from group to group. By washing their hands on first arriving and on leaving the child care area, caregivers can minimize the role that they play in spreading disease from one group to another, as well as to themselves and to their own families.

As anyone who has ever worked with children knows, caregivers can catch some of the illnesses the children have. Caregivers can catch infectious

Caregiver Illness

diseases from family members, from other people in the community, and from any child in child care. The caregiver can then pass these infections to any contact. Promoting caregiver health is important not only to caregivers but also to the stability of the program and to prevention of disease in all of the caregiver's contacts.

Child care operates within constraints imposed by the design of the program's physical facilities and by the limited resources available to make changes.

ENVIRONMENTAL AND ECONOMIC FACTORS

Child care is labor intensive, involving many close physical interactions among children and adults: toileting, diapering, multi-meal and snack service,

High Level of Physical Interaction

shared objects, affectionate kissing, touching, lap sitting, use of water tables, and shared moist art materials. For very young children, frequent body contact is an essential part of care. Each of these contacts is an opportunity for transfer of the germs that cause infectious diseases. Special effort is required to reduce the risk of infection without losing the loving, caring, and developmentally appropriate activities required for good-quality child care.

Only a few child care programs have the luxury of designing a building from scratch. Even in a building designed for child care, many compro-

Design of Child Care Facilities

mises are required because of site limitations, cost, building code requirements, and conflicting demands. Older buildings that are converted for child care use frequently lack sufficient plumbing to supply enough hand-washing sinks and toilets in the right places. Retrofitting buildings with plumbing is extraordinarily expensive. An alternative to running water is the use of a water reservoir and collecting device where running water is needed. Drinking water machines and picnic coolers with collecting basins can be used, but they require at least daily refilling and weekly sanitization with bleach to be maintained in a hygienic condition.

Inadequate Staffing and Inadequate Staff Compensation

Efforts to upgrade the quality of child care are hampered by the relationship between caregiver compensation, the primary determinant of the cost of care, and the affordability of care. Because many parents cannot afford to pay what good child care costs, child care programs limit caregiver compensation and the number of caregivers, often with unhealthy results. For example, when caregivers have too many children to look after, they find it difficult to allocate time for hand washing. More public and corporate involvement in funding child care will help, but the change is not happening quickly or easily.

Unfortunately, the majority of parents and purchasers of child care find it hard to justify the high cost of the service. Few understand that the cost of child care is the cost of competent, skilled workers caring for small groups of children. Like many other traditionally female roles, child care is undervalued in American society. Few adults in other professions have the opportunity to experience the requirements of caring simultaneously for three or four infants or four or five toddlers for the duration of the workday. As women become more assertive in the work place, caregiver compensation should improve. Caregivers who do not receive adequate incomes, health benefits, vacation, and sick leave understandably leave child care for other jobs. Those who stay are stressed by their unfair burden and struggle to maintain the standards for safe, healthy child care.

PRESSURES TO BRING SICK CHILDREN TO CHILD CARE

When children become ill, parents who work are faced with difficult choices. As responsible adults, they are expected to be at work. As responsible parents, they want to provide good care for their children. In many work settings, and in our culture in general, employees are rewarded for coming to work despite personal demands. Use of sick time for anything other than significant illness is seen as undesirable. Tolerance of absence for care of a family member is marginal and limited. Co-workers who must pick up the slack and bosses who evaluate performance rarely view such absences compassionately.

In reality, few parents have jobs from which they can be absent for the number of days that young children are ill. Preschoolers average six to eight common respiratory infections and one or two gastrointestinal infections a year; infants are ill between a quarter and half of the time. The reality of frequent illness has led to the development of child care for ill children whose parents must work.

Generally, children in child care experience the same types of infections as do children who receive care only at home. Occasionally, children are exposed to unusual infections which then

have an opportunity to spread and cause outbreaks of disease. However, outbreaks of unusual infectious diseases in child care are exceptional.

Table 8.1 lists the types of germs thought to be spread in the child care setting.

TABLE 8.1

TYPES OF INFECTIONS THAT MAY SPREAD IN CHILD CARE SETTINGS

Respiratory
  Bacteria
  Strep throat, scarlet fever (group A *Streptococcus*)
  Whooping cough (*Bordetella pertussis*)
  Tuberculosis (*Mycobacterium tuberculosis*)
  Meningitis (*Haemophilus influenzae* type b, *Neisseria meningitidis*)
  Viruses
  Measles (rubeola)
  Chickenpox (varicella)
  Cold and flu (respiratory syncytial virus, adenovirus, influenza A and B viruses, parainfluenza, rhinoviruses)
  Fifth disease (parvovirus B19)
Gastrointestinal (diarrhea, vomiting, dysentery)
  Bacteria
  Shigella
  Salmonella
  Campylobacter
  Escherichia coli
  Viruses
  Rotaviruses
  Hepatitis A virus
  Enteroviruses
  Parasites
  Giardia lamblia
  Pinworms (*Enterobius vermicularis*)
  Amebic dysentery (*Entamoeba histolytica*)
  Cryptosporidium
Skin
  Bacteria
  Impetigo (group A *Streptococcus*, *Staphylococcus aureus*)
  Viruses
  Cold sores (Herpes simplex virus)
  Parasites and fungi
  Lice (*Pediculus humanus*)
  Scabies (*Sarcoptes scabiei*)
  Ringworm (*tinea capitis, tinea corporis*)
Other
  Viruses
  Cytomegalovirus (contact with urine or saliva)

Respiratory Tract Infections

Infections of the respiratory tract include the common cold, ear infections, throat infections, croup or laryngitis, bronchitis, bronchiolitis, and pneumonia. Respiratory tract infections are spread by direct contact with infected secretions, contaminated hands, and any substances that can carry germs (fomites). As anyone who reflects on his own experience realizes, respiratory infections are the most common type of infectious disease for children and adults.

Data on the incidence of respiratory infection among children in child care versus those who receive care only in their own homes are used to assess the relative risk of respiratory infection in these two settings. Unfortunately, data on the incidence of respiratory disease are usually collected by asking parents or other family members to report whether or not a child has been ill or has taken medication for a respiratory illness in a preceding (usually two-week) period. Several sources of bias affect the data collected by this method. First, working parents whose children are in child care may be more observant of minor symptoms of illness because of the potential implications of the child's illness for the parent's ability to work. Second, depending on the type of care the parent is using, the likelihood that the child will be excluded from care may affect the parent's recall of symptoms. A parent whose child will be excluded for illness may be much more attentive to minor symptoms than a parent whose child care program accepts ill children. Third, participation of the child in care may affect the frequency with which the parent consults a medical professional for advice or seeks medication to relieve symptoms. Many pediatricians feel that parents who work call for medical advice and seek medication more readily than do other parents. Child care staff may also encourage parents to seek medical advice or obtain medication to alleviate the child's symptoms.

Given that the data may be biased, current research using information collected by the National Center for Health Statistics during 1981 shows that parents of infants who use child care centers report that their children have had a recent medicated respiratory infection more often than do parents of infants who receive care in family day care homes. Parents of children who receive care in their own homes and who have no siblings report least frequently that their children had medicated respiratory infections. This difference in reported frequency of respiratory infection between family day care homes and child care centers persists into the toddler age group but disappears by around 3 years of age.

The frequency of reported respiratory disease among young children is high in any setting. Infants who receive care in their own homes are reported to be ill with medicated respiratory infections about a fourth of the time; those in child care centers, about half the time. By 3 years of age, 26 percent of families of children receiving care only at home, 39 percent of families using family day care, and 37 percent of families of children in child care centers report that their children have medicated respiratory illnesses.

The main consequence of all this respiratory disease is the incidence of middle ear disease among young children. Because of evidence that frequent or persistent middle ear disease may affect language development and learning in some children, medical professionals worry about children who have frequent middle ear problems. The data on middle ear disease suggest that infants in child care versus those receiving care at home have an increased burden of middle ear disease. This difference disappears by 6 years of age. However, research shows that the magnitude of child care as a risk factor for middle ear diseases is about the same as the increased risk from having siblings, a parent who smokes, low socioeconomic status, or crowding in the child's home.

Studies of children who are in the same child care program over several years have shown lower rates of respiratory infection after the first year in care than for children who receive care only at home. These studies suggest that stability of children in the group and of caregivers may play an important role in the incidence of respiratory disease in the child care setting. New reports of studies of infection must be closely scrutinized for bias. Bias may be introduced by failing to look at the length of time children have attended the program, the age of the children involved, having the information gathered retrospectively or by someone whose observations could vary because of outside factors, and failing to distinguish among different types of child care for which the measurements were made.

Meningitis is an inflammation of the covering of the brain. The symptoms of meningitis are a relatively sudden illness, with the child looking very ill, irritable, and usually febrile. Older children may have a stiff neck and be unwilling to look down (at a toy or their bellies), but children under 2 years of age may not show any sign of a stiff neck and still have meningitis. Although some meningitis is caused by viruses, life-threatening meningitis is caused by bacteria. Two kinds of bacterial meningitis have been found to be more common among children in group care: *Haemophilus influenzae* type b (Hib) and meningococcus.

Children in child care centers have a two- to threefold-increased risk of Hib disease compared with children who receive care only in their own homes. In addition to meningitis, Hib germs can cause life-threatening infection of the epiglottis (the flap that covers the windpipe during swallowing), infection of deep tissues (cellulitis) and joints (septic arthritis), pneumonia, and infection of the blood (sepsis). Most of the children who get Hib infections are under 2 years of age, but the disease may appear in children up to around age 5. Vaccines to prevent this disease have been developed and should be given to children in child care beginning at 2 months of age, the youngest age when the vaccine is effective. Public health authorities should always be consulted when a case of Hib occurs in child care so that decisions can be made about whether special measures are needed to prevent other cases from occurring.

The other respiratory tract bacteria that can cause meningitis is meningococcus. Clusters of meningococcal infections in child care centers have been reported but are rare. In addition to meningitis, this germ can cause blood infection (sepsis), shock, and rapid death. One of the most important warning signs of this type of infection is the appearance of petechiae, which are red (not pink) spots on the skin caused by small amounts of bleeding into the skin, or larger areas of bleeding into the skin. Because the progression of this disease without treatment can be rapid and fatal within hours, the appearance of petechiae must be treated as a medical emergency. When a case of meningococcal infection occurs in a child in a child care program, public health authorities should be consulted about whether medication should be used to prevent others from developing the disease.

Gastrointestinal Infections

Germs that cause gastrointestinal infections are spread by the fecal-oral route. The bacteria, viruses, and parasites enter the mouth through food or from hands, table tops, or toys that are in contact with food or put into the mouth. Swallowing only a few of some of these germs (especially *Shigella* and *Giardia lamblia*) may be enough to start an infection.

Studies of child care programs repeatedly show that living germs from feces are found in great numbers on caregivers' hands, cots and cribs, table tops, toys, floors, diapering areas, sinks, and counter tops, especially in rooms where infants and toddlers are in care and in food preparation and serving areas, including kitchens. Areas with flushing toilets, places expected to harbor fecal material, are usually maintained well enough so that fecal contamination is low compared with other areas of the program. Air samples taken at the same time show that few of these germs are in the air. Of all the surfaces, caregivers' hands are the most heavily and most frequently contaminated. In one study, 67 percent of samples taken from the caregivers of infants were positive for bacteria found only in feces.

Diarrhea occurs more commonly among children in child care than those who receive care only in their own homes, especially among toddlers. The rates of diarrhea among children in child care centers where no special diarrhea control program has been instituted are higher than the rates in family day care homes. This finding probably reflects the control achieved by limiting the size of the group of children who can exchange germs with one another. When hand washing is routinely practiced in child care, the incidence of diarrhea among the children in care falls precipitously and stays low as long as the strict handwashing routines are followed. The use of disposable gloves during procedures that require handling of body fluids may be helpful but is no substitute for good hand washing.

Diarrhea is usually defined as increased frequency of production of unformed, watery stools. An unformed stool is one that takes the shape of the container that it is in. Some children have unformed stools most of the time. Unformed stools are normal among infants and may persist for long periods of time after a bout with diarrhea in toddlers. Because stools always have germs in them, and because infection-causing germs may be in stool in children who do not appear ill and for several days before any symptoms of diarrhea appear, all stool material should be regarded as possibly infective. Any surface touched by hands that touched stool can spread disease.

Another germ, the virus that causes hepatitis A, is a special problem in the child care setting. Hepatitis A is transmitted via the fecal-oral route and usually does not make young children appear ill. When an adult becomes infected with hepatitis A, an illness associated with nausea, vomiting, fever, and jaundice usually occurs. Child care programs have been shown to be an important route of spread of hepatitis A in communities. Hepatitis A is most likely to spread via child care programs where infants and toddlers are in care and where good hand washing is not routine. Because the virus may survive on objects for weeks, routine sanitization of surfaces is essential. When a case of hepatitis A occurs in staff or a family contact of someone who is involved with a child care program, public health authorities should be contacted immediately so that they can decide who should receive a gamma globulin shot to halt the spread of the disease.

The spread of germs involved in infections of the skin and mucous membranes comes primarily from direct person-to-person contact and less commonly from indirect contact with a surface contaminated by an infected person. Although these illnesses are generally not serious, they are common problems in child care.

Infections of the Skin and Mucous Membranes

Impetigo Any opening in the skin may become secondarily infected. Superficial infection of the skin by staphylococcal and streptococcal bacteria are the cause of impetigo. Impetigo is usually treated with frequent cleaning of the skin and antibiotics applied to the skin or taken by mouth.

Ringworm Ringworm is caused by a fungus growing on the skin or scalp, and is spread by contact with someone or an animal who is infected or with an article carrying the spores of the fungus. Scaling and redness are common symptoms. Ringworm of the scalp is caused by a different fungus than ringworm of the body, and the two are treated differently. Ringworm of the scalp is treated with oral medication, while ringworm of the body is treated with medication applied directly to the infected skin.

Lice Lice are usually recognized when children are seen scratching their heads or when eggs (nits) or small crawling adult insects are seen on the scalp or in clothing. Nits are most often seen behind the ears and around the hair roots on the scalp near the nape of the neck, but they may be found throughout the hair. Children who have only a few lice may not have any symptoms.

Lice appear among all socioeconomic groups, even among clean, well-groomed children. Length of hair does not seem to be a factor in whether or not an infestation occurs, although girls get lice more often than boys, and Caucasian and Oriental children get lice far more often than black children. Lice are transmitted by direct contact with an infested person or with infested articles such as clothing, hair brushes, or combs. Infestations spread by books in public libraries have been reported.

Lice do not jump or fly and cannot live away from a blood meal for more than 12–15 hours. The insect feeds on the host's blood about every five hours. The female louse deposits about three or four eggs each day on hair close to the scalp. Called nits, these eggs are tiny cases that are attached to the hair shaft by a cementlike substance. Nits are visible to the naked eye and look like grains of sand attached to the hair (hence the expression nitty gritty). The eggs usually hatch in 7–10 days and then live as nymphs for two weeks before becoming sexually mature adults. Since hair is often held near the scalp by barrettes, ponytails, or hair styling, viable eggs may be found anywhere along the hair shaft.

Lice are treated by using pesticides. The better treatments kill the eggs as well as the insects. Because pesticides are toxic drugs, treatment of lice should be done strictly according to the manufacturer's instructions, after which all of the nits should be combed out of the hair. Unless the nits are combed out completely, reinfestation is hard to distinguish from the persistent nits on the hair. Environmental cleanup is also necessary by machine washing and hot air drying of all articles. Dry cleaning or storage of nonwashable articles in plastic bags for about 14 days will also work. Carpets, mattresses, pillows, and upholstered furniture should be carefully vacuumed, not sprayed. Sprays sold to kill lice on furniture and other objects are too toxic and dangerous to be used.

Close contact between children, sharing of clothing or close contact of articles of clothing, and shared use of surfaces in contact with children's heads or hair allow lice to spread easily in child care. Common routes for transmission of lice include closely stacked cots, shared dress-up clothes, and coat hooks or cubbies that allow clothing and blankets from one child to touch another child's.

Pinkeye Infections of the mucous membranes of children in child care are common. When the membrane that covers the eyeball and the inside of the eyelid is involved, the condition is called conjunctivitis or pinkeye. Because the membrane of the eye can become irritated and inflamed by air pollutants, allergy, material in the eye, and infections that also involve the nose and throat, it is often difficult to decide the cause of a red or pink eye. Children with conjunctivitis may have to consult a health professional. Germs growing in the eye may be easily spread by hands that touch the area around the eye. Caregivers should encourage children to avoid rubbing their eyes. Itching can be overcome and healing fostered by continual rinsing of the eye with salt water (saline) solutions for use in the eye.

Infections Preventable by Immunization

Diphtheria, pertussis, tetanus, poliomyelitis, measles, mumps, rubella, and *Haemophilus influenzae* type b (Hib) infection are all preventable through immunization. The immunization status of adults who work in child care, including volunteers, is as important as immunization of the children. Exposure of infants in child care to measles, mumps, rubella, and Hib infection are potentially serious problems during the period between entry into child care and the age at which immunization against these infections can begin. Whenever a case of one of these infections occurs, public health authorities should be contacted as soon as possible.

Other Types of Infections

Chickenpox Chickenpox is the disease that comes from the first infection with the varicella-zoster virus, a member of the family of herpesviruses. The rash of chickenpox consists of red bumps that become blisters and then scab. The rash comes in crops over a period of four to seven days and is usually widespread over the body and very itchy. Sometimes the rash is preceded by cold symptoms and a fever. After the first infection recognized as chickenpox, the virus stays in the body and can be reactivated to cause a disease called shingles. Chickenpox is highly contagious, spreading from person to person by direct contact and by airborne particles. The incubation period is 14–21 days, and the disease is most common in the late winter and early spring. If the ventilation system brings air from one child care area to another, susceptible children in the entire facility are likely to come down with the disease.

Younger children generally have less severe cases of chickenpox; some infants may only have a few blisters. Children are no longer contagious when the last blister is scabbed, usually no later than six days after the rash begins. Although exclusion of children with chickenpox from child care has been traditional, there is no absolute reason for it. By the time the symptoms are recognized, the child has already spread the disease to all susceptible children who share the same space and air. In mild cases, children do not have to be excluded at all. Cases of shingles can be handled by allowing the child or adult to come to child care with the sores covered.

Herpes Simplex Virus and Cytomegalovirus Herpes simplex infections are of two types. Type 1 is caused by the cold sore virus, transmitted by contact with infected secretions, usually from the mouth. Type 2 is caused by the genital herpesvirus, transmitted by sexual activity. Cytomegalovirus (CMV) is a member of the herpesvirus group that causes an illness in adults that is like mononucleosis but often produces no symptoms at all in children. Once children are infected by either CMV or herpesvirus, they may continue to excrete the virus for extended periods of time.

Oral herpes infections are common among young children. Most of these infections cause no symptoms, and many children shed the virus in their saliva without any sign of disease. For this reason, saliva should always be viewed as potentially infected and handled by washing and sanitation as for any other body fluid. Sometimes children get lesions from herpes on fingers they suck or on other parts of the body, usually spread by saliva. Children with cold sores or herpes sores elsewhere present no greater risk than children who are excreting the virus without symptoms.

When children are infected by CMV before puberty, their bodies make antibodies that may offer at least partial protection later in life for themselves and, in girls, for their future children against congenital infections with these viruses. Women who did not have a CMV infection before becoming pregnant may be at risk for this infection during pregnancy, and their fetuses may be damaged by CMV. For this reason, women who plan to become pregnant while working in a child care facility should discuss with their obstetricians the possibility of having a blood test to determine whether they are already immune to CMV. Mothers of children in child care who have not previously been infected with CMV and become pregnant may also be at increased risk. Women who are susceptible or who do not know whether they are susceptible should be especially careful about good hand-washing techniques when they are pregnant to protect against this disease during pregnancy.

AIDS Few modern health problems have mobilized as much public concern as acquired immunodeficiency syndrome (AIDS). The disease is caused by Human

Immunodeficiency Virus (HIV), which has been shown to pass from one person to another by sexual contact or by contact with blood or blood products. The disease is most often spread to a child from an infected mother during gestation, which is essentially a blood contact route. Although transmission seems limited to these two routes, people who are infected by the AIDS virus are feared to the point of hysteria and treated as outcasts.

The emotional response to AIDS is based on the fact that once the virus infects an individual, a fatal loss of function of the immune system develops over time. The majority of people whose blood tests for HIV are positive will show no disease symptoms and may not manifest the disease for many years. No danger exists from routine contact with adult caregivers who have positive tests for HIV. Those who have positive tests for HIV should be responsible about their sexual contacts and about proper hygiene in situations that involve possible blood transfer between individuals.

Many people find it hard to believe that a virus that can cause such a cruel and fatal disease is not easily caught from people who are infected. Although the virus that causes AIDS has been isolated from many body fluids, including saliva, tears, urine, blood, breast milk, semen, and vaginal fluid, the presence of the virus in these fluids does not mean that the disease can be caught by contact with all of them.

Medical experts have warned that increasing numbers of people are expected to contract the disease via blood and sexual contact, the two major routes of infection. Absolute proof cannot be provided for the absence of risk from any other means of spreading the disease, but in the thousands of cases of AIDS in the United States reported to the Centers for Disease Control, the disease has been transmitted only by blood, sexual contact, and breast feeding (perhaps by blood from the nipple rather than by breast milk). It has not been shown to be transmitted in any other way, not even to close family members of patients with AIDS. A reasoned response to AIDS requires knowledge about how the disease is transmitted, not just an awareness of the seriousness of the disease.

AIDS is usually suspected because someone either has one or more of a list of "indicator" diseases or is an infant of a mother with AIDS. Indicator diseases include several unusual infections that do not occur in normal healthy individuals. These are the same illnesses which doctors see in people who are treated with drugs that suppress the immune system (e.g., to help prevent rejection of transplanted tissue). Most of the people who have been diagnosed as having AIDS are illicit intravenous drug users or sexual contacts of intravenous drug users, homosexuals or bisexuals, and infants born to mothers who are infected with HIV. By the end of the 1990s, the number of children with AIDS is expected to rise into the tens of thousands. Most of these will be infants and toddlers infected in utero; relatively few will remain without symptoms past age 3.

Currently, the risk of spread of AIDS by children in child care is only hypothetical. No case of AIDS in the United States has been transmitted in the school or child care setting. Since sexual contact with children or adults with AIDS in child care is confined to the rare case of child abuse, we are most concerned with blood transfer as a means of transmission.

Some health professionals suggest that children who are infected with HIV and are still exhibiting biting behavior should not be allowed to be in child care programs. Biting occurs frequently among young children in child care and rarely breaks the skin. Since saliva has not been shown to transmit AIDS, transmission by a child who is infected with HIV would require that the infected child bleed from a sore in the mouth while biting someone else. This is an unlikely event. The only proven case in which biting spread the disease occurred when the biter had a bloody mouth. The concern about biting should be reversed to address whether other children are likely to bite the child who carries HIV and draw the infected child's blood into their mouths. Thus, the "AIDS Policy" for the child care setting should concern itself with the biting habits of the healthy children who share child care with an infected child at least as much as with the biting habits of the infected child.

Theoretically, AIDS could be transmitted by the small amounts of blood lost by children and adults when they have minor scrapes, cuts, and nosebleeds. Prompt wound cleaning to prevent infection of any type is always appropriate. Anyone who cares for bloody wounds should try to wear gloves in situations when contact with blood is possible. Since adults are more likely to be unwitting carriers of the AIDS virus, these precautions are especially important when cleaning up blood from an adult. Wearing of gloves followed by careful hand washing is a good practice whenever contact with potentially infected body fluids is involved. Many child care programs already require use of gloves during routine diaper changing to augment hand-washing procedures. Similar practices should be instituted for cleaning of wounds that may involve infected blood or pus.

Contact with urine, stool, nasal secretions, vomit, tears, or saliva has not been shown to be associated with transmission of AIDS. No transmission has been documented in the intimate contact of foster homes where young infants have been placed with healthy families when their natural parents are unable to care for them. AIDS has not been spread by wiping noses, sharing mouthed toys, hugging, coughing, sneezing, using common eating utensils, or touching surfaces used by someone infected with HIV.

If reason can overcome fear of spread of HIV by infected children who participate in child care, appropriate energy can be focused on the primary health issue: the infected child's ability to resist common infections in the face of increased exposure in the child care setting. Not all children with positive tests for HIV exposure are sick; some have only a positive blood test and no evidence of illness. Exclusion of such apparently well children from usual activities is not warranted by current knowledge about AIDS. However, children who have symptoms of illness associated with AIDS may need special protection.

Because of close physical contact, suboptimal hygiene, and the larger pool of infectious possibilities characteristic of child care, a child who has symptoms of AIDS may be at increased risk in this setting. The decision to allow children who have AIDS to attend a child care program should be based on a medical evaluation of how they are likely to be affected and whether the child care program personnel can provide the minimal additional hygenic measures to manage situations in which blood loss occurs. The child care program's policies should provide for input from the child's physician based on specific information about the child's condition and the expected exposures the child will have in the particular arrangement offered by the program. Knowledge of an HIV infection should be shared only as necessary for care of the infected child and the other children.

Anyone who is infected with HIV has a right to privacy about this sensitive health problem. Because of the stigma that has been associated with AIDS, many adults who have tested positive for HIV will not disclose this fact to others. To exclude someone who admits to having a positive blood test for HIV because of unfounded fears is unfair and discriminatory.

The child care program's policies must allow for the fact that children who have symptoms of AIDS should not be given live virus vaccines but can and should receive other vaccines [diphtheria-tetanus-pertussis (DTP), killed poliovirus, and Hib preparations] to be protected. Routine notification of all parents about outbreaks of infectious diseases such as chickenpox is especially important for the child with AIDS or any other condition in which the immune system is weak, because these infections can pose a special threat to such children. As safe vaccines against common infections become available, child care programs should expect children with immune system disease to be first in line to receive additional protection.

Hepatitis B Hepatitis B is another infection spread through contact with blood and sexual contact. Unlike hepatitis A, hepatitis B can cause chronic infection. People with hepatitis B can develop serious liver disease; a few develop liver cancer years after the infection. No special precautions other than those that should be practiced routinely for blood spills are required for children with hepatitis B who are in child care.

THE RIGHT TO CHILD CARE AND PRIVACY FOR CHILDREN WITH CHRONIC INFECTIONS

Like children with any chronic disease, those who are infected with HIV, CMV, herpesvirus, or hepatitis B virus need to be able to lead as normal a life as possible within the limitations of the illness. Child care professionals have a responsibility to help provide for the needs of these children and of the other children in the program in a reasonable, sensitive fashion.

Those involved with the care of a child with a chronic infection should be informed of the child's infection status so that appropriate precautions can be taken. However, the information should only be shared on a need-to-know basis. Hard policy issues must be faced in deciding who has a right to this private information. The parents of the child, the child's health provider, and the child's caregivers and caregiver supervisors should discuss each case to develop a plan. Like all plans, the suitability of the decisions and the success of implementation should be monitored on a periodic basis.

SUGGESTED ACTIVITIES

1. Observe hand-washing behaviors in a public restroom or a child care program for 30 minutes or so. How many people wash after contact with sources of disease-causing germs? How many do not? How many wash before eating or handling food?

2. Observe children in a child care program. How many times in one hour do you see mouth, nose, and other body fluids get on surfaces where other children can pick them up? How often do the children put their hands or objects in or near their mouths? How often do the adults?

FOR MORE INFORMATION

American Academy of Pediatrics. *Report of the Committee on Infectious Diseases,* 21st *ed.* Elk Grove Village, IL: American Academy of Pediatrics, 1988.

Kendrick, A., Kaufmann, R., and Messenger, K., eds. *Healthy Young Children, A Manual for Programs.* Washington, DC: National Association for the Education of Young Children, 1988.

Pickering, L., ed. Infections in Day Care Centers. *Seminars in Pediatric Infectious Diseases.* Philadelphia, PA: W. B. Saunders, 1990.

9

Preventing and Managing Infectious Diseases in Child Care

Infectious disease results from the interplay of people, places, and germs. Preventive measures are designed to strengthen the resistance of people to germs, reduce the dose of germs people have to resist, and change the places where people and germs can come together to make it more difficult for germs to infect people. This relationship is called the epidemiologic triangle (Fig. 9.1).

MODIFYING PEOPLE, PLACES, AND GERMS

Hand Washing

Hand washing is the single most important measure to use to stop the spread of disease in child care. Hand washing reduces the number of germs on hand surfaces. As a consequence, fewer germs are spread around the environment, and fewer germs are available to be introduced into the body when the hands come in contact with the mouth, nose, eyes, or food.

When to Wash Hands Hand washing should be routine for adults and children at the following times:

- on arrival in the child care area
- before touching food or objects used to prepare or serve food
- after using the toilet or assisting a child with using the toilet
- after diapering a child (caregiver's hands) and being diapered (child's hands)
- after having contact with any body fluid (nasal secretions, drool, vomit, urine, stool, or blood)

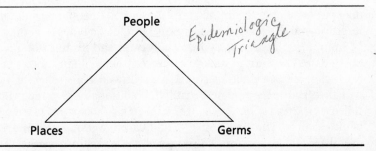

FIGURE 9.1

The Epidemiologic Triangle: People, Places, Germs.

How to Wash Hands Effective hand washing will dilute the load of germs on the hands by using soap to loosen the oily substances and dirt that hold germs on the hand and then using a flow of water to rinse the loosened material away. All other methods, including special chemicals, foams, and wipes, are less effective than soap and running water. Liquid soap is more hygienic than bar soap because the bars serve to pass germs from one person to another and frequently remains in pools of water that support the growth of germs. Sinks designed to be operated without touching the faucet handle with the hands are preferable to those that require touching the handle after hands are clean. Faucet handles pass germs from dirty to clean hands. If a foot-, knee-, or photoelectrically operated sink is not available, a paper towel should be used to turn the faucet off after hand washing.

The following procedure for washing the hands of adults and children should be systematically followed:

- Check the location of the soap, paper towels, and waste receptacle.
- Turn on the water.
- Moisten the hands with water.
- Apply liquid soap.
- Lather the fronts, backs, between fingers, and under fingernail areas of the hands for about 15 seconds.
- Rinse well under running water, holding the hands downward so that water runs off the fingertips. Unless the water automatically turns itself off, leave the water running.
- Use a disposable towel to dry the hands and then to turn off the water.
- Discard the towel into a waste receptacle.
- Apply hand lotion, if desired, to keep hands from becoming excessively dry.

Infants and Toddlers When infants and toddlers are not able to have their hands washed at the sink, use a disposable towel moistened with water with a little bit of liquid soap or a disposable commercial diaper wipe to clean the child's hands and then rinse off the soap with a clean, water-moistened paper towel or a second wipe.

Immunization

Maintenance of age-appropriate routine immunizations for all children and staff is the first line of defense against the diseases for which immunizations are available. Immunization strengthens people by building the immune response and thus improves resistance to specific types of germ. Children should be immunized before entry into child care, and immunizations should be kept up-to-date. The current schedule of recommended immunizations of the American Academy of Pediatrics should be followed. This schedule is published as a part of a routinely updated manual, traditionally covered with a red binder, called The *Report of the Committee on Infectious Diseases* or, more popularly among pediatricians, "The Red Book." Child care programs will find The Red Book a useful reference because it lists specific information on the cause, incubation

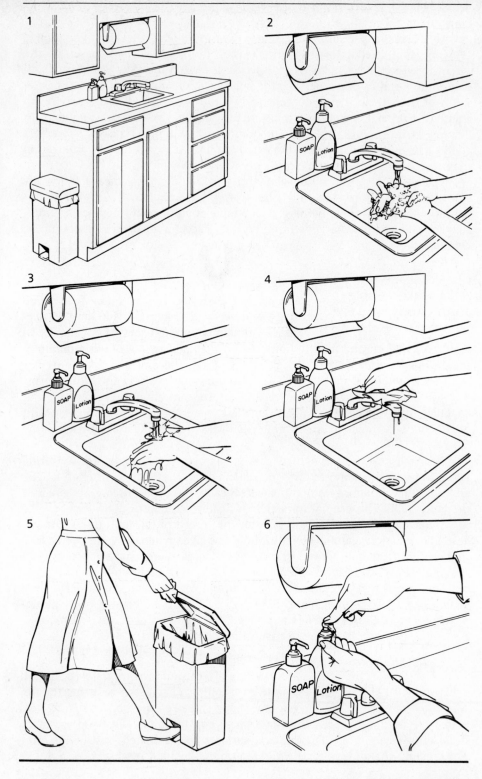

FIGURE 9.2
*Step-by-step se-
quence for
proper hand
washing.*

period, spread, control, care of contacts, and treatment for each type of infectious disease of children.

All vaccines cause some adverse reactions in some people, and none protect everyone completely. However, the decision to use a vaccine is based on the extent to which the benefits of the vaccine outweigh the risks. Child care staff play an important role in checking the immunization and well-child supervision status of children in their care and steering those who need health services to health care providers. Because child care providers have done such a good job in helping to make sure children are immunized, national statistics show that children in child care are better protected against disease through immunization than are children who receive care only at home.

New vaccines are being developed that will add control measures for diseases that can be spread in child care. Currently, vaccines are available to prevent diphtheria, tetanus, pertussis (whooping cough), polio, measles, mumps, rubella, and *Haemophilus influenzae* type b. Vaccines to prevent chickenpox, cytomegalovirus, and rotavirus are being tested.

Other Measures to Make People More Resistant to Infectious Diseases

Good nutrition, including vitamin C-rich fruits and juices, breads and cereals, milk, meat group foods, and vegetables, help provide the fuel necessary for maintenance of healthy body tissues. In addition, children and adults should try to maintain enough fluid intake that their urine does not become dark yellow. Urine can become a dark yellow color from taking vitamins or having a disease, but usually a dark yellow urine means that the body is trying to conserve fluid by concentrating the urine. Without adequate fluid, the body will not be able to keep all tissues as well supplied with blood and with the infection-fighting chemicals and cells that are carried in the blood.

Rest and exercise strengthen the body's ability to handle stress. During periods of rest, the body restores and repairs damaged tissues. Although fatigue and upsetting situations do not themselves cause infectious disease, they reduce the body's ability to use natural defenses against infection.

Medications can be used to prevent the spread of infection of certain diseases. For example, gamma globulin should be given when there has been a case of hepatitis. Rifampin may be recommended if there has been a case of *Haemophilus influenzae* type b meningitis. Treatment of all the children in a group with pinworms may stop the reinfestation that commonly occurs. Whenever a serious illness occurs in a child care setting, or if more than one or two children develop the same disease, a health professional who knows or can obtain public health information about the disease should be consulted.

General Environmental Hygiene

Maintaining a clean and appropriately sanitized child care facility is effective in reducing the development and spread of infections. Ongoing programs are needed to teach the importance and techniques of hand washing, disposal or cleaning of materials and surfaces contaminated with body secretions, diaper changing and toileting, food handling, and meal service.

Diaper-Changing Techniques Routinely, diaper-changing should include:

- the location of diaper-changing areas adjacent to a sink and as far away as possible from where food is prepared or served
- the use of disposable diapers, unless a child is unable to use them
- placing soiled clothing, unrinsed, in a plastic bag to be sent home to be washed
- disposal of diapers, changing paper (used to cover the changing table), wipes, and gloves (if used) in covered containers operated by a foot-pedal
- cleaning of the child's hands, cleaning and sanitizing the changing surface, and cleaning of the caregiver's hands

The surfaces that are used for diaper changing should be nonporous, smooth, and easily cleaned. They should be kept clear of all other objects, and they should be washed to remove visible soil and then sanitized after each child is changed. Diapers, wipes, and a bottle of bleach water or other sanitizing agent should be kept off the diapering surface but not behind cabinet doors, which would themselves become contaminated during use. The use of gloves for diaper changing does not substitute for hand washing but can reduce the level of contamination that washing must remove from the caregiver's hands.

Wipes that are used to clean the children should be disposable. Wet paper towels are acceptable if they are freshly moistened at the time of use. Keeping a stack of wet towels around invites the growth of germs. Commercial disposable diaper wipes are a more expensive but easy-to-use alternative.

Potty or Training Chairs Receptacles for excrement that do not flush are built-in sanitation problems. Without flushing toilets, the staff must handle the germ-laden body fluids and must clean the potty in a sink somewhere. If portable potty or training chairs are used, a separate sink or commercial bedpan washer should be provided and used for no purpose other than to wash and sanitize the potty chairs. The chair must be made of nonporous material that can be washed and sanitized (with a bleach solution, 1 tablespoon of bleach to 1 quart of water, made fresh daily) after each use. The staff time required to wash and sanitize this type of equipment and the potential for contamination of the environment make potty chairs impractical in child care.

Washing Toys and Surfaces Keeping toys and surfaces clean is essential to reduce the sharing of germs. Dishwasher-proof toys for infants need to be available in sufficient numbers so that a toy that has been slobbered on can be removed from service when a child puts it down, before other children put the toy into their mouths. An ordinary dishpan with soapy water labeled "soiled" can be used for soaking these toys until they can be washed in the dishwasher or by hand. If the toys are washed by hand, the sanitary dishwashing procedure must be followed: soapy wash, rinse, soak in diluted bleach water (¼ cup to a gallon), and air dry. Cuddly toys should also be washable and individually assigned to children. Many stuffed toys can be washed in a clothes washer. Toys that cannot stand up to frequent washing should stay at home.

Soiled toys from a child care classroom must be washed either by hand or by dishwasher to reduce the sharing of germs.

Crib rails, seat bars, tabletops, and any other surface that children handle or drool on need to be cleaned with soap and water to remove visible soil and then sanitized with the diluted bleach solution before another child has contact with that surface, especially before food is served. Use of disposable table mats for eating may reduce the incidence of diarrhea. Certainly the predilection of children to eat off the table no matter how big a plate they have makes table cleaning and covering before meals appropriate.

Care of Blood-Contaminated Surfaces Simple washing with soap and water to remove blood is the first step. Then, any surface contaminated by blood should be sanitized with the same bleach solution that is used to sanitize other surfaces in child care (1 tablespoon of bleach to 1 quart of water).

Maintaining Healthful Humidity and Temperature

When the air is excessively dry, water is drawn from the mucous membranes into the air. The loss of fluid from the membranes interferes with the protective functions that take place in the mucous barrier. Keeping rooms too warm when outdoor temperatures are low makes it more difficult to maintain humidity at the comfort level of 40–60 percent. Cold outdoor air holds very little water, but when it is brought inside and warmed, it can hold much more. Unless humidifiers are used, the dry air will pull moisture out of anything—people, plants, rugs. Static shocks received from walking across a carpet in winter are evidence of inadequate moisture. Excessively hot environments increase the loss of body fluid by evaporation of sweat from the skin.

Caregiver Assignments and Cohorts

In good-quality child care, each child is assigned to one caregiver, who is the primary adult responsible for that child in the child care program. Other adults will share in the child's care, but when more adults interact with a larger group of children, the opportunities for transfer of germs from one to another are increased. Keeping children together in small groups (cohorts) cared for by the same caregivers is a public health strategy for reducing the spread of infection.

One infection control measure commonly recommended is the establishment of cohorts of children at the same developmental level. This strategy is designed to prevent infants and toddlers from spreading disease to older children. However, mixing children of various age groups may have some curricular advantages. Such groups are more like the normal family structure in which younger children learn from older children, and older children can develop nurturing skills by assisting in the care of younger children. In situations where children of different developmental levels are in the same child care group, strict adherence to sanitary routines is essential.

Practicing Healthy Behaviors

Despite the social convention, children who are taught to cover the nose and mouth when they sneeze and cough are learning to increase the risk of the spread of disease. Unless they wash their hands after each sneeze or cough, they will transfer the germs now concentrated on their hands to every surface that they touch. Children should learn to turn away from other people, or to turn their heads toward their own shoulders when they sneeze or cough.

Use disposable tissues and washcloths and discard them immediately after use into plastic-lined receptacles. Hankerchiefs gather germs; reused nasal tissues are no better. Washcloths collect and grow germs. If they are used, each should be restricted for use by one child (a tough rule to monitor in child care) and laundered daily.

Even in winter, windows need to be opened at least once daily to dilute breathed air with fresh air that has fewer germs. If an internal ventilation system is used, the air flow should be from the child care space to the outdoors, not from one child care area to another. Spacing of cots and cribs at least 3 feet apart allows the germs breathed into the air by one child to fall to the floor or die before reaching an adjacent cot or crib. While it is true that the children are closer to each other when they are awake, by separating them while they sleep, the dose of germs donated by one child to another is reduced at least for that period of time.

When water play and manipulation of moist art materials are a part of the curriculum, children should have their own water pans and art materials to use whenever possible, rather than have a group of children share germs through this type of play. When shared use is essential to the activity, close supervision to prevent introduction of nasal mucus or mouth secretions is necessary. Hand washing should precede and follow such shared activities.

PREPARING PARENTS FOR THE INEVITABLE

Before enrolling children in child care, parents need to know that some illness from infectious disease is inevitable and that when children first enter care, these illnesses occur fairly frequently. Because every child is likely to experience some illness that will require exclusion from day care, parents should be helped to plan, maintain, and evaluate their alternative child care arrangements at enrollment and on an ongoing basis.

Parents need to know from the time of enrollment who will decide whether an ill child can come to child care or can stay if the child becomes ill during the day. Because the parent is ultimately and legally responsible for the care of the child, the child care provider has the right to accept or reject the transfer of this responsibility for care from the parent. Within the program, disputes over whether the child can remain in care are best handled by someone other than the child's own caregiver to preserve the close relationship between caregiver and parent as much as possible.

For their part, child care providers must consider the dilemma faced by parents whose alternative care arrangements are tenuous or inadequate. Because of the number of variables to consider and how these factors will differ from one instance to another, the best policies are those which outline the factors to be weighed and provide for consideration on an individual basis. The needs of the other children and the staff in the program as well as the needs of ill children and their parents should be considered, but the final decision belongs to the program.

Parents not only should have plans for alternative care when their children are too sick for the child care program to meet their needs or when their illness poses a risk to the other children in the group but also should be prepared to call the child care program if a child cannot come and to let the program know about the problem. Sometimes, the child care program staff or the program's health consultant will need to speak to the child's health provider directly to obtain clear information about the nature of the problem. If the child has an infection that could spread to other children, the staff and the other parents need to know about it. Sample letters for parents are provided in Appendix D.

When an infectious disease known to be a potential problem for others occurs in the child care program, public health authorities should always be notified and expert advice obtained. Caregivers should be informed as soon as possible and should be given as much specific information about the disease as possible.

Parents will ask caregivers questions about the disease and about the situation of the ill child. Unless the parents of the ill child have authorized the program to share information about the child's status, this information must be treated as confidential. The essential information to be shared with parents is that a case of the specific infection has occurred, what causes the infection, how it is spread, what parents should watch for, and what parents should do.

Several questions must be addressed in considering when a child is too sick to come to child care: What criteria will be used? Who will have the last

EXCLUSION GUIDELINES

word if parents and caregivers disagree? When and how promptly must an ill child leave the program?

Parents who need child care generally have difficulty maintaining and using alternative arrangements. The alternative care available to many parents is inconvenient, makeshift, and inadequate. Parents who are reluctant to lose work time may keep a school-age sibling home as caregiver, leave the child at home alone under remote supervision by a neighbor, or supervise the child themselves from work by phone.

Programs experience frequent conflicts between parents and child care professionals over the care of ill children. From the child care provider's point of view, the other children in the group must be protected from exposure to a child who can spread a contagious disease. Further, ill children may demand more staff time and attention than well children. Child care providers must also consider whether they are able to provide the measures that will help the child to recover as quickly as possible.

If the purpose of excluding an ill child is to prevent the spread of infection to others in the group, this action is rarely appropriate. The few instances where exclusion is required are limited to infectious diarrhea and vomiting, untreated conjunctivitis, impetigo, ringworm, head lice, and scabies. For most of these conditions, exclusion can be limited to a day or two, during which time the child receives treatment to bring the condition under control.

Children with infectious diarrhea or vomiting spread the disease by contaminating the environment with infectious viruses or bacteria. Unless the environment of the well children in the group can be adequately protected by careful hand and surface sanitation, vomiting children or children with frequent loose stools that cannot be contained in a diaper probably should be cared for in a setting where only a few individuals are exposed to the infection.

Children with bacterial or fungal infections of the eyes, skin, or hair are usually not infectious about 24 hours after treatment has begun. Because determining contagiousness involves review of technical information, child care programs need ready access to the advice of a knowledgeable medical professional. Public health officials traditionally provide this advice, but many practicing pediatricians have the needed skills and references.

Even for health professionals, decisions about the extent of risk for spread of infectious diseases are judgment calls. Children with no symptoms of illness may carry virus particles that can spread infection in the nose, mouth, stool, and urine. Most children who develop symptoms of illness shed infectious material several days before developing any symptoms; some shed this material for many days after the symptoms are gone. Because the contagious phase of respiratory illness is so difficult to predict, reputable scientists question the value of exclusion to prevent exposure of other children for any infection that is transmitted through the respiratory system, even chickenpox. The exclusion criteria shown in Table 9.1 are based on current understanding of infectious disease risks.

Even though it is rarely possible for providers or parents to know when a child has a communicable illness, about half of all state regulations require that children who have such an illness be sent home. Many child care programs and some state licensing agencies require that a child with a temperature over a specified level must be excluded from care.

Levels of temperature used by child care providers as an exclusion criterion vary widely and are generally inappropriate. Normal children may have temperatures of up to 100 degrees Fahrenheit rectally, especially during the late afternoon and early evening. Moreover, research studies have shown that the presence or absence of fever in an ill child is not correlated with the amount of infectious material being shed. Therefore, fever is not a good indicator of the need to exclude a child to protect others from exposure to infectious disease.

T A B L E 9.1

EXCLUSION GUIDELINES

Disease	Exclusion required
Infectious respiratory diseases except strep throat	No
Infectious diarrhea, not contained in a diaper	Yes
Varicella (chicken pox)	No, if only those children already exposed remain in contact with the infected child.
Cytomegalovirus	No
Hepatitis B carriers	No, but avoid shared secretions.
Lice, scabies, impetigo, ringworm	Yes, until day after treatment.
Infectious conjunctivitis (with pus)	Yes, until day after treatment is initiated.
Giardia lamblia carriers	No, if asymptomatic unless there is a child in the group with diarrhea.
Hepatitis A	Yes, if known. Use gamma globulin to stop outbreaks.
Haemophilus influenzae type b	Yes, for illness. Consider use of rifampin to eliminate organism from carriers. Use vaccine in all day care children 18 months–5 years.
Vaccine-preventable diseases (measles, mumps, rubella, diphtheria, tetanus, pertussis or whooping cough, *Haemophilus influenzae* type b)	Yes, until judged not infectious by a physician. Report every case to the health department.
Strep throat	Yes, until day after treatment is initiated.

There is no rationale for requiring instant isolation of a symptomatic child from the rest of the group. Separation is inappropriate unless the child will receive better care elsewhere or unless

ISOLATION OF ILL CHILDREN

the attention required exceeds the resources available in the child's usual group. Furthermore, studies comparing child care centers in which stringent policies are followed for excluding ill children with centers that are less stringent about exclusion show no difference in the amount of illness.

If the reason for excluding an ill child is for the comfort and health of the child, the decision about exclusion will focus on different factors. Of course, the needs of other children in the group

WHEN ILL CHILDREN CAN REMAIN IN CHILD CARE

must also be considered. A child who is clinging to the caregiver or coughing so often that the sound disrupts all other activity may unfairly tax the resources available to the other children in the group.

Child care and health professionals struggle to establish reasonable, scientifically supportable policies for excluding children with transmissible infections. There is no evidence to suggest that the exclusion of children with respiratory infections from child care makes any difference in the wellness of others in the group. The decision about permitting a child with a respiratory illness to remain in child care should depend on the availability of the parent to provide the needed care and the ability of the child care staff to provide the extra attention that an ill child requires. On the other hand, most programs find it prudent to exclude a child with frequent loose infectious stools because stool running out of a diaper or let out by accident in a child's underwear poses a significant risk for spread of infectious disease if the ill child remains in the program.

More liberal use of stool cultures and parasite evaluation for children in child care may be indicated to identify cases that pose a public health risk. Not all loose stools are caused by infectious disease agents. For practical purposes, exclusion might be considered when a child is having twice or more the usual frequency of stools with a liquid consistency that are not easily contained by toilet habits or in a diaper. If the pattern persists or appears in other children in the child care group, laboratory investigation to identify the type of germ causing the problem is appropriate.

Except in cases of unusual diseases, children who have been excluded from care due to illness can be readmitted when they feel and act well. Requesting a note from a physician for readmission

Readmission of a Child Who Has Been Ill

is both unnecessary and costly. Physicians generally determine whether a child has recovered by asking the parent about the child's behavior and by the child's loss of physical signs of illness. When in doubt, a physician who is a consultant to the program can be asked whether further evaluation is required before the child's is readmitted to the program. Every child care program needs to have easy access to a health professional for technical advice about the nature of an infectious disease problem and suggested control measures.

INSPECTIONS

At least yearly inspection of every day care facility (not just the kitchen) by a qualified sanitarian can help pinpoint problems before they cause significant disease. Some sanitarians can provide suggestions on inexpensive ways to modify problems identified at the child care site. There should be no exemptions from health and safety inspections because of religious affiliation or any other reason. Religious affiliation does not immunize against infectious disease. Sanitarian inspections help programs prevent infectious disease in children and staff.

SUGGESTED ACTIVITIES

1. Observe hand-washing behaviors in a child care program for 30 minutes or so. How many people use appropriate technique when they wash their hands?
2. Observe diaper changing in a child care program. What common breaks in technique are evident?
3. Observe surface sanitation practices in a child care program. When does the routine get ignored?
4. Check the immunization records of children in a child care program against the recommended schedule. Are the children up-to-date? How hard is it to work with the schedule? How hard is it for parents to make sure their children are kept up-to-date?
5. Write an exclusion policy for a child care program. How reasonable is it from the caregiver's point of view? How reasonable is it from the point of view of the parent of the child who is ill and from the point of view of the other parents?

FOR MORE INFORMATION

American Academy of Pediatrics. *Report of the Committee on Infectious Diseases*, 21st ed. Elk Grove Village, IL: American Academy of Pediatrics, 1988.

American Red Cross. *Child Care Course, Health and Safety Units*. Washington, DC: American National Red Cross, 1990.

Kendrick, A., Kaufmann, R., and Messenger, K., eds. *Healthy Young Children, A Manual for Programs*. Washington, DC: National Association for the Education of Young Children, 1988.

CHAPTER

10

Managing Illness
in Child Care

IN THIS CHAPTER:

CARE OF CHILDREN WITH SHORT-TERM ILLNESSES
CARING FOR CHILDREN WITH CHRONIC ILLNESSES AND DISABILITIES
ALLERGY
MEDICATION
WRITTEN POLICIES AND PROCEDURES FOR CARE OF ILL CHILDREN
SUGGESTED ACTIVITIES
FOR MORE INFORMATION

Because young children are ill often, the care of ill children is a major issue for early childhood professionals. Illness is recognized by a change in bodily function or behavior. These signs or symptoms are clues to diagnose the problem, not diseases in themselves. For example, a change in a child's behavior can be a subtle sign of illness, but it can also occur because of a new baby in the family.

Children respond differently to illness than adults. Their behavior during illness depends on their developmental stage and on the nurturance they receive from trusted adults. Unlike adults, children do not take time off when they are sick. Instead, they integrate their illness experience with other current routines. Pain is endured with or without complaint and then managed emotionally through play and behavior during and after the illness. When ill, children may regress to a less mature level. The amount of behavioral change observed is related to the amount of disruption in the child's usual routines. Nurturance from a familiar caregiver in a familiar place minimizes the disruption and stress of illness.

Parents respond to their child's illnesses on the basis of their own experiences with illness, their resources, and the demands that their other roles place upon them. Parents inevitably have conflicts as they struggle to fulfill simultaneously their responsibilities to children, jobs, and spouses, and meet their own needs. When an ill child is brought to the early childhood setting, parents are rarely deliberately evading their child care responsibility. They are choosing what they believe is the best coping strategy for the circumstances. Sometimes, parents feel that sharing the care of the child with their child's regular caregiver will provide better care than the parent can give the child alone. Sometimes, parents do not realize that the child is ill because subtle signs of illness were not recognized during a hurried morning departure routine.

Caregivers also view illness on the basis of prior experience. In addition to their concern about meeting the needs of an ill child, caregivers tend to worry about the possibility of the spread of contagious diseases to themselves, to their families, and to other children in care. Furthermore, experienced caregivers know that ill children may require extra attention, which may make the caregiver's job harder. Since the course of illness is not absolutely predetermined, caregivers also worry that an ill child might become worse while in their care.

In contrast with caregivers and parents, child health professionals tend to be more relaxed about illness in children. Studies of ill children have shown that

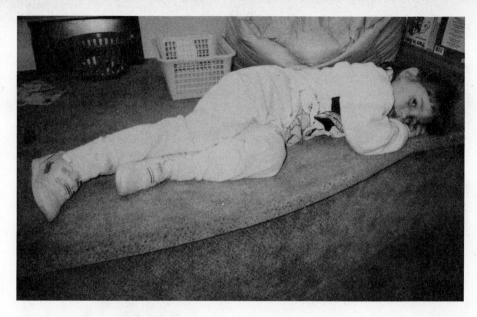

Children may develop signs of illness during the child care day.

behavior is a good indication of the severity of disease. Kids who can play and interact well are unlikely to be severely ill. Health professionals know that most illnesses are self-limited and that the maximum period of contagion is usually early in the disease, before and shortly after the first symptoms appear. Despite close daily contact with ill children, child health professionals do not experience an excess rate of common illness. They know that their own immunity and conscientious hand-washing practices are good protectors.

CARE OF CHILDREN WITH SHORT-TERM ILLNESSES

Toddlers and preschoolers experience a yearly average of six to eight respiratory infections, the most common type of illness of childhood. Of parents surveyed at home, about a third report that their children under 5 years of age have been ill with a medicated respiratory infection within the previous two weeks. For infants in child care, parents report that as many as half have had a medicated respiratory infection in any given two-week period. The frequency drops off as children grow older; adults average four infections per year.

The next most common illness is gastrointestinal infection. The average child experiences one to two bouts of diarrhea or vomiting each year. Noninfectious illnesses occur less frequently, but for some children often enough to pose a problem for caregivers and parents.

Helping Parents to Plan Ahead

Every child is likely to experience some illness that requires exclusion from an early childhood program. When a child becomes ill, many parents face the prospect of disrupted schedules and feel guilty about their need to use

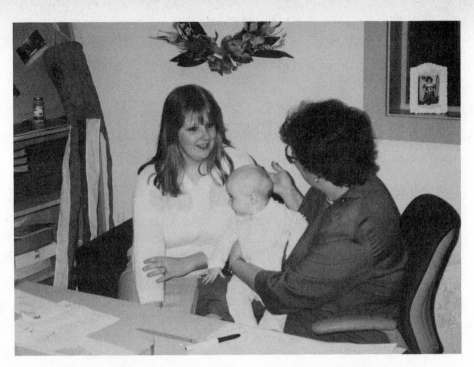

At an intake interview, parents should discuss specific plans and program policies in the event of child illness.

child care. Some parents feel that they have failed to protect their children from illness by allowing them to be exposed in the child care setting to other children who are ill. Parents often feel that by sending their sick child to child care, they are not responding to the child's illness personally, not "giving the best care," as a "good parent should." From the parent's perspective, a child's illness is a source of stress.

Before each child's first entry into day care, the intake process should include a discussion of program policies and parent plans for child illness. Usually, parents will want to be with a child who is seriously ill, regardless of the demands of other responsibilities. Parents need to understand their employer's policies on use of sick days and personal leave. Can a parent use sick leave when a child is ill but the parent is well? Is advance notice required for taking personal days?

Most working parents need an alternate person to care for a child who is too ill to attend the day care program but not so ill that the parent must stay home from work. Parents need to find a dependable adult whom the child knows and likes, someone who can be comforting and reassuring when the child does not feel well.

At enrollment and periodically thereafter, parents should be helped to plan, maintain, and evaluate an alternative child care arrangement for times when their children are ill. Parents need to know what criteria will be used and who will have the final say about whether an ill child can come to the program or can stay if the child becomes ill during the day. Because employer and peer expectations for meeting career and job responsibilities are so strong, parents need ongoing support to balance parenting responsibilities against job pressures. For some parents, the choice to care for the child themselves can result in a lower performance evaluation, lower pay, or even a need to find a job that offers more flexibility.

Deciding When Ill Children Can Remain in Child Care

The determination of how sick is too sick to be in the early childhood program differs from one program to another, depending on the resources of the program and the needs of children, staff, and parents. Exclusion from child care of children whose parents do not have good alternative care can result in spread of disease in the community. Parents faced with job pressures may choose to place ill children in another child care program, take the children to work with them, or leave the children at home to care for themselves. Child care professionals need to play an active role in helping parents plan for and manage these dilemmas. A sample letter to parents about preventing infections and planning for illness is provided in Appendix D.

Mildly ill children who can carry on normal routines with only a little extra attention can and should receive care in their regular child care arrangements. Children with common colds can go outside in good weather, and may only need to be encouraged to drink extra fluids. Seriously ill children and children who pose a risk of spreading disease to others should receive care from parents and health professionals. Mildly ill children who cannot carry on normal routines but who are not sick enough to need care only from their parents can receive child care in specialized child care settings. Early childhood programs should consider the following key planning and policy issues to decide when ill children can remain and when they need care elsewhere:

- communicability of infections
- needs of ill children
- staffing demands
- parent needs
- established procedures for management of illness, including administration of medication
- health professional advice
- who decides whether an ill child can receive care in the program

Communicability of Infectious Diseases Communicability of infectious diseases is an essential factor in deciding whether an ill child or adult can remain in the program. Some basic understanding of the course of infectious diseases is required to know when a disease can be spread to others. For common respiratory infections, the period of communicability usually begins a few days before and ends a few days after symptoms such as a runny nose or fever first appear. Often, by the time the secretions are thickened, the battle of the body over the original infection has been won. Since thickened secretions provide a good environment for bacterial growth, noncontagious complications such as ear infection, bronchitis, and pneumonia may occur after the initial contagious period of a common respiratory infection is over.

Although infections associated with diarrhea or vomiting are usually highly contagious, some individuals may be carriers of gastrointestinal infections and seem perfectly well. On the other hand, because young children often have loose stools for noninfectious reasons (e.g., reaction to foods), it may be hard to tell when loose stools mean infection. Three criteria of gastrointestinal infection are (1) stools are unformed and watery, with a frequency twice or more what is usual; (2) more than one person in the same group has diarrhea; and (3) the diarrhea is associated with temperatures of 101 degrees Fahrenheit or more.

Other types of infections must be diagnosed to determine whether they are contagious. Fever alone indicates illness, but not necessarily infectious disease. Immunizations, reactions to medications, inflammatory diseases such as juvenile rheumatoid arthritis, and many others can cause fever but pose no risk of contagion.

Needs of Ill Children Some children with moderate temperature elevations are able to function with no apparent impairment, whereas others without fever seem gravely ill. Many children are happy to curl up with a book or rest quietly while normal activity continues around them. Others who are disturbed by noise and light need a darkened, quiet place to rest. Of course, the needs of the other children in the group must also be considered.

Staffing Demands Contagious or not, sick children often require more attention than well children. Time and attention must be taken from the other children and activities of the program. When children are ill, classroom staff can be supplemented by paid substitutes, volunteers, or administrative personnel, but children need care from adults whom they know well. When staff from outside the classroom help out, special hand-washing and clothing precautions should be observed so that infectious diseases are not transmitted from one group to another.

Parent Needs In deciding whether an ill child may remain in the program, the needs of parents must also be considered. Child care program staff should ask the following questions:

- Will parents be able to take care of the child? Can either parent rearrange his or her schedule at work or school or bring work home? If both parents have flexible schedules, can both share in caring for the child during an illness? Might each take a half day off from work?
- Will absence from work to care for a sick child result in loss of pay? Will the parent who is faced with a pay loss choose to leave the child in an unsafe child care situation, even alone?
- For school-age children, is the child competent enough to be left at home, to convalesce with only telephone supervision from a parent?

Established Procedures for Management of Illness Because young children are ill so often and their symptoms linger long after they pose no threat to others, all programs need to have procedures for management of illness. If all children were excluded for all symptoms of illness, one-third to one-half of the children

Early childhood programs should consult with health professionals about management of illness.

would be absent. These procedures should address the types and severity of symptoms that the program can handle, what adaptations can be made by the program when a child is ill in activities, use of the facility, diet, and medication administration, as well as when and how medical advice will be obtained.

Health Professional Advice All early childhood programs need several types of health professional consultation about how to handle ill children:

□ technical advice for development of policies and procedures, including how to handle specific symptoms of illness and how to define the limits of the program's ability to care for ill children

□ technical interpretation and advice from the child's routine source of health care when the significance of symptoms or a diagnosis is unclear

□ readily accessible consultation to the program administrator about what to do when a child's illness is not addressed by the program's policies and procedures

One or more health professionals may provide these three different types of consultation. In the event of a difference of opinion that cannot be resolved by having the health professionals talk to one another, the local public health authority by law has the last word.

Since few health professionals fully appreciate the resources and constraints of the operation of early childhood programs, they cannot easily evaluate whether or when a sick child's needs can be met by the program or when a child is well enough to participate in the program's activities. Doctors usually determine wellness by asking patients whether the signs of illness are gone. For a few gastrointestinal infections, communicability is determined by sequential cultures of stool to determine that the infecting organism is no longer present. Except for these specific gastrointestinal infections, requiring a note from a doctor to certify wellness is of limited value and generates a needless office fee. Decisions about child or staff readiness to participate in early childhood program activities are best made by program staff, reserving contact with health professionals for technical input into policy development and advice about the significance and management of illness.

Who Decides Whether an Ill Child Can Receive Care in the Program Caregivers, parents, and pediatricians have different views about when children with fever or other signs of illness need to be excluded from child care. In studies of caregiver, parent, and pediatrician responses about the need to remove children from child care programs for various symptoms (Fig. 10.1), the majority of caregivers and parents use much lower elevations of temperature as a criterion for immediate pick-up than pediatricians think is necessary. The percentage of pediatricians, parents, and caregivers who think that immediate pick-up is appropriate increases when fever is accompanied by other symptoms. However, significantly fewer pediatricians than parents or caregivers think that such action is necessary for minor signs of illness. Among the three groups, caregivers are most ready to suggest immediate pick-up of febrile children, for any other symptom, or for any combination of symptoms. Bringing the views of parents, care-

FIGURE 10.1

Views of caregivers, parents, and pediatricians on the need to exclude immediately children with certain symptoms.

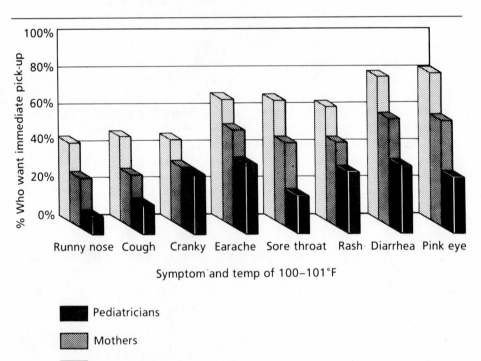

(Adapted from Landis, S. et al. *Pediatrics*, 1988, p. 665, Figure 3.)

givers, and health professionals together about care of ill children challenges every early childhood program.

If parents know from the outset what the resources of the program are for sick child care and how decisions about this issue will be made, many conflicts can be avoided. On their part, child care providers must consider the dilemma faced by parents whose alternative care arrangements are tenuous or inadequate and whose jobs are placed in jeopardy by absence to care for an ill child. Because of the number of variables and consequences to consider, the best policies are those which outline the criteria for inclusion of an ill child in the program as well as those that weigh special factors for consideration on an individual basis. However, the final decision on this matter belongs to the program.

Providing Care for Mildly Ill Children

Some parents may be willing to pay a surcharge to obtain short-term special care when their children are ill. Services that might be provided by a child care program for parents of sick children to use include:

- □ Additional staffing in the classroom of the ill child so that the child's usual caregiver can provide extra nurturance without shortchanging other children.
- □ A "Get Well Room" where ill children can spend a quiet day with a familiar caregiver in a familiar setting.
- □ Substitute caregivers who help at a center-based program who are available for one-on-one care in the child's own home for a fee to be paid by the parent.
- □ Linkages with homemakers in the vicinity of the child care program, where ill children may go for care with caregivers whom they have previously met and visited.
- □ Liaisons with a sick-child care center that the children visit often enough to feel comfortable with the caregivers and the setting.

Symptoms of Illness

Children may show the same symptoms for a variety of illnesses. Caregivers are not expected to diagnose what is wrong with a child, but they are expected to accurately observe that there is something wrong and to describe the symptoms. The chronology of the appearance of symptoms and their relationship to one another are important clues to the nature of an illness.

For most illnesses, the same questions apply. Programs can record the answers to these questions on a checklist that is completed each time a child is ill, so parents have the information to take home and discuss with a doctor if health professional advice is needed. This type of checklist is available in the materials from the National Association for the Education of Young Children and the American Red Cross listed at the end of this chapter. The questions to ask are:

1. How can you describe the symptoms? What symptoms does the child have at this time? Symptoms to note include changes in behavior, fever (note the temperature), sore throat, pain (have the child point with one finger to define the location clearly), type of pain (sharp, dull, steady, crampy), cough, wheezing, nausea, vomiting, diarrhea, headache, rash, and stiff neck.

When and how did symptoms begin?
How often are the symptoms happening?
What makes symptoms better? Worse?
How have the symptoms changed?

2. What else has happened that might contribute to the child's illness?
Did the child have any injury recently?
Has the child had any immunizations or medications in the past two weeks?
Has the child been exposed to other people who are ill at home or in day care or to new foods, animals, insects, soaps, and the like?

3. Does the child have any chronic illness such as asthma, allergies, anemia, or diabetes?

4. What is the child's intake and output?
How much has the child had to eat and drink in the past eight hours?
How many times has the child urinated?
Has the child had a bowel movement?

5. What care has been given so far?
What medications, fluids, or other efforts to make the child more comfortable have been tried?

Health professionals make diagnoses from information revealed by taking a careful history of the illness, supplemented by objective findings and appropriate laboratory data. Of these sources, the history of the illness is by far the most important. For a child in a child care setting, health professionals need the history of the illness while the child was in child care as well as the parents' report on the current status of the child when the parents seek advice. Information on onset, duration, amount, frequency, behavior-associated symptoms, intake, output, exposures, complicating illnesses, and remedies already attempted is important in establishing diagnosis and determining care. Child care programs should document this information for the child care record and for the parent to take home.

Caring for Children with Minor, Short-term Illness

The arrangements needed for care of ill children vary by the severity of the illness. Removal of children from the child care group to an isolation area is rarely appropriate. First, young children may consider isolation a form of punishment. Second, the isolation area is often in a central location in the child care facility, such as the director's office. Because of frequent contact between the staff who use these areas and other staff and children in the program, the practice of isolation may result in increasing the exposure of other children and adults to a child's disease. Contact with new susceptible individuals may be most effectively limited by having an ill child remain with the group already exposed to the illness until the child is able to leave the child care facility.

Some children have illnesses that do not require exclusion for control of contagion or parental care. If their care requires more change in child care routines than their regular child care program can easily provide, some special arrangements should be made. Children who are excessively cranky and demanding and those who are unable to keep up with child care routines and need significant program modifications or special supervision are candidates for "get well" care.

Caregivers may be the first to recognize something unusual. After taking stock of all symptoms that the child displays, caregivers can assess the seriousness of illness and the need for further action. The child's parents must always be notified, but other possible actions include:

- adjusting routines to accommodate the needs of an ill child while still meeting the needs of other children
- contacting the program's health consultant for advice about whether the child's problem requires exclusion and how to manage the condition
- giving medications according to the instructions of parents and doctors
- implementing exclusion criteria
- arranging for emergency transport for medical care

Staff can make some simple adjustments for ill children. In general, children are more irritable when they are ill than when they are well. Planning for slower transitions and decreased activity levels is helpful. Although different illnesses require different approaches to management, some common strategies for symptoms are useful.

When children have fever, increased fluid intake is advised because more fluid is lost than usual with increased body temperature. Even when an infection is not accompanied by fever, increased fluid intake helps all body systems to fight infection and heal damaged tissues. Lukewarm, clear fluids are best because they are rapidly absorbed. Clear fluids (e.g., water, tea, jello, soda, apple juice, grape juice, and chicken broth) are defined as those that are transparent. Adequacy of hydration can be judged by checking the frequency of voiding and color of urine. Infrequent voiding of dark yellow, concentrated urine is an indication of a need for more fluid intake.

With vomiting, getting fluid in can be quite a trick. It requires patience to find the volume small enough that the stomach will not throw back. Start with 1 teaspoon at first. This amount can be repeated every 5–15 minutes, increasing the amount slowly so long as no further vomiting occurs. With diarrhea, the opposite strategy is used. Since there is a reflex that stimulates bowel activity every time something goes into the stomach, fluids are given to a person with diarrhea in as large a quantity as can be tolerated, but only every three or four hours. Special fluids with the right amount of sugar and salt are sold for treatment of children with vomiting and diarrhea. These oral rehydrating solutions, not juice or soda, should be used.

Fever is a common response to infection or reaction to conditions such as immunization in children. The height of the fever bears little relationship to the seriousness of the illness. Body temperature is regulated by the brain within limits that rarely exceed 106 degrees Fahrenheit (41.1 degrees Centigrade). Although a high fever may be a sign of significant illness, a temperature of up to 106 degrees Fahrenheit does not by itself damage the body.

The body establishes a temperature level (set point) that tends to be maintained as the environmental temperature varies. The set point of a healthy person is that person's normal temperature. When the body temperature drops below the set point, muscle tone and chemical activity in the body are increased, surface blood vessels constrict, and sweating decreases. The person feels cold and seeks more clothing or covering to retain body heat. These responses result in a rise in body temperature up to the set point. When infection or some other stimulus causes the body to release a chemical that raises the set point for temperature in the brain, these same mechanisms result in a rise in the body temperature over the normal levels, which we call a fever.

Fever is not a disease; it is a symptom. The significance of a rise in body temperature depends on the stimulus that triggers the body's adjustment of the set point.

Acetaminophen (Tylenol, Tempra, etc.) and other fever-reducing medications work by blocking the action of the body chemical that raises the set point for temperature, thus restoring the set point to normal. Lukewarm tub bathing works by dilating constricted surface blood vessels and substituting for sweating as a means of transferring body heat to the environment. If the water in a fever-reducing bath is too cool, the child will further constrict the blood vessels and shiver to raise the body temperature instead of lower it.

When should fever-reducing medications and lukewarm tub baths be used? Minor elevations of body temperature (under 102 degrees Fahrenheit) may enhance some of the body's infection-fighting mechanisms and interfere with multiplication of germs. Higher temperatures are associated with significant loss of fluid from the body by evaporation through the skin and can cause significant discomfort. With these considerations in mind, physicians usually recommend only treating children for fever whose temperatures are over 102 degrees Fahrenheit or seem uncomfortable.

Acetaminophen is the most commonly used medication for temperature reduction. The appropriate dose is 6 milligrams per pound of body weight every four hours. Because of a suspected relationship between aspirin and Reye's syndrome in individuals infected by the influenza and chickenpox viruses, aspirin is not usually recommended for use to reduce fever, especially in these two conditions.

When lukewarm tub bathing is used in addition to fever-reducing medications, 30–40 minutes of contact with the water is often needed to permit enough loss of body heat into the water to lower the temperature several degrees. In a program without a child-size sink, a temporary tub can be made by lining a cardboard box with a plastic garbage bag and pouring lukewarm water from a pitcher over the child. A few toys in the water can make the experience more pleasant.

Many programs include temporary management of fever in their procedures. In consultation with a health professional, a generic physician's instruction or "standing order" can be written so that staff can administer fever-reducing medication and tub bathing with parental consent for children with temperatures of over 102 degrees Fahrenheit. Even for children who are being sent home, using these measures usually makes the child much more comfortable by the time the parent arrives to take charge. Bringing a high temperature under control also makes it easier for a physician to assess the remaining symptoms of the illness.

Activity Ideas for Children Who Are Ill

Plan to use disposable materials for children who have illnesses that might be transmitted. Homemade playdough, fingerpaint, crayons, egg cartons with macaroni and yarn, and paper bag puppets make excellent toys for children who may have a contagious disease. Removing sick children from their toys adds an extra burden to illness because the children think that they are being punished for being sick. Receiving special playthings, love, and reassurance from those who know them best is especially important to children when they are ill. Isolation has little utility in a setting where intimate exposure has already occurred.

CARING FOR CHILDREN WITH CHRONIC ILLNESSES AND DISABILITIES

Families of children who have chronic illnesses or disabilities are more like other families than they are different. They share the needs and aspirations of all families with young children. They too need child care so that parents can work and participate in other adult activities. Early childhood education programs help families of children with special health needs by providing (1) activities that promote the development of the children, (2) respite from the demands for constant care of the children, and (3) opportunities to share planning and caring for the children with other adults who understand the day-to-day burdens of parents and have the children's interests at heart.

Even when few adaptations are required to accommodate children with special needs, many early childhood programs are reluctant to enroll them. The key to accepting children with chronic illnesses or disabilities is planning for their enrollment and reevaluating their needs on a periodic basis. Some children require intensive services that are beyond the resources of the usual program. Many have only mild manifestations of their impairment and require only intermittent or minor adjustments of the program's curriculum.

Federal Funding of Services for Children with Special Needs

As a result of public recognition of the need for supplemental services for children with special problems, federal funding of special services is available in every state. Chronically ill and disabled school-age children are eligible for services under Public Law 94-142. This federal law requires states to provide services to all children of any age to whom any services are given. In all states, these services have been extended into infancy by Public Law 99-457, signed by President Reagan in 1986. Public Law 99-457 requires that children with potentially handicapping conditions be identified, evaluated, and placed in the "least restrictive environment" or with their healthy peers wherever possible. In practical terms, many disabled infants, toddlers, and preschool children can be integrated into normal settings if supplemental services appropriate to their disability are provided. Child care programs often require little adaptation to respond to the needs of infants or toddlers with developmental delays. However, for children with significant sensory impairments (blindness or deafness), specialized services to augment a regular child care program are essential.

Supplemental services can be provided through the agencies and consultants who are paid by funds administered by the states. Multidisciplinary early intervention service teams are available in many communities. These teams establish and support individualized education plans (IEP) for preschool and school-aged children. They also provide individualized family service plans (IFSP) for infants and toddlers with special needs. Although funding is never adequate to meet the entire need, some services are available in almost every community. Information about how to obtain these services is available from the special education departments of most school districts.

Benefits of Enrolling a Child with Special Needs in an Early Childhood Program

When consultants work with an early childhood program to plan and manage a child with special needs, the involvement of the consultant often benefits the entire program. When children with chronic illnesses and disabilities participate in early childhood programs, the children and families benefit in many ways. Children with special needs who enroll in early childhood programs spend more hours outside the family in the early childhood program than in clinics or in special treatment programs. In these hours, caregivers have opportunities to implement stimulation and treatment programs and to make observations that can be instrumental in decisions about medical and rehabilitative service needs. Activities once left solely to parents such as administration of medication and implementation of physical, occupational, speech, and language therapy can involve providers who incorporate prescribed activities into the curriculum. These activities may also benefit other children in the group. As for healthy children, the child care provider has a potential role both as extended family and as a member of the child's professional service team.

Types of Disabilities

Children with disabilities include those who are developmentally delayed or mentally retarded; those with hearing problems, visual disabilities, emotional disturbances, or orthopedic impairments; and those with health problems such as heart conditions, tuberculosis, rheumatic fever, nephritis, asthma, sickle cell anemia, hemophilia, epilepsy, lead poisoning, leukemia, diabetes, immune system diseases, or diseases of any other body system that adversely affect development and education. Nationally, for all age groups from 3 to 21, about two-thirds of all children with disabilities are in regular environments; slightly less than half of these children are orthopedically impaired; the others have other health problems. Often, a physician will be called upon to define the extent and nature of a child's illness, but it is up to the educators who care for the child to determine how the illness affects developmental opportunities. Effective developmental enrichment can be achieved when parents, medical professionals, and educational professionals work together.

To assess the extent to which the routine program requires augmentation and to plan daily management, early childhood educators should ask the child's health provider some questions:

Questions to Ask the Child's Health Provider About Children with Special Needs

- □ What physical restrictions are needed because of the child's condition?
- □ Does the child require medication either continuously or intermittently? If so, how is this need determined and adjusted? What is required to administer the medication? What possible adverse effects can be seen? How will home and child care administration of the medication be coordinated?
- □ What course is expected for the child's condition?
- □ What adaptations in the usual schedule are needed for the child? (It helps if the usual schedule of program activities for this child's group accompanies this question.) Does the child need shortened activity periods or more frequent rest periods? What kind of rest period is needed?
- □ Does the child require any special diet modification?
- □ What special care or emergency procedures might be required for this child? How will early childhood program personnel be certain about their skills in performing these procedures? How will parents be assured of about the competence of their child's caregivers?
- □ Does the child need any special equipment such as protective helmets, wheelchair, adaptive furniture, or utensils for eating or activities of daily living? Under what circumstances and for how long can the child be out of braces or special seating equipment?
- □ What changes in routines are needed for the child to get the most from planned activities (e.g., having light fall on the speakers' face or having the child separated from distractions to complete a task)?
- □ What special therapy does the child require? How will the therapy be incorporated into the child's routines?
- □ Does the child require special assistance with toileting?
- □ What do the child and other family members understand about the child's condition? What goals have been set for the child and other family members in the near and distant future?

Disabled child being transported in a special seat. Copyright © J. A. Preston Corporation, 1990, Bissell Healthcare Corporation. Reprinted by permission.

Labeling of Children with Special Needs

Traditionally, labeling of disabilities has been avoided to minimize stigmatizing and stereotyping children. Especially for very young children, disability labels may be difficult to assign and may be inaccurate. However, some use of labels is an inevitable result of the need to identify resources and special expertise required to cope with the disability of the child. Every effort must be made to avoid considering such labels as fixed or final. Rather, think of each child as *a child* among whose unique characteristics is a disability that may change over time. Wherever possible, children with special needs should be included in every phase of care, making adaptations as needed to accomplish the fullest participation possible.

Transportation of Children with Special Needs

Special efforts may be needed in transportation planning. Children with disabilities may require special safety restraints for use while traveling. Emergency plans may be needed to handle any problem related to the child's disability which occurs in transit. Drivers must be as skillful and knowledgeable as other caregivers while they are in charge of the child. Whether transport is provided by car pool, bus, or parental vehicle, planning for pick-up, transit, and drop-off routines is needed.

Coordination of Care for Children with Special Needs

Each child in an early childhood program needs to have a responsible staff member who coordinates all inputs for the child's involvement in the program. For children with chronic illness, this coordination requires more time. Communication linkages must be maintained among family members, health providers, sources of evaluative and therapeutic services, and all staff who are involved with the child's care.

Medical care services for a child with a chronic illness are often fragmented, requiring that someone in the health care system coordinate medical care services for the child. The child's pediatrician, a nurse clinician, or a special patient care coordinator may have this role. Otherwise, someone else must be found who will help parents shoulder this burden.

Within the early childhood program, linkages are needed which involve transportation, food service, regular and substitute child care, and administrative personnel. Multiple individuals may need to have training to understand the nature of the child's illness, to learn the skills required to handle potential emergencies, and to know where needed equipment and supplies are kept.

The Financial Burden to Families of Children with Special Needs

Children with disabilities not only drain their family's emotional and physical resources, but they are often a financial burden as well. Any request that might result in loss of work or pay is especially difficult for these parents. Extra visits to health care providers for evaluation and therapy stress parents, as do the difficulties in finding suitable child care for employment and social needs. Health care services are often inadequately funded by insurance or public health resources, requiring outlay from family funds. In addition, coordinating health care financing programs to get the most from what is available is a time-consuming and frustrating endeavor. Commonly used sources of funds for medical care for children with chronic illnesses include Medicaid, state crippled children's services, categorical state programs for children with specific diagnosis, private insurance, disease-oriented voluntary organizations, and out-of-pocket payments.

Medical technical advancement in the care of children with chronic illnesses continues, but the human element of support to families and coordination of services lags far behind. Early childhood education programs have an opportunity to help by providing support services. The investments required are significant, but the reward is long-lasting. There is a certain undeniable satisfaction derived from helping children master their disabilities and from helping family members weather continuing stresses. A child with disabilities has unknown potential. The reward for unlocking the barriers to the fulfillment of that potential is the opportunity to admire the child's and family's accomplishments.

ALLERGY

Allergy is so common among people of all ages that every early childhood program can expect to have some children and adults with this problem. While a person can become allergic to any substance at any time, allergic problems occur infrequently among young infants and become more prevalent with increased opportunity for exposure to allergic stimuli. Allergic reactions are the result of an abnormal or increased response of the body's immune system to certain substances.

The immune system makes and mobilizes defenses against foreign substances such as germs that cause infectious diseases and is an essential protective mechanism. The system involves both chemical responses and cellular responses that work both independently and together. Generally, a foreign material is recognized by the body in the nearest lymph node (sometimes mistakenly called glands) or by cells of the immune system. A whole series of responses is then set in motion which help to tag the foreign material for destruction and elimination from the body. Some of these responses cause an increase in blood supply, tissue fluids, and secretions in the part where the offending material is encountered. These chemical responses cause discomfort when the immune response is triggered too easily or when the magnitude of the response is too great. This reaction often involves the release of a body chemical called histamine. Often, the exposure to the offending substance is in the nose, eyes, throat, chest, or skin, and these areas become congested and irritated. Such people are said to suffer from allergy.

Although the best allergy management is avoidance of the offending substance, sometimes complete avoidance is not possible, particularly with respiratory allergies. For people who are sensitive to substances that are difficult to avoid and who have trouble with histamine-mediated reactions, medications called antihistamines may be recommended.

The most common substances that cause allergy trouble are pollens, smoke, house dust, house dust mites, animal danders, molds, feathers, drugs, cosmetics, perfumes, fumes or air pollutants, dyes, insect stings, and certain foods such as shellfish, eggs, and nuts. Some of these substances are also direct irritants and cause reactions that are not allergic. However, since people with allergies are often sensitive to more than one substance and their symptoms may be made worse by irritating substances, allergic symptoms are usually improved by avoiding as many of the problem substances as possible.

The best way to tell what someone is allergic to is to note when the symptoms occur and what types of contacts the person had before experiencing symptoms. Many people put more faith in allergy tests than is appropriate. At best, most laboratory and clinical tests for allergy only supplement the observations about what makes the person worse or better in the real-life setting. Offending substances can be identified by noting when the symptoms are worse, for example: morning, afternoon, evening, or night; in wet or dry weather; in the spring, summer, fall, or winter; while visiting a household with pets or where someone smokes; when the heat is on.

It may be impossible to avoid all contact with substances that cause allergic symptoms in the child care setting, but by careful management of a few potential problem areas, it is possible to improve the environment significantly.

Smoking should not be permitted anywhere in the child care facility at any time. Smoke moves with the air in the facility and lingers for a long time. Passive smoking by children is a cause of illness both for allergy sufferers and for those without allergies.

Steam or hot-water heat is preferable to hot-air heat. Radiators of any type must be kept free of dust. Forced-air heating is satisfactory if suitable filters are used and kept clean. An electrostatic air cleaner on the main duct of the furnace is best, but special cleanable filters are also available to replace the disposable type that do not take out small particles. Room deodorizing air purifiers do not do the job. Fuel-burning heaters (e.g., kerosene or wood stoves) should not be used in a room, or where their fumes can reach a room, where people will breathe.

Periodically, the child care room, including all closets and shelves, should be emptied of all objects: floor coverings, drapes and curtains, upholstered furniture, toys, and books. Holes or cracks in the floor around heating or other pipes should be sealed off. If linoleum is used, it should be cemented to the floor. Clean drawers and closets with a damp cloth and store only cleaned and dusted objects.

The child care room should be cleaned thoroughly with a dust-holding cloth, including walls, ceiling, floor, woodwork, and closets, as often as possible. For rooms used by people with asthma or severe allergic symptoms, this cleaning should be done no less than twice a week. The floor should be waxed with a paste wax or silicone sealant. No cleaning materials that have fumes or strong scents should be used. Pay special attention to window frames and sills. Clean the floor daily with a damp mop.

Outside the room, the cots should be thoroughly washed, aired, or vacuumed at least once a week. No feather or foam pillows, mattresses, or comforters should be used. Once cleaned, rest equipment should be covered when it is not being used.

Use cotton or cotton/synthetic fiber washable sheets and blankets as free of fuzz as possible. Do not use quilts, comforters, or bedding that can hold dust. Launder curtains, blankets, and mattress pads at least every two weeks.

Plain wooden furniture is best; upholstered pieces should be avoided. Any soft furniture should be thoroughly vacuumed and covered with a frequently washed synthetic fabric that has a smooth surface. Washable cotton throw rugs may be used on the floor if they are washed every week. Plain washable drip-dry curtains or drapes may be used, but they too need frequent washing. Venetian blinds should not be used unless they are cleaned daily.

Keep only those toys, magazines, books, papers, and other objects that can gather dust on shelves that can be cleaned often.

All furred and feathered pets, including dogs, cats, hamsters, guinea pigs, and birds, should be kept out of the rooms of those that are allergic to them. Since animal dander is the problem, allowing the animal to be in the room at any time introduces the offending material, even if the allergic person is not present when the pet visits.

Plants should be kept out of rooms where children are in care who have plant or mold sensitivity.

To keep the dust down in the rest of the building as much as possible, mop the floors and vacuum the furniture in the other rooms as frequently as possible. Such cleaning should be done when allergic children and adults are out of the room.

Special attention should be paid to storage areas and basements, where dust and mold may accumulate in large quantity. If an area below grade is used for child care or if the below-grade part of the building is damp, musty, or moldy, use a dehumidifier to reduce dampness and wash the floors, walls, and furnishings at least monthly with a solution of Clorox-2 or other color-safe bleaching agents to kill mold spores.

Avoid odorous substances such as room deodorants, paints, perfumes, camphor, mothballs, tar, gasoline, kerosene, and cleaning fluids. If pesticides are used by an exterminator, be sure that they are applied only to cracks and crevices, not sprayed on surfaces in the child care area. If there is any detectable odor, ventilate until the odor is gone before letting anyone use the room.

Keeping the environment clean can often make a big difference in the need for antihistamines and other medications to control allergic symptoms. However, some medications used for allergies may be needed. Many of these require frequent administration and may not be able to be given only at home. Use of medications in the child care setting can make the difference between a child's being disabled by allergy or feeling and acting normally. Since allergic responses may change as body chemistry changes, some children do outgrow their allergies, but they may also develop new ones. With some understanding of the mechanisms of control, allergic problems can be handled.

MEDICATION

Deciding whether the program can accept responsibility for giving medication to children should be part of establishing the program's general health policies and procedures. The dosage schedule for many medications may be adjusted to limit or eliminate the need for giving the medication during the time the child is in child care; if such an adjustment is not possible, usually the dose schedule can be arranged so that medicine can be given in conjunction with the midday meal. This way, if more than one child needs medication, all doses can be prepared in the kitchen, each labeled and administered before or at mealtime.

Medications that are kept in the kitchen refrigerator must be stored in a separate, closed (preferably locked) container to prevent an overturned bottle from accidentally spilling onto food stored on a shelf below and to prevent a child from having access to any medicine. Most medicines can be safely stored in the refrigerator. By setting up routine procedures for handling and storing all medicines, there is less likelihood that improper handling or accidental ingestions will occur. All medicines that are available only by prescription are dispensed by a pharmacist and should bear the original prescription label with the doctor's dosage instructions, date of the prescription, and child's name. Medications that are available without prescription (over-the-counter drugs) still should require a health professional's written instruction to ensure safe and appropriate use in the early childhood program. If the drug has not been recommended by a health professional, the program cannot be sure that administration of the medication is sufficiently important to the child's health to justify the extra burden to the staff.

The common cold is the most frequent illness that children experience. When parents see signs of a cold in their children, many seek a quick fix, a magic cure, something to take away the symptoms of illness and avoid the disruption that illness brings to daily life. This urge leads parents to drugstore shelves to try medications that often promise more than they can deliver. Many of the over-the-counter drugs given to children for common colds are either ineffective or contraindicated because they increase the risk of complications from minor self-limited illnesses. Strict exclusion of all children with any symptoms of illness from child care fosters inappropriate use of medications that may control symptoms but may also increase the risk of more serious illness.

The majority of colds follow a natural course that may be shortened slightly by attention to fluid intake, respiratory hygiene, and rest. Decongestants and cough remedies do not shorten the course of the illness and may alter the body's natural clean-up mechanisms, predisposing a child to ear infections and other complications of thickened, retained secretions. Decongestants generally work by causing the blood vessels in the mucous membranes to constrict, reducing the flow of blood that carries infection-fighting cells and antibodies to the infected tissues. Antihistamines make children sleepy, reducing or enhancing crankiness by dulling the senses. Blocking the release of histamine has not been shown to have any beneficial effect on the course of a cold. Cough suppressants reduce the body's ability to raise phlegm and secretions from the air tubes in the chest and throat. When coughs are merely irritative and disrupt rest, cough suppressants may be helpful, but those circumstances must be separated from the more common situation when cough suppression is not helpful.

In all cases when medication is given to children, written consent should be obtained from the parents, and a written record of the name of the child, the name of the medicine, the amount of the dose, and the time given should be recorded for the parent to see at the end of the day.

Every child care program needs written policies and procedures for care of ill children. These policies should address:

WRITTEN POLICIES AND PROCEDURES FOR CARE OF ILL CHILDREN

1. Any state regulations that define how care for ill children must be handled.

2. A plan to review, at enrollment, the parents' arrangements for care of their children during inevitable illnesses.

3. The program's resources and constraints in caring for ill children.
   - *What physical restrictions can be accommodated by the child care program (e.g., for nonambulatory children, those who cannot go outdoors, those who need privacy, rest, or care apart from the group, and those for whom sanitization of equipment and toys will be required before others can use them)?*
   - *Can the program provide medication? What types? At what times? By whom? Using what procedures? (Note that a program may be able to give a single dose of oral medication around the noon hour but be unable to interrupt the flow of other activities to administer medication at other times.) Can the program administer eye drops, nose drops, inhaled medication, or suppositories? Can the caregiver change dressing?*
   - *What adaptations in the curriculum can be made for ill children (e.g., can an ill child be allowed to nap in the corner of the room)? Can extra fluids be provided throughout the day? Can diet modifications be accommodated? What happens if a trip is scheduled for the child's group on an illness day?*

- *What special equipment does the facility have for children with minor illnesses (e.g., is a humidifier available?)?*
- *Is bathing possible for children with high fevers or vomiting?*
- *Can a separate diapering or toileting area be established?*
- *Are there special disposable toys for those whose illnesses might still be somewhat contagious?*
- *Does the facility have positive ventilation (whereby the air is steadily pumped from a clean source through the child care area to the outside)?*
- *What special care skills or emergency procedures does the staff of the program have (e.g., can someone suck out mucus from a stuffy nose?)? Is someone skilled in cardiopulmonary resuscitation always in the facility?*
- *Do the staff know what to do if a child has a febrile convulsion?*
- *How would the emergency transport arrangements work for an ill rather than an injured child?*

4. Signs of illness that will be used to signal worsening of the child's condition and the need for parental or medical attention.

5. The health consultant(s) with whom the program will review the program's health policies initially and at regular intervals and those who will be contacted for technical advice on health problems as they arise.

6. The exclusion/inclusion decision:
- *Who among the day care program staff will handle requests for care of ill children?*
- *How do parents reach this person early in the morning and late in the evening?*
- *Who in the day care program has the final say if parents and caregivers disagree?*

7. The conditions and circumstances for which the program will require exclusion.

SUGGESTED ACTIVITIES

1. Ask participants to recall all of their own illnesses for the previous six months or year. For how many days did they restrict their activities to staying at home? How many days did they work or go to school with some symptoms? How did they decide whether to limit their activity? What measures did they take to hasten recovery?

2. Ask participants to recall a childhood illness. Ask them to discuss what they remember about it. What gave them comfort? Why do they remember the particular aspects of the illness experience that comes to mind easily?

FOR MORE INFORMATION

American Academy of Pediatrics. *Health in Day Care.* Elk Grove Village, IL: American Academy of Pediatrics, 1987.

American Academy of Pediatrics. *Report of the Committee on Infectious Diseases,* 21st ed. Elk Grove Village, IL: American Academy of Pediatrics, 1988.

American Academy of Pediatrics/American Public Health Association. *National Reference Standards for Health and Safety in Child Care* (in press).

American Red Cross. *Child Care Course, Health and Safety Units*. Washington, DC: American National Red Cross, 1990.

Fewell, Rebecca. Child Care and the Handicapped Child. In *Group Care for Young Children*, Johnson and Johnson Roundtable No. 12. Ed. Caldwell, Bettye. Lexington, MA: Lexington Books, 1987.

Haggerty, Robert, ed. Chronic Disease in Children. *The Pediatric Clinics of North America*, vol. 31, no. 1. Philadelphia: W. B. Saunders, 1984.

Healthy Young Children, a Manual for Programs. Washington, DC: National Association for the Education of Young Children, 1988.

Lorin, Martin I. Is fever a friend or foe? *Contemporary Pediatrics*, February 1986.

Osterholm, M., Klein, J., Aronson, S., and Pickering, L., eds. *Infectious Diseases in Child Day Care: Management and Prevention*. Chicago: The University of Chicago Press, 1987.

Child Abuse

IN THIS CHAPTER:

DEFINITIONS
RECOGNIZING CHILD ABUSE AND NEGLECT
REPORTING CHILD ABUSE AND NEGLECT
RECRUITING STAFF TO PREVENT CHILD ABUSE IN EARLY
CHILDHOOD PROGRAMS
POLICIES AND PROCEDURES
WORKING WITH ABUSIVE PARENTS AND ABUSED CHILDREN
SUGGESTED ACTIVITIES
FOR MORE INFORMATION

Because children are vulnerable and dependent, they are easy targets for abuse and neglect. Some children, by temperament or because of special needs for care, are more vulnerable to abuse than others. Some adults, because of their own upbringing or circumstances, are more likely to become abusive than others. When a vulnerable child and a potentially abusive or neglectful adult come together in a stressful, isolated situation, child abuse or neglect is likely to occur.

During times of socioeconomic stress, the number of reported deaths from abuse and neglect climbs. Although the frequency of death from child abuse and neglect is lower than that from unintentional injury, even the latter may be considered the result of neglect since most unintentional injuries are preventable. Child abuse and neglect can occur in any setting, but wherever they occur, they must be stopped. Early childhood educators and caregivers have a duty to recognize and prevent abuse and neglect and must not be perpetrators.

The true meaning of discipline is teaching, not punishment. A child does not have to suffer pain, terror, embarrassment, isolation, restraint, or corruption to learn how to behave in civilized society. Indeed, a child who is taught by such methods learns that adults are allowed to behave in these brutal ways. Alternative,

more effective means of teaching desired behavior are available and should be used. Positive reinforcement for good behavior works much better than negative sanctions. In general, diversion, or adult interruption of the offending behavior with verbal expression of disapproval and an offer of an acceptable alternative, is all that is required for most situations.

Toddlers Once children become verbal, simple contracts produce good results. A 2-year-old can be told that while the adults are busy now, they will soon be free. If the child can wait quietly for a short time (less than five minutes at age 2), the adults will attend to his or her concern. Both the adults and the children must keep their bargains. Two-year-olds need firm limits, and they are very literal. Giving young children a way to gain control, such as counting to three before the adult steps in, helps them feel in control and behave. When a 2-year-old loses control, adult discipline must provide and teach control, not respond in kind. Ignore inappropriate behavior to avoid reinforcing it. When the child is in danger of injury, hugging the child snugly (not painfully) and talking quietly to overcome a temper tantrum often work. Brief explanations, not lengthy discussions, are appropriate for toddlers. Adult-supervised time-out should be used when a few words have not worked.

Preschoolers As cause-and-effect reasoning develop around the age of 3, children can be told in advance about what consequences to expect from inappropriate behavior. As in the adult world, the consequences should be related to the offending behavior. For example, if you take things that are not yours, you will not be trusted to be left alone with other people's possessions. You must give back what is theirs to them. If you lie, you are not believed and will need to have your word backed up by other means.

School-age Children When older children lose control, adults must calmly show how anger can be expressed in words to achieve a resolution of the problem. Adults are most effective when they discipline older children by talking out problems and making contracts with children to which both the adults and the children must be faithful.

Physical Abuse

Physical abuse is application of force that produces pain or injury. Spanking, beating, holding hard enough to bruise, cutting, scraping, burning, and tying up a child are forms of physical abuse. Some people have a firm belief in corporal punishment—"Spare the rod, spoil the child." Corporal punishment is a means of control by torture that is neither civilized nor effective. Corporal punishment teaches children that physical power should be used to control the behavior of others, an antisocial approach.

Corporal punishment works only when the recipient feels or is less powerful than the person who inflicts the pain. Inevitably children learn to respect power, not reason. They do not gain the inner control necessary for consistent, responsible adult behavior. Corporal punishment often is delivered in anger, when the potential for serious injury to the child is significant. When corporal punishment is inflicted in a cool, deliberate manner, it is sadistic and teaches a value inconsistent with our cultural expectation for resolution of conflict. Usually, adults believe in corporal punishment only if they were physically punished as children.

Abuse via use of corporal punishment must be distinguished from the rare (but inappropriate) episode of physical punishment without resulting injury that many parents admit to. Most parents lose control of reason at one time or another and spank a child. A parent who recognizes this behavior as undesirable, avoids it, talks about it with the child, and seeks alternative means of discipline is less likely to seriously injure a child than is one who believes that hurting a powerless child is the right thing to do.

Emotional Abuse

Emotional abuse occurs when adults treat children in developmentally inappropriate ways, damaging their spirit and self-esteem through belittling, verbal abuse, or excessive demands. Some adults inflict emotional abuse by ridiculing the lesser abilities of a child as a way to bolster their own low self-esteem. Many adults think that such abuse is just "kidding around," but a young child does not understand the subtlety in sarcasm.

Sexual Abuse

Sexual abuse of children is the use of a child for sexual gratification. Unlike physical abuse, which usually occurs as an unpremeditated, angry outburst, sexual abuse is often carefully planned and is carried out only after the confidences of the child and others have been gained. Generally, privacy and secrecy are necessary for sexual abuse to occur. Sexual abuse of children may go undetected for a long time because the child does not know that the relationship and acts of the trusted adult are inappropriate.

Efforts to teach young children to distinguish between appropriate and inappropriate adult behaviors place a heavy and unreasonable burden on the child for self-protection. The child may incorporate the prohibition against touching of genitalia and sexually sensitive body parts to form attitudes that can interfere with normal sexual behavior or, more immediately, with necessary medical examination and care. Children must know that adults will keep them safe. Most sexual abuse is carried out by male relatives or by male relatives of caregivers. Opportunities for unsupervised intimacy between young children and staff members of either sex should be avoided. Special efforts should be made to protect males, especially adolescent males, from situations in which they will be alone and responsible for body care of young children.

A national study of sexual abuse in child care found that there were four times as many allegations of abuse as substantiated cases. The study estimated that there were 5.5 children sexually abused for every 10,000 children enrolled in child care centers. For children in their own homes, the rate is 8.9 per 10,000 children under the age of 6. Three- and 4-year-old children were the most common victims (the largest age group of children in child care); 62 percent of the victims were girls, and 38 percent were boys. The most common symptoms exhibited by the sexually abused children were fears and sleep problems. Other clues included genital irritation and unusual sexual knowledge.

The people who perform sexual abuse in child care are not usually known sex offenders. They may or may not be college educated, and they are usually married with children of their own. By far the most common situation is for sexual abuse to occur in child care toileting facilities during times when fewer caregivers are present—naptime, early morning, or late evening.

In the national study, the most common form of sexual abuse was fondling of a child's genitals, including a high incidence of penetration with a finger, object, or genital organ. In one-fifth of the cases, children were induced to sexually abuse other children.

Given these findings, child care staff must be vigilant in avoiding circumstances that can lead to opportunities for sexual abuse or the suspicion of improper behavior. Staffing patterns should include having at least two caregivers present at all times, even in the early morning and late evening. In family day care, there is an unavoidable risk that requires unannounced visits by parents and regulatory staff to be monitored as well as possible.

Facilities should be designed to provide for adult viewing of all spaces where a caregiver could be with a child, including the bathroom. A half wall or a wall with a window from adult waist height to 5 or 6 feet above the floor can be provided in the bathroom wall to permit viewing of adult activity while affording some privacy to preschool children whose parents feel that this privacy is important. The children's bathrooms should have the stall doors removed and no locks on the room doors. Adult bathrooms should have stalls around the toilet with walls that do not reach the floor so that the occupant's feet are visible from the toilet room door. The door to the staff bathroom should also not have a lock.

Caregivers are legally responsible for reporting suspected child abuse of any kind. Despite the tendency to cover up or avoid making trouble for a co-worker, children must be protected by reporting suspected abuse to the authorities, not just to the administrator. If the situation is handled within the program by terminating the employment of the abusive person, some other child care setting may unknowingly employ the individual and expose additional children to risk.

Neglect

Neglect is the absence of reasonable care for a child that puts the child at risk for or causes harm. Neglect may be obvious by looking at a child and seeing inappropriate clothing, lack of hygiene, or malnutrition. More subtle forms of neglect are detectable as delayed development that can be corrected by developmental stimulation.

RECOGNIZING CHILD ABUSE AND NEGLECT

Conditions That Predispose to Abuse and Neglect

Victims of abuse are more likely to be abusive, usually during times of stress when other adults are not available to help. Isolation and stress are the most common factors that favor abuse. Adults who do not feel nurtured, those who were abused themselves and accept violence as a way of solving problems, and those who suppress frustrations until they explode in anger are more likely to be abusers. Abuse most often occurs when a single caregiver, particularly a male, is alone with a child.

Stress can come from many sources. In child care, the most common source of stress is understaffing—too many children for one caregiver to manage well. Marital difficulties, job problems, and alcohol or chemical abuse are also frequent factors in the abuse of very young children. Parents or staff who smell of alcohol, even if they seem to function normally, or those whose behavior is unusual at any time should not be ignored, not only because they need help but also because of the possibility of abuse or neglect of children in that adult's care.

Recognizing Abuse and Neglect That Occur Outside the Early Childhood Program

The signs of abuse of young children can be shocking or subtle. Some of the indicators are found in other conditions. This fact makes people wary of voicing their suspicions without evidence. A child may be particularly difficult because of inherent temperamental characteristics and may lead adults to be abusive. On the other hand, young children who have been chronically abused often seek abusive behavior from adults because it is with such behavior that they expect to interact.

Signs of physical abuse include injuries that are inconsistent with the story about how the injury occurred. Bruises on the face, abdomen, or backside of an infant and welts in the shape of a belt buckle, tree limb, cord, rope, or hand are suggestive of physical abuse. Children may report or act out acts of violence, be unusually fearful of adults, or be absent without explanation.

Emotionally abused children are unhappy, often emotionally unresponsive, and fearful. They are recognized by the extremes of behavior that they display: unusual aggressiveness, unusual shyness, or low self-esteem with an inability to accept praise.

Sexually abused children often show no indication other than an unusual interest in or knowledge of sexual matters. Interest in body parts, especially genitalia, is age appropriate for 3-year-old children, but simulation of the act of sexual intercourse is not. Children who have been sexually abused often reenact the experience in their play. Children who have been violently sexually assaulted may show more obvious signs related to physical injury sustained. Such children may exhibit difficulty walking, stained or bloody underwear, bruises or infections unusual for children, and extreme changes in behavior.

Abuse and Neglect That Occur in Early Childhood Programs

Physical abuse occurs in early childhood programs under the same circumstances in which it occurs in the child's own home—during periods of stress, while the abuser is without other adults to help. Such abuse is rarely premeditated, except by advocates of corporal punishment. Usually, someone other than the abuser recognizes injuries that are inconsistent with the account of how the injuries occurred. A parent may see them first when undressing the child after a day in the program. Often a conflict arises over when and where the child was injured, at home or in the program. Since several adults are often involved in the care of an individual child, responsibility for the abuse may be difficult to assign.

Sexual abuse in early childhood programs may go unrecognized unless there is some physical indication of the abuse. Usually, the abuser binds the child in secrecy and has gained the child's trust. Often the physician will suspect the problem because of signs of infection or changes in the child's body that suggest sexual abuse.

Sexual abuse in early childhood programs is usually planned and performed by someone who is sexually attracted to children. This person works to gain the confidence of children, parents, and staff and then begins clandestine sexual acts with the children in care. Sexual abuse in child care centers is less common than in family day care homes because it is more difficult to ensure privacy in the center setting.

Sudden infant death syndrome (SIDS) is the death of an infant who dies for no apparent reason. These cases often raise suspicion that abuse has occurred, even when autopsy findings confirm no known cause of death. When a SIDS death occurs during the time a child is in an early childhood program or when the child is at home, local SIDS support programs should be contacted to help everyone through the difficult grieving process. When more than one SIDS death occurs in the same early childhood program in a short period, close supervision of the program by the licensing agency and an inevitable reluctance of parents to use the program should be expected.

REPORTING CHILD ABUSE AND NEGLECT

In most states, a report must be filed by certain "mandated reporters" whenever child abuse or neglect is suspected. Early childhood professionals are usually mandated to report suspected abuse. No proof of the allegation is required, and the reporter is protected from legal redress for an erroneous report. However, reports must be made with some caution. Although individuals who report suspected abuse cannot be successfully sued for erroneous allegations, legal costs to defend against the suit may be incurred. Furthermore, erroneous reports are damaging and stressful to those who are wrongly accused. Overburdened workers who follow up on reports are often associated with less than fully professional handling of every case. Because of these concerns, early childhood providers should receive training and have access to professionals who have experience with recognizing, reporting, and managing child abuse.

Usually, the parent should be told before a report is filed. The parent needs to be told that the report is being filed as a legal obligation of the reporter, to involve helpful professionals who can determine whether the family needs assistance, and to help mobilize that assistance. Parents often are grateful that someone has recognized their plight and sought help for them. On the other hand, some are angry. Even though the reporting process does not require identification of the reporter, parents who do not know who initiated the process will suspect everyone and may distort the reasons that led to the filing of the report.

As part of being a professional who is responsible for children, all early childhood staff must find out how to report suspected child abuse and how the agency that receives the report will respond. Find out who will investigate the report, what type of evidence is needed to consider the report founded, and how to follow up on what is being done about a report.

Early childhood programs need a systematic process to fill vacancies. This process should be overseen by a personnel committee so that the burden of evaluation and selection is not limited to one person. The process includes:

- ▫ announcing and advertising vacancies
- ▫ reviewing the credentials of candidates
- ▫ interviewing qualified individuals
- ▫ checking references, background, public and criminal records
- ▫ closely observing the potential employee on a trial basis on the job

Applicants who have been previously found guilty of child abuse or neglect should not be hired as caregivers or teachers.

Whenever possible, written references should be checked by a telephone call to the person who gave the reference. On a one-to-one basis, the tone of voice and innuendos that can be discerned in conversation about a candidate may prompt further questioning. The quality of the responses received from the person giving the reference will also help to determine the extent to which the answers provided should be relied on. The questions to ask in checking an applicant's references include the following:

1. How long have you known the applicant?

2. In what capacity have you seen the applicant work?

3. How does the applicant relate to children, parents, peers, and supervisors?

4. Have you witnessed the applicant's behavior in an emergency?

When hiring adult caregivers, written references should be checked by a telephone call to the person who wrote the reference.

5. What kind of judgment and behavior have you seen the applicant demonstrate with respect to health and safety issues?

6. Have you observed the applicant communicating program policy to parents?

7. What does the applicant do to practice and communicate sound nutrition principles to children and parents?

8. Have you witnessed the applicant discipline a child for inappropriate behavior? If so, what was the situation and how was it handled?

9. Is the applicant often late or absent for illness, personal business, or other reasons?

10. What is the applicant's greatest strength in relation to the type of job being considered?

11. What is the applicant's greatest weakness in relation to the type of job being considered?

12. Would you hire the applicant for a similar job?

13. Would you feel uncomfortable leaving your own child in this person's care?

POLICIES AND PROCEDURES

Before the situation arises, every early childhood program should have a set of policies and procedures to address suspected child abuse or neglect. These policies and procedures should spell out the following:

1. Conditions considered possible abuse or neglect

2. Requirements for reporting suspected abuse or neglect in the state

3. Procedures to follow in reporting incidents of suspected abuse

4. Procedures to follow when staff or volunteers in the program are accused of abuse or neglect

5. Acceptable methods of discipline

6. Acceptable methods of restraint

7. Procedures for screening prospective staff and volunteers for previous history of abusive treatment to themselves by others or by them to others

8. Procedures for supporting parents who are reported for suspected abuse or neglect

9. Procedures for obtaining legal counsel for anyone suspected of abuse or neglect

10. Insurance coverage for costs involved in responding to an accusation of abuse or neglect

In addition, certain practices should be followed to prevent the circumstances and stresses that lead to abuse. These practices include:

- avoiding isolation of caregivers with children
- providing for visibility and supervision of all child care areas at all times
- maintaining sufficient numbers of competent staff
- providing supervision of children at all times in all areas of the facility
- protecting children from unsupervised intimacy with family members of caregivers or parents of other children
- maintaining confidentiality of records

Child abuse is usually thought of as willful acts of violence against children; neglect is the failure to provide what a reasonable person should provide to prevent an adverse outcome. Thus, child care providers may be subject to accusations of neglect and to legal action for failing to protect children from injury or to take actions to meet their needs. Having written policies and procedures is one step toward compiling the documentation necessary to protect against such accusations, but there must also be evidence that the policies were implemented, such as minutes of meetings at which the policies were reviewed and statements signed by incoming staff to confirm that they have read, understood, and agreed to abide by the policies and procedures. Periodic monitoring to ensure compliance with the policies and procedures is appropriate. Documentation of monitoring efforts can be very useful in the event the program is sued.

Early childhood programs can help prevent abuse by reducing the stresses of families, decreasing isolation, and modeling appropriate, effective discipline for parents. Families that are prone to abuse or neglect can sometimes be identified by

WORKING WITH ABUSIVE PARENTS AND ABUSED CHILDREN

their previous lack of appropriate use of services such as prenatal care, neglecting recommended follow-up for illnesses, substance abuse, or family violence. High-risk families may benefit by involvement in an early childhood program that serves as a family support center.

Taking on the care of a child and family at risk for abuse is a heavy burden. Children from families of violence often reproduce the situations that evoked the violence against them at home, provoking caregivers and seeking interactions like those to which they have become accustomed. Abusing parents often need considerable nurturance themselves but may not accept care and support when it is offered. Working with such families will not always be successful, but when a stronger, healthier family emerges from a sustained relationship with an early childhood program, a lifetime of good can come of it.

Child care routines should involve at least a visual inspection of each child every morning for illness and signs of injury. Parents and caregivers need to be sure about when and how any injuries occurred and symptoms appeared. Parents who are belligerent, who get behind in child care payments, or who talk about suing others must be treated with extreme care. These are parents who may accuse the early childhood program of abuse.

Child care programs have a key role to play in preventing, identifying, and

A visual inspection of every child each morning should be part of the child care routine.

treating child abuse and neglect. The sensitive issues related to child abuse and neglect are best handled by planning in advance with the help of community agencies. No matter what type of clientele is served by the child care program, early childhood educators will inevitably find a role as part of the community support network to protect and nurture children at risk for abuse and neglect.

SUGGESTED ACTIVITIES

1. Determine how the state handles child abuse or neglect reports. What does the state require for reporting of child abuse and neglect? What follow-up occurs when a report is filed? What type of professional investigates? What type of professionals are available to help a stressed family? What is the caseload for workers in the local agency that would handle reports of child abuse and neglect?

2. What are the staff to do according to the manuals and procedures used by the agency that receives reports and does follow-up? What portion of reports made in the previous two years have been considered founded versus those that have been dismissed?

Deitch, Selma, ed. *Health in Day Care: A Manual for Health Professionals*. Elk Grove Village, IL: American Academy of Pediatrics, 1987.

Kendrick, A., Kaufmann, R., and Messenger, K., eds. *Healthy Young Children, a Manual for Programs*. Washington, DC: National Association for the Education of Young Children, 1988.

National Center on Child Abuse and Neglect, U.S. Department of Health and Human Services, Washington, DC 20201.

Strickland, J., and Reynolds, S. *The New Untouchables: Risk Management of Child Abuse in Child Care*. Redmond, WA: Exchange Press, 1989.

Implementation
Making It All Happen

IN THIS CHAPTER:

USING STANDARDS
HEALTH POLICIES AND PROCEDURES
HEALTH RECORDS
THE HEALTH ADVOCATE
HEALTH CONSULTANTS
TRAINING EARLY CHILDHOOD PROGRAM STAFF
COMMUNICATING WITH HEALTH PROFESSIONALS
LIABILITY FOR HEALTH AND SAFETY IN CHILD CARE SETTINGS
FUNDING AND GETTING ALONG WITH WHAT YOU HAVE
SUGGESTED ACTIVITIES
FOR MORE INFORMATION

Few would disagree that ensuring health and safety is a basic responsibility of an early childhood program, but knowing how to do it is less clear. Preceding chapters have covered the principles of health and safety. This chapter addresses how to use these principles to make child care safe and health promoting.

USING STANDARDS

Some programs have access to consultants who provide the needed expertise, leadership, and motivation. More often, child care professionals do the best they can to gain access to the best advice, using written material combined with whatever other resources they can find. Authoritative written material is available as standards, regulations, and guidelines.

How Standards, Regulations, and Guidelines Differ

The term "standard" is used differently by different people. A standard is a measure used to assess the level of performance. Some define standards as the minimum requirement, but minimum requirements are those commonly expressed in regulations. A regulation is the floor below which no one is allowed to fall. Generally, standards are broader than regulations and describe the performance criteria from the minimum to the ideal. Both standards and regulations may be interpreted by guidelines that suggest ways to meet the requirement.

Well-written standards and regulations are measurable criteria that can be used as tests of performance. Standards provide an authoritative reference base for defining approved practices. Many standards that apply to early childhood programs are available. They can be found in building codes, recommendations of the American Academy of Pediatrics, criteria for accreditation for child care centers and nursery schools of the National Association for the Education of Young Children, a similar set of accreditation criteria from the National Association of Family Day Care Providers, the standards of the Child Welfare League, the performance standards of the Head Start program, and the Health and Safety Standards for Child Care of the American Academy of Pediatrics and the American Public Health Association. Standards are not etched in stone. As new information becomes available, standards are reevaluated and revised. By using current standards to evaluate programs, the strengths and weaknesses of a program can be identified and areas needing correction can be targeted.

Using Standards to Write Program Policies

Standards are good references for writing program policies and a basis for setting priorities for training. When new staff come and when current staff are being evaluated, program policy review helps to establish a common understanding of how the program operates. Regular program policy review also helps to identify areas that need to be changed because the way the program decided to implement a particular standard does not seem to work.

Using Standards for Program Evaluation and Resource Allocation

Standards help promote improved quality of care by developing shared goals and objectives among providers, parents, licensing inspectors, and consultants. They also provide an objective means of determining how the program is doing. By using standards to evaluate the performance of the majority of programs in a given community, new resources can be mobilized for early childhood programs that no one program could easily develop. Policy makers can use comparative data on the levels of compliance with standards to decide where to invest resources and to determine how well the investment of resources is paying off. Wise application of standards can also prevent unscrupulous programs from providing lower-cost, substandard care.

Scarce training resources are best used by focusing them on areas where the program is weak rather than merely enhancing areas where the program staff enjoy learning more but already perform well. The effectiveness of focused training and technical assistance can be judged by measuring improved performance.

HEALTH POLICIES AND PROCEDURES

In the press of day-to-day operations, important elements of health and safety are easily forgotten. The process of drafting and reviewing health policies provides a focus for thinking about health issues and how they influence other aspects of the program. Used well, health policies and procedures facilitate orientation of new staff and parents, evaluation of the ongoing performance of staff, and consistency in the program's approach to health matters. Site-specific health policies and procedures bring together the thoughts of staff, parents, and experts on health issues based on consideration of the past experience of the particular program at a given location and current information about optimal practices.

The best thinking of staff, parents, and experts changes over time. Circumstances change, new information becomes available, and the skills and attitudes of the people who are expected to implement the policies vary. As a result, routine, annual review and revision of policies and procedures are vital parts of a good quality program.

Although model health policies and procedures can be suggested that are likely to fit many programs, adjustments will be needed for each program

site. The policies should be written as specifically as possible, stating what is to be done, how it is to be done, and why it is to be done. A good test of a written policy is to have someone who is not familiar with the program read the draft to see whether the written material can be understood with little or no additional explanation.

During the process of drafting policies and procedures, the material should be circulated for review, revision, and final approval by those who will be administratively responsible for them, those who will be affected by them, and those who have special expertise in the areas covered. When the final copy is prepared, each reviewer and each new and veteran staff member should initial the final draft to indicate agreement and willingness to follow the policies and procedures. Copies of the policies and procedures should be widely disseminated—to staff, parents, administrators, and consultants. By encouraging reference to the document whenever a concern is raised about a health issue, everyone will become more familiar with it. Areas that need revision will be identified. If an issue is not covered or is not addressed clearly, mark a master copy so that the deficiency will be corrected the next time the document is revised. Color coding of policies that affect urgent matters facilitates access to these instructions under stressful circumstances.

Although health policies from other programs may offer a useful starting point, policies and procedures must be tailored to fit each early childhood program and each site. For programs with multiple sites, generic policies can be drafted that are designed to be supplemented by specific procedures to fit the circumstances at each site. For easy reference, the health policies and procedures should be organized topically, logically, and referenced by a table of contents. Because health should be integrated with the other components of the program, many of the health policies can and should be integrated with other written policies that the program uses. The rationale for each policy should be given, not just the rule. Knowing why the required procedures are important to health and safety is likely to help staff see such requirements as desirable rather than burdensome. Through this process, the program will become a safer, healthier place for children and adults.

Good health policies are a reflection of the combined thinking of the staff, consultants, and parents. They should be reviewed and modified on a

regular basis. When a situation arises that is not covered in the program's policies, a new policy may be written. Health policies can be combined with the program's general policies and procedures, as many topics overlap with policies that are not specifically related to health. However, certain basics must be covered:

- □ statement of services
- □ personnel policies

- enrollment
- routine health care
- daily arrival and departure
- nutrition; food and formula handling
- supervision
- curriculum, activities, and discipline
- care of ill children
- exclusion of ill children
- emergency preparedness
- management of injuries
- surveillance for environmental problems
- sanitation and hygiene
- medication administration
- bathing and swimming
- sleep, nap, and nighttime care
- dental hygiene
- health education
- transportation
- mechanism for routine review of health policies and procedures

Statement of Services This section should describe the types of services that the program offers, including any health screening services, meals and snacks, care for ill children, and reference to all the other services covered elsewhere. Include the philosophy of the program, its commitment to cultural and ethnic diversity, promotion of different points of view, and similar matters.

Personnel Policies This section should include qualifications for each position, wage structure, benefits, working conditions, staff health policies and procedures, health promotion activities for staff, occupational hazards, and training requirements. Describe initial and ongoing requirements for health assessments for all who work in the program (staff and volunteers). Include requirements for health history review, tuberculosis screening, immunization, and determination of diseases or medications that might affect the individual's role in the program or that would be relevant in the event of an emergency. Describe the practices to be followed to prevent occupational injuries and illnesses.

Enrollment This section should include the basis for enrolling or excluding children with health problems such as deafness or chronic illness that might require modification of the program. Describe how children will be evaluated before admission and how a management plan will be developed for children with health problems who are to be enrolled. List the types of information to be gathered before children are enrolled and the transitional activities planned to help children and parents prepare for regular attendance.

Routine Health Care This section should describe the routine health assessments (screenings, examinations, and immunization) to be required and how compliance with requirements will be verified. Describe how information about health care will be communicated between health providers and program staff for both routine and special health concerns. Specify how the program will assist in making referrals where appropriate. State how health records will be established, reviewed, and updated. Indicate who will have access to confidential records.

Daily Arrival and Departure This section should describe the routines for the beginning and the ending of the child's day in care. Address how notification of symptoms of illness will be shared between parents and the program staff and who will be responsible for receiving this information. Specify who will greet children on a daily basis, who will be responsible for recognizing potential health problems, and who will communicate this information to parents during and at the end of the day.

Nutrition; Food and Formula Handling This section should include how information of the children's usual feeding schedule will be obtained, updated, and used; how information on use of vitamins or mineral supplements will be obtained and whether the program will assist in providing supplements (e.g., fluoride if it is not in the drinking water); and how information on the children's food habits and home feeding practices will be obtained and used. Specify how responsibility for food ordering, food service management, and menu planning will be handled. Describe procedures for maintaining foods at safe temperatures, protected from pest infestation. Describe procedures for transport and storage of perishable food items from home to day care (formula, food for parties, brown bag lunches, etc.). Specify how nutrition education will be integrated into the program's activities.

Supervision This section should define the program's policy on the extent of supervision of children required (e.g., within view or within earshot), making distinctions where appropriate for naptime, playground play, and independent activities for older children.

Curriculum, Activities, and Discipline This section should describe how the activities of the program day will be planned and individualized for each child. Include developmentally appropriate methods to be used by staff to control and modify behavior. Specify clearly that corporal punishment, fear, intimidation, shaming, and demeaning of children are not permitted.

Care of Ill Children This section should include how symptoms will be evaluated, how parents will be informed about the status and care of their children, how health professional advice will be sought when needed, and how supervision and interim management of ill children will be provided.

Exclusion of Ill Children This section should describe the rationale for exclusion or inclusion of ill children, a list of symptoms or illnesses that will be used as evidence for a decision in an individual case, the person who is responsible for the decision, and any additional factors to be weighed in the decision.

Emergency Preparedness This section should describe how emergency evaluation will be handled, where the children and adults will gather for temporary shelter if they cannot return to the building, how verification of complete evacuation of the building will occur, how often evacuation and emergency drills will be held, and who will be responsible for planning and conducting drills.

Management of Injuries This section should describe requirements for competence in first aid and expectations for training for staff and volunteers. Specify the type and location of first aid supplies, the requirement for emergency supplies, and information to be taken on trips.

Include responsibility for first aid, care of other children in the group, notification of parents, and emergency medical transport. Specify what emergency facility and emergency transport arrangement will be used, who, in addition to a driver, will accompany a child to the emergency medical facility with the program's medical record for the child, and who will stay with the child until the parents arrive. Describe under what circumstances and how other appropriate individuals (e.g., the licensing agency) will be notified about the injury. Specify who is responsible for completing injury reports. Identify what information must be recorded, where it will be kept, and how it will be reviewed to identify common injury problems.

Surveillance for Environmental Problems This section should specify a mechanism for routine, total facility surveillance and correction of hazards, heat, light, ventilation, humidity, noise, and other maintenance problems. Specify safe locations for storage of potentially toxic materials.

Sanitation and Hygiene This section should specify a requirement for hand washing for staff and children before handling any food, after diapering or assisting with toileting, and after any contact with potentially infectious materials such as nasal discharge, vomitus, feces, wounds, or infected eyes. Indicate procedures for disposal of contaminated materials and cleaning of potentially contaminated surfaces. Include responsibility for providing changes of clothing and diapers and responsibilities for laundering soiled articles. Specify acceptable locations and equipment away from food preparation and handling areas to be used in diapering and toileting activities. State who is responsible for identifying an infectious disease problem and notifying health authorities.

Medication Administration This section should state the program's policy on use of over-the-counter medications. If medications can be administered, specify requirements for parental consent, physician instructions, labeling, safe storage, and maintenance of a dose record. Alternatively, state a policy of refusing to administer medication at the site. Indicate that parents are responsible for communicating with staff about any medicine being given to a child, even if only at home, in the event of a reaction or emergency occurring while the child is in the program.

Bathing and Swimming This section should designate areas for bathing and clothes changing away from food preparation and service areas. Specify staff/

child ratios for swimming or wading supervision. State a requirement for the presence of staff qualified in advanced life saving for swimming or wading activities.

Sleep, Nap, and Nighttime Care This section should include issues of supervision, transitions, and handling of children who are not ready for rest. Describe cleaning, storing, and labeling of individual rest equipment. Indicate responsibility for cleaning of linen if used, including the required frequency of laundering.

Dental Hygiene This section should describe the requirement for tooth brushing for children. Include supervision of the activity and sanitary storage of individually labeled toothbrushes. (Toothpaste is unnecessary). Indicate who has responsibility for supplying of fresh toothbrushes.

Health Education This section should describe how health-related topics will be discussed in routine scheduled meetings and incorporated into activities planned for children, parents, staff, and volunteers.

Transportation This section should include a requirement for availability and use of safety restraints for all vehicular travel except via public transit. Establish safety precautions for walking trips and trips away from the program site. Describe limitations on staff as drivers for children in the program. If the program provides drivers, indicate training requirements and expectations for safety precautions for them. Specify safe pick-up and drop-off locations at the program site for parents and drivers. If children are transported by the program to and from home, describe what places are considered safe pick-up and drop-off sites and how the responsibility for care of the child is to be transferred to someone at home.

Mechanism for Routine Review of Health Policies and Procedures This section should describe how the program's policies and procedures will be routinely reviewed as part of preenrollment orientation for parents, preservice orientation of new staff, and evaluation of staff performance. State how often and by whom (parent committee, staff, consultants, administrators, etc.) revision of the health policies and procedures will be undertaken.

Keeping health records up-to-date is important only if you use the information stored in these records. Record keeping is time-consuming and tedious, but it provides the memory for facts and details, an opportunity to systematically provide each person with the full array of needed services, and the means of communicating information. Information in health records should be confidential, open only to those to whom the responsible adult gives consent. Adults and parents of minors always have the right to view the records of their own information, even though the material on which the information is recorded is the property of the program. Parents have the right to request copies, but the program may charge for the copying cost.

HEALTH RECORDS

*Health records should
be kept up-to-date.*

Content of the Health Record

The data to be collected in the health record include growth information, significant items from the health history or examination, a list of current health problems, the results of screening tests, and immunization data. Immunization data include dates, special restrictions, or instructions about the health of the person. In addition, the health or general record for each individual should contain medication and special diet instructions, emergency information, injury/ incident reports, reports of observations of behavior or performance, reports of conferences, referrals, and follow-up, and individualized plans for education.

Storing and Using Health Record Data

Health records for staff and children should be kept in a consistent and usable form within the program, in a manner that requires the least amount of duplicate entry and facilitates easy recognition of items that require action. Many good forms are available for health record data. Some sources for health forms are listed at the end of this chapter.

Highlight or extract information that needs attention and note when the next services are needed. Some useful tracking systems for medical records have been developed by the Head Start program with forms, instructions, and guidance about how medical record data can be used on an ongoing basis. These manual-entry systems are beginning to be replaced by computerized data bases that easily identify children and staff who are due for services or who need special care.

Because health record information is cumulative and often difficult to retrieve retrospectively, the information should be passed to the child's next source of care when the child leaves the program. Remember that transfer of such information always requires parental consent. Coordination and sharing of information about the child with the child's source of health care is also helpful (with the parents' consent). Too often, sharing of information between health professionals and early childhood programs is one way, from the health professionals to the program via routine forms. However, the early childhood program's information can be of great value to the child's physician. Records of observations made by caregivers about a specific problem can be a clue to a diagnosis and almost always offer a view of the child that the health professional cannot obtain in a brief encounter in the office.

The concept of a Health Advocate for each early childhood program is derived from the management principle that responsibility must be clearly

THE HEALTH ADVOCATE

assigned to one individual. This person should be someone who is interested in the health aspects of the program and understands the importance of maintaining a healthy environment. The Health Advocate should also be someone who has access to the program's ongoing planning and functioning on a day-by-day basis and who is held accountable for the program's success in achieving the health component's goals and objectives.

A Health Advocate may have other roles in an early childhood program. The Health Advocate can be a teacher, a family day caregiver, an educational supervisor, an administrator, or, if available as a member of the staff, a nurse or other health professional. The Health Advocate has responsibility for increasing the awareness of fellow workers, parents, and health service providers in the community about the potential of the early childhood program for health promotion and the need for specific actions to fulfill this potential. The Health Advocate is not necessarily the person who implements every health activity, but is the one responsible for seeing that health-related tasks are done. An effective Health Advocate has good group process skills as well as the knowledge, attitudes, and diligence to persist against frustrating obstacles.

Because Health Advocates are responsible for seeing that health concerns are integrated with the other priorities of the program, they need support from other members of the staff. Some programs select the Health Advocate by having this person nominated by the staff as a group. Others programs hire the person who will be the Health Advocate with this role in mind. In either case, the administration and the other staff must support the Health Advocate's work by sharing in planning and implementation of the health component as defined by the health policies and procedures of the program. To demonstrate administrative support, the Health Advocate should be officially appointed to this position by the director of the program and should be called upon at staff meetings to contribute items for discussion and to report on progress with tasks that are ongoing.

HEALTH CONSULTANTS

Child care operations are affected by many medical technical issues and by frequently changing views about health. Information about these issues is available to child care professionals from publications, professional meetings, and peer exchange. However, even the most conscientious child care professional cannot be fully informed about all health matters that affect the program, the staff, the children, and their families. Health professional input is needed for the following:

□ to help define health goals and identify health problems and hazards
□ to help establish and periodically review health policies and procedures
□ to provide linkages to other health professionals
□ to identify appropriate and qualified community health resources
□ to identify authoritative sources of information about technical issues such as sanitation, immunization, and first aid procedures
□ to provide an immediate opinion about a health problem
□ to participate in training of staff on health issues and help identify health training resources
□ to provide advice about the management of children with special health problems
□ to provide "standing orders" (detailed instructions) for medical procedures that can be performed with parental consent for predictable situations (e.g., medical authorization to administer acetaminophen to children with temperatures over 102 degrees Fahrenheit)
□ to provide a "medical home" for children who lack a source of pediatric health care
□ to broker disputes among health professionals regarding the child care program
□ to assist in providing surveillance and solutions for health and safety problems in child care

One health consultant may not be able to provide all of the services listed above but should be able to identify other health professional resources that the child care program can use. When more than one health consultant is involved, communication among medical professionals is essential to avoid putting the child care staffer in the middle.

Where to Look for a Health Consultant

Local organizations called child care information, resource and referral agencies may be aware of health professionals who have been found to be skillful, knowledgeable health consultants for other child care programs in the community. However, a practicing physician's patient care schedule may make it difficult to assume a consultative role outside the office setting. Practitioners who are unable to take on additional consultative roles personally may be able to recommend colleagues. Local health departments may be able to provide health consultation. Many public health authorities have become aware of the public health impact of child care program operation and have started to be more responsive to requests for help from early childhood programs than in the past. Funding and personnel limitations can be overcome by advocacy for inclusion of child care consultation among other public health priorities. Other potential resources for health consultants include community nursing services, visiting nurse associations, local pediatric societies, state chapters of the American Academy of Pediatrics, pediatric departments of medical schools and hospitals, and the pediatricians who provide health care for the children in the child care program.

How to Choose a Health Consultant

Child care program health consultants need both knowledge of pediatrics and the skills required to provide consultation to a program. The credentials of the health consultant should be reviewed with these two areas in mind. Examples of eligible child health professionals are pediatricians, family practice physicians with significant pediatric training, public health nurses with pediatric training, pediatric nurse practitioners or pediatric nurse associates, and physician assistants with significant pediatric training. Because this role is relatively new to health professionals, only a few candidates will have had specific training in how to be a health consultant to a program as a part of their formal educational preparation. The child care program may need to provide on-the-job training to a health consultant with no previous experience with this role.

In addition to formal credentials (training and experience), a health consultant for child care should be someone whose experience as a parent or as an advisor to parents who use child care indicates a positive or at least neutral attitude toward out-of-home child care. Furthermore, good health consultants should be willing to visit and learn more about the early childhood programs that seek their advice.

How to Use a Health Consultant

The first step is to establish the program's priorities and needs for health professional input. Identify current areas of health concern faced by the program. Review the list of potential roles for the health consultant and rank them in order of importance to the program.

Consider how to gather the health consultant's input and how to implement pertinent advice. Effective change is achieved by involving those with authority to implement a decision, those who are affected by a decision, and those who have expertise to bring to the decision-making process. Be sure all the elements are present in working through health related problems. Orient the health consultant to:

- the philosophy of the child care program
- staff roles and relationships
- types of families served by the program
- the program's relationships with other sources of health professional advice and services

- licensing requirements
- existing child care program documents (policies, handbooks, and forms) with any health implications for the program
- the facility via a site visit

If possible, site visiting should include a day-long visit so that arrival and departure, food handling, diapering and toileting, and activity periods can be observed. Lulls in activity and naptime can be used to review site records and documents and to meet with the staff to review previously identified concerns. If a day-long site visit is not possible, the child care program must give the consultant vivid descriptions of the program's operation so that the consultant's advice can be relevant.

Ensuring Accountability of the Health Consultant

Financial arrangements will need to be decided in advance. Budgeting to pay reasonable charges for health professional time required to provide needed consultation is best. After identifying the tasks for the health consultant, project how many hours of on-site meeting, telephone consultation, and independent document review will be needed and are affordable. Payment should be based on the usual hourly compensation of the health professional whose services you wish to engage.

In some settings, health consultation will be available at no cost to the program. Physicians who are seeking to expand their practices may view their role as a health consultant to child care programs as part of an overall marketing program. Others may simply feel that health consultation is part of their commitment to the community. However, be wary of completely volunteered services. Despite good intent, accountability is linked to remuneration.

Whether the services are compensated or donated, write a contract that includes deadlines for work to be performed, accessibility, and commitments to attend meetings and review documents. Have the contract signed by the parties involved.

What to Do When Consultants Disagree

In the real but imperfect world, absolute answers are rare. In health-related matters, equally authoritative sources may offer different opinions. An issue that affects just one child or one staff person can be decided by that person's physician. If the issue involves more than one child or adult in the program, the opinion of the program's health consultant should be sought. If the opinion of an individual's physician differs from the opinion of the program's health consultant, the issue must be resolved by negotiation between the health consultants or decided by a designated representative of the public health department. As with health professional opinions about personal health decisions, second and even third opinions can be sought, but ultimately the action chosen must be the one that makes most sense to the program and conforms with applicable legal restrictions of public health and licensing requirements. Once an action plan has been chosen, all those who gave input should be informed of the decision and why other recommendations were rejected. This feedback leaves the door open for future input and helps generate support for the action plan.

Getting the Health Consultant Relationship Off to a Productive Start

Health professionals play many roles. Traditionally, health professional training is focused on the care of an individual child and family as a patient. The health professional is taught to gather background information (health history) and objective information (physical examination and laboratory data), from which an assessment and a plan are developed. The plan consists of further information to be gathered, actions to be taken, and a checkpoint for follow-up. This approach can be easily adapted to the role of the health consultant to an early childhood program. Health consultants can be as systematic in their approach to their relationship with a child care program as they are in their approach to patient care. Using these familiar concepts to view what may be an unfamiliar role can help the health consultant be more comfortable and effective.

Ultimately, just as people must search for the "right chemistry" in their patient-health provider relationships, child care programs must seek a health professional with whom a good working relationship can be established for health consultation. The time is past when child care programs can simply apply home remedies to all health problems. Health professional input is essential to provision of safe, healthy child care.

TRAINING EARLY CHILDHOOD PROGRAM STAFF

Child care staff come from diverse backgrounds and levels of preparation. Some are college graduates, while others are paraprofessionals who have no special training other than life experience. Because of high turnover rates among staff of early childhood programs, ongoing preservice orientation, inservice training, and continuing education must be planned for every early childhood program. Although many courses emphasize a holistic approach to children, health, safety, and nutrition are often only superficially addressed. The unmet need for information on these subjects is extensive.

Workers in the early childhood setting have limited resources to promote health and safety while attending to many other issues and priorities. Often staff want to learn about issues that worry them, even though these areas may not be significant problems for the child care program. These worries must be addressed to some extent, but the program must not consume all available training resources with issues of little relevance. For example, the aspect of cardiopulmonary resuscitation (CPR) skills most likely to be needed for care of children is that involving rescue breathing and care for choking. Except for medically fragile, handicapped children, children's hearts rarely stop before irreversible brain damage occurs. Current CPR courses take four to eight hours to complete, while the American Red Cross Unit on infant and child first aid, which includes rescue breathing, choke-saving, and first aid for the injuries that are likely to occur, generally requires five to seven hours to complete. Unless time is available to do both, child care programs should choose the first aid training over CPR for every member of the staff.

In deciding what topics to address in staff training, caregivers should be asked what they want to learn, but the training should be based primarily on the training needs identified by an evaluation of the program against recognized standards and the program policies and procedures. On-site training usually requires short sessions that can be held during naptime, in the evening, or during days when the program is closed. Use of time outside regular work hours is an added burden to already overworked, undercompensated workers. Thoughtful planning, provision of a meal, overtime pay, or other compensation is appropriate when personal time is used for training. Continuing education credit or academic credit should be offered whenever possible.

Topics to Cover in Training

The range of issues that could be covered is broad. Some of the key issues are:

□ recognizing and managing minor illness
□ caring for children with special needs
□ pediatric first aid, with rescue breathing and choke-saving
□ preventing injury
□ preventing and managing infectious diseases
□ caring for ill children
□ medication administration
□ emergency response practices
□ nutrition and food practices
□ occupational health and safety
□ transportation safety
□ child abuse prevention, detection, and reporting
□ growth and development
□ guidance and discipline
□ planning the curriculum
□ child care administration
□ linkages with community services
□ communication with families

Methods of Training

One of the least expensive forms of training is preparation for and participation in an on-site evaluation of the early childhood program. By reviewing the standards and trying to meet them, early childhood staff members become engaged in a learning process of immediate significance and benefit.

Formal coursework related to the health component of the child care program is beginning to become more available at the community college and university levels. These courses have the advantage of providing credentials that can lead to a degree. However, because they are designed for a diverse group of participants with different work sites, the content must necessarily be generalized.

Effective training is planned with the techniques of adult education in mind. Training sessions should be started with a warm-up activity that gets the participants involved in the topic and at ease with one another. Active and passive methods of teaching should alternate in the same session using liberal and varied audiovisual aids (films, slides, handouts, and demonstrations). It is best to pace training to involve no more than 30 minutes of passive activity.

Whenever possible, training should result in some finite task, preferably one that improves the quality of the child care setting where the trainee works. Thus, when general information is provided about the theory and factual basis to motivate change, participants should be asked to identify how they will put this information to work. A good tool is a "Plans for Change" sheet on which the participants note ideas during the training. At the close of the training activity or the beginning of the next gathering, asking all trainees to contribute an idea from their "Plans for Change" lists reinforces their commitment to making the changes and builds a library of good ideas from which everyone can draw. To ensure that everyone contributes, a master list for the group can be developed by asking for one idea from each person until all available ideas have been exhausted.

Adult education skills are delineated in numerous texts on the subject. Organizations like the Literacy Council and the American Red Cross have instructor-training courses that provide brief reviews of instructional principles to trainers of volunteers. In addition to didactic instruction about instructional methodology, prospective trainers need hands-on practice in developing a training agenda, preparing behavioral objectives, delineating the concepts to be conveyed, determining the methods, materials, and timing to use, and evaluating whether the behavioral objectives were achieved.

Structuring the Physical Environment to Promote Learning

Comfortable seating, good lighting, and absence of ambient noise are conducive to active learning. Tables provide surfaces to lean on and to hold any papers being used in the session. Groupings of chairs in a "U" shape or semicircle promote interaction as well. Limiting group size to between 10 and 20 participants enables each person to be involved in discussions in a meaningful way. Larger groups tend to foster passivity.

COMMUNICATING WITH HEALTH PROFESSIONALS

Health professionals are busy people with set approaches and mechanisms for dealing with requests for information and service. Through many years of training, physicians learn to listen for "the problem" and to filter out the essential details that help to formulate the issue clearly. First, they want to hear what needs attention, not the background information that led to the problem. When leaving a message for a health professional, give the name and position of the person to be contacted, the problem, the urgency of the problem, and the best time for the health professional to call back. If the message consists of only a name and telephone number, the call will get lowest priority among all demands for attention.

Most health professionals have secretaries, receptionists, answering services, or other "gatekeepers" to handle the flow of calls. Different weight is given to different types of calls. If time permits, a letter sent before a call is made can pave the way if no previous relationship exists.

LIABILITY FOR HEALTH AND SAFETY IN CHILD CARE SETTINGS

The concern about being sued is a powerful motivator. Documentation is a strong countermeasure to employ against unfounded accusations but is not a sure defense. Keep good records and have written procedures. Records for individuals should be retained for the period of liability specified in the applicable state law. For children, the statute of limitations is often extended to the age of majority. As a result, children's records may have to be retained for as long as 21 years. Records must never be modified after an incident has occurred. When documentation is requested by an attorney, consult your own attorney about how to proceed.

Some insurance companies offer risk management information and training for early childhood programs that they insure. Attorneys and early childhood program associations can also provide guidance. Studying past litigation can prevent future suits.

FUNDING AND GETTING ALONG WITH WHAT YOU HAVE

Money helps finance improvements, but not all improvements require money. Many changes are behavioral. No additional cost is involved in practicing exit drills. Even structural changes can often be done with donated money, supplies, and volunteer work. Local foundations can often give one-time grants to a child care program for a structural improvement. Share the problems with as many of those who are affected by it as possible. Someone may have a new and creative solution.

SUGGESTED ACTIVITIES

1. Draft a set of model health policies for an early childhood center or for a family day care home. Divide the task among class members with each having responsibility for one topic, and then put the set together for all participants in the class to review and critique. Alternately, this task can be done by each student as a term paper for the entire course. A complete set of health policies will cover most of the topics related to health and safety in the early childhood setting and will be a useful tool for an early childhood program.

2. Ask participants to contact a pediatric health professional in the community to ask whether that professional is currently a consultant to an early childhood program. If so, ask what roles that person has been asked to play and what type of compensation is offered. If the person

is not a health consultant, ask if she or he would be willing to be one, what roles could reasonably be played of those listed in this chapter, and what compensation would be required.

3. Ask the participants to work in small groups to prepare a staff-training activity. Have the small groups discuss and develop behavioral objectives and evaluation measures for each behavioral objective for the topic they chose. Then have the groups exchange their work and discuss whether the other groups' behavioral objectives are appropriately defined. To carry the exercise further, have each small group define the concepts, methods, materials, and timing needed to conduct the training activity, then conduct the activity for the other members of the class.

FOR MORE INFORMATION

Deitch, Selma, ed. *Health in Day Care: A Manual for Health Professionals*. Elk Grove Village, IL: American Academy of Pediatrics, 1987.

Kendrick, A., Kaufmann, R., and Messenger, K., eds. *Healthy Young Children, a Manual for Programs*. Washington, DC: National Association for the Education of Young Children, 1988.

Mager, Robert F. *Preparing Instructional Objectives*. Palo Alto, CA: Feron, 1962.

Mager, Robert F. *Developing Attitude Toward Learning*. Belmont, CA: Feron, 1968.

Mager, Robert F. *Measuring Instructional Intent*. Belmont, CA: Feron, 1973.

Appendixes

The Content of Routine Health Supervision for Children

HEALTH HISTORY

A comprehensive and regularly updated health history, developed from a health profes-sional's interview with the child and the parents, will reveal about 90 percent of health problems. Input from caregivers other than the parents should be brought by the parents to the health professional. Parents should be encouraged to bring a list of symptoms or concerns to discuss at the child's checkup, including those of concern to the child's other caregivers.

MEASUREMENTS OF PHYSICAL GROWTH AND BLOOD PRESSURE

Because variation from the normal growth pattern is often an early sign of a serious physical problem, measurements of height and weight for children of all ages and of head circumference for children up to 1 year of age should be taken and compared with data on healthy children. Body measurements correlate closely with nutritional status.

Recent evidence suggests that children with blood pressure measurements in the upper ranges of normal for their age group may be at risk for hypertension and associated diseases. After 3 years of age, blood pressure is measured concurrently with other growth measurements. Treatment is reserved for significant aberrations, but early identification of children with elevated blood pressure permits closer observation and attention to factors thought to contribute to hypertension, such as obesity and excessive salt intake.

SENSORY SCREENING

Vision

Between 5 and 6 percent of preschool children have one or more vision defects, and this proportion increases to 20–25 percent during school age. Because uncorrected visual defects in preschoolers may result in blindness, vision screening should be performed early and frequently. Follow-up diagnosis with correction for any problems is important at any age.

Hearing

Children with hearing impairments may suffer profound and long-lasting effects; such children are often mislabeled slow learners. The reported prevalence of hearing problems varies from 3 to 20 percent, depending on the age of the children and screening method used. The disability caused by hearing impairment justifies routine hearing screening for all children from age 3 through adulthood.

DEVELOPMENTAL AND BEHAVIORAL ASSESSMENT

Mental retardation, seizure disorders, neuromotor disabilities, learning problems, and emotional disturbances are common problems that can be seriously disabling. The type of screening method used is not as important as ensuring that the method provides systematic, ongoing comparison of the child's progress with that of normal peers. Early detection of significantly abnormal development or behavior provides the greatest opportunity to benefit from interventions.

PHYSICAL EXAMINATION

The physical examination is a look-and-touch procedure that is conducted on the unclothed child to search for abnormalities and to clarify concerns raised by the health history. Body build, maturity, posture, gait, coordination, and examination of head, ears, eyes, nose, mouth, neck, chest, abdomen, genitalia, extremities, and back are included. Relative to the other procedures included in the checkup visit, the physical examination is a low-yield procedure. The detection of a new finding in the physical examination that was not suspected from the health history is unusual.

OTHER PROCEDURES

Immunization

Immunizations usually are given at the checkup visit. Child care program personnel can help parents to assemble and maintain records of routine immunization so that full immunization of each child can be ensured. Child health professionals frequently see children who have used several other sources of health care and whose parents have no immunization records. The importance of retention of immunization records needs constant reinforcement. Immunizations should be updated using the current schedules of the U.S. Public Health Service and the American Academy of Pediatrics.

Tuberculin Testing

The frequency of tuberculin testing varies by community and is determined by the prevalence of tuberculosis. Local public health departments should be consulted to determine the appropriate frequency of tuberculin testing for children in child care. Screening of children who have been exposed to an adult with tuberculosis is very important; adults with tuberculosis are the usual source of spread of the disease.

Anemia Screening

Anemia affects up to half of poor children in some preschool populations. Anemia may reduce resistance to infection, attention span, motivation to learn, and overall intellectual performance, and it can cause apathy and fatigue. The detection of anemia is simple and inexpensive, using the hematocrit test (percent of whole blood occupied by red blood cells) or the hemoglobin test (grams of hemoglobin per 100 milliliters of blood). The most common cause of anemia is iron deficiency. This condition occurs when the child's growth is not matched by an adequate intake of iron. When iron deficiency anemia is present, oral iron therapy is usually effective. Correction of iron deficiency anemia is correlated with an increase in energy and resumption of normal growth and development.

Cholesterol and Blood Lipid Screening

Blood testing to detect elevated cholesterol and blood lipid levels should begin at age 2, at least for children with a positive family history. A positive family history includes parents, grandparents, aunts, and uncles who have had an early heart attack, stroke, or elevated blood cholesterol. An early heart attack is defined as one occurring before age 60 in females and before age 50 in males. Some physicians believe that all preschoolers and preteens should be screened for cholesterol and blood lipids.

Urinalysis

Unlike adults, children rarely develop diseases that might be detected in the urine without first developing some symptom of disease. The value of periodic checking of the urine in the absence of symptoms of a problem in the urinary tract has been questioned. For this reason, current recommendations suggest that routine urinalysis be performed for children sometime during infancy and again in early childhood, late childhood, and adolescence. Routine urinalysis usually includes checking the urine for color, clarity, concentration, acidity, presence of sugar and protein, and enzymatic evidence of infection. Other chemical tests may also be included. Further evaluation of the urine may be performed by looking at samples under the microscope, both as the urine came from the body and after centrifugation to concentrate the cellular elements. Normally, the kidneys will have kept cellular components from entering the urine. Detection of cellular elements in the urine is an indication of improper function or a problem in the urinary tract that is putting cells into the urine after the kidneys have made the urine.

ANTICIPATORY GUIDANCE

Parents need to have the opportunity to ask questions and, within the practical limitations of a busy office schedule, to received unhurried answers. The child health professional has an opportunity to educate parents about parenting, about intervention for identified problems, about health-promoting behaviors, and about care appropriate to the needs of the specific child and family. Sometimes this counseling can be provided in the course of the routinely scheduled visits required during childhood. However, when special needs are identified, appointments for the purpose of extended discussion must be scheduled.

DENTAL CARE

By age 3, every child needs dental services. Routine preventive dental services of proved effectiveness include once- or twice-yearly cleaning, evaluation for risk factors for development of caries (cavities), application of topical fluoride, and use of fluoride supplements for children who drink water that is not fluoridated. The requirement for fluoride intake begins at birth. Fluoride supplements must be prescribed by a health professional for breast-fed infants who do not take significant amounts of water, since fluoride does not cross into breast milk, and for all infants and children who do not drink fluoridated water. By being incorporated into tooth development from birth onward, fluoride can reduce dental decay by more than half over a lifetime.

Children's Books on Health and Safety

Many good books for children on health and safety topics are available. Consult a children's librarian for those available locally. The following are some examples that belong in the library of every early childhood program.

SLEEP

Brown, M., *Good Night Moon*, Harper & Row

Zolotow, C., *Sleepy Book*, Harper Junior

Fujikawa, G., *Sleepy Time*, Grosset & Dunlap

Hoban, R., *Bedtime for Frances*, Harper & Row

Sendak, M., *Where the Wild Things Are*, Harper & Row

NUTRITION

McQueen, L., *The Little Red Hen*, Scholastic Inc.

Titherington, J., *Pumpkin, Pumpkin*, Greenwillow

McCloskey, R., *Blueberries for Sal*, Viking Press

Hayes, S., *Eat Up, Gemma*, Lothrop

Carter, A., *Bella's Secret Garden*, Crown

Ehlert, L., *Growing Vegetable Soup*, Harcourt, Brace Jovanovich

Sendak, M., *Chicken Soup with Rice*, Harper & Row

FIRST EXPERIENCES

Rogers, F., *Going to the Doctor*, Putnam Publishing Group
Going to the Potty, Putnam Publishing Group
Going to Day Care, Putnam Publishing Group
The New Baby, Putnam Publishing Group

Where to Send for Child, Staff, and Parent Educational Materials

GENERAL

Consumer Information Center
Pueblo, CO 81009

American Academy of Pediatrics
141 Northwest Point Blvd.
Elk Grove Village, IL 60009-0927
(Ask for the AAP Publications Catalog and the "Pediatric Patient Education Audio-Visual Resource List")

American Red Cross
(contact local chapters listed in the telephone directory)
National ARC Headquarters
17th and D St.
Washington, DC 20006

March of Dimes Birth Defects Foundation
1275 Mamaronek Ave.
White Plains, NY 10605

National Association for the Education of Young Children
1834 Connecticut Ave., N.W.
Washington, DC 20009-5786

National Center for Clinical Infant Programs
2000 14th Street North, Suite 380
Arlington, VA 22201-2500

State, county, and municipal departments of health
(consult local telephone directories for contact information)

Superintendent of Documents
Government Printing Office
Washington, DC 20402
(especially materials from the Department of Health and Human Services, Office of Human Development Services, Bureau of Head Start; and the U.S. Public Health Service, Maternal and Child Health, Centers for Disease Control, National Institutes of Health, Health Services Administration)

National Health Information Clearinghouse
P.O. Box 1133
Washington, DC 20013

SAFETY EDUCATION MATERIALS

U.S. Consumer Product Safety Commission
Washington, DC 20207

National Safety Council
444 North Michigan Ave.
Chicago, IL 60611

North County Health Services
348 Rancheros Dr.
San Marcos, CA 92069
(an Injury Prevention Program for Head Start)

Statewide Comprehensive Injury Prevention Program
Division of Injury Epidemiology and Control
Center for Environmental Health
Centers for Disease Control
Atlanta, GA 30333

Child Passenger Safety

National Highway Traffic Safety Administration
400 7th St., S.W.
Washington, DC 20590

Insurance Institute for Highway Safety
Watergate 600
Washington, DC 20037

American Automobile Association (contact local clubs)

National Association for Pupil Transportation and National School Transportation Association; National Association of State Directors of Pupil Transportation, National Safety Council; School Bus Manufacturers and Suppliers. Contact:
Raymond F. Kroll
Chairman for National School Bus Safety Week
11001 2nd Ave. North
Minneapolis, MN 55405

Building and Fire Safety

National Conference of States on Building Codes and Standards and Council of American Building Officials
481 Carlisle Dr.
Herndon, VA 22070

Local electric utility company

National Fire Protection Association
Battermarch Park
Quincy, MA 02269

American Society of Safety Engineers
1800 East Oakton St.
Des Plaines, IL 60018-2187

Federal Emergency Management Agency
U.S. Fire Administration
Washington, DC 20472

Drowning Prevention and Water Safety

U.S. Coast Guard and National Safe Boating Council
U.S. Coast Guard HQ (G-BBS-4)
2100 2nd St., S.W.
Washington, DC 20593

The California Drowning Prevention Network
Suite 100
321 North Rampart St.
Orange, CA 92668

Poison Prevention

Poison Prevention Week Council
P.O. Box 1543
Washington, DC 20013

U.S. Environmental Protection Agency
Washington, DC 20460
(see telephone directory for regional offices)

Occupational Safety

U.S. Department of Labor Occupational Safety and Health Administration
Washington, DC 20213

Child Care Employee Health Project
P.O. Box 5603
Berkeley, CA 94705

NUTRITION EDUCATION MATERIALS

The American Dietetic Association
216 West Jackson Blvd.
Chicago, IL 60606-6995

American Home Economics Association
2010 Massachusetts Ave., N.W.
Washington, DC 20036

Society for Nutrition Education
1736 Franklin St.
Oakland, CA 94612

Food and Nutrition Information Center
Room 304
National Agricultural Library Bldg.
Beltsville, MD 20705

U.S. Department of Agriculture
Food and Nutrition Service
Office of Public Information
Room 823
Park Office Center
3101 Park Center Dr.
Alexandria, VA 22302

Cooperative Extension Service (consult telephone directory for state college listing and local government section)

VISION

American Foundation for the Blind
15 West 16th St.
New York, NY 10011

TEETH AND DENTAL CARE

American Association of Orthodontists
460 North Lindbergh
Dept. KD
St. Louis, MO 63141

BREATHING AND LUNG PROBLEMS

American Lung Association
GPO Box 596-RB
New York, NY 10001

American Cancer Society (local offices are listed in the telephone book)

CHILD ABUSE AND NEGLECT

Clearinghouse on Child Abuse and Neglect Information
P.O. Box 1182
Washington, DC 20013

CHILDREN'S DISABILITIES

Clearinghouse on the Handicapped
Room 338-D
Hubert H. Humphrey Bldg.
200 Independence Ave., S.W.
Washington, DC 20201

National Information Center for Handicapped Children and Youth
Suite 600
1555 Wilson Blvd.
Rosslyn, VA 22209

Forms

Sample Letter to Parents About Outdoor Play

Dear Parents:

As long as the temperature is above 40 or below 80 degrees Fahrenheit, and it is not raining, we take the children outdoors to play every day, even in winter. Daily outdoor play gives children a change of scene, an opportunity for large muscle play, and fresh air. In fresh air, children do not breathe in each other's germs as much as they do when they share the same air indoors. After playing outdoors, children eat better, sleep better and feel better.

Exposure to cold, to wind, or to dampness does not make children sick. Children become ill when they are stressed by exposure to conditions for which they are not prepared and when they are exposed to germs that are new to them in a quantity that is too large for them to fight off. Regular outdoor play prepares children to handle stressful conditions that occur unexpectedly. While children play outside, we will ventilate the rooms so that there are fewer germs in the air when the children return from outdoor play.

When the weather is very cold or very hot, we will take the children outdoors for shorter periods of time or plan trips so that the children can benefit from the change of scene and new experiences with limited exposure to inclement weather. We will let you know when we plan trips and ask for your consent for your child to participate.

Children should be dressed appropriately for the weather so they can enjoy our daily outdoor activities. Use the following guide to decide what your child should wear or bring to the program:

For Damp, Cold Conditions: *Underpants, undershirt, long pants, long sleeve shirt, socks, shoes, rubber boots, water-repellant coat with a warm lining and hood or cap, and mittens with a water repellent surface. Be sure we have a complete change of indoor clothing available in case your child finds a puddle to splash in. Plastic bags worn over the shoes inside boots help keep feet dry and make it easy to get boots on and off.*

For Dry, Cold Conditions: *Add layers of medium-weight clothing to trap body warmth. Have the child wear an extra pair of socks, a sweater, snowpants over long indoor pants, long underwear if it is really cold, an extra pair of mittens, a wool cap inside the hood of the jacket, and a long scarf to cover the nose and lower part of the face. Clothing should be dry and clean to provide maximum warmth.*

Children need about the same number of layers to keep warm as adults; they just become colder and warmer faster when they are under- or over-dressed. Overdressing should be avoided because it leads to sweating. When clothing becomes wet with perspiration, it no longer keeps the child warm and the child may become chilled.

For Warm Weather: *Keep underwear to a minimum and select outer garments that are loose and light-weight. Since young children cool themselves by losing heat from their heads and necks more than do adults, avoid closely fitting clothing in these areas in hot weather.*

Sample Handout for Parents:
How to Keep Children Healthy

You can help your child stay well by following some healthy routines:

1. Teach and practice good hand washing.

   Everyone should wash to prevent germs from going from one person to another. Hands should be washed routinely before eating, after toileting, and whenever there is contact with a body fluid from the nose, the mouth, the genital area, or any other source.

2. Make sure your child has a regular bedtime and regular routines that help the child prepare for sleep.

   A firm, regular bedtime helps children get the rest they need to meet the challenge of another busy day. Children need time to calm down before they drop off to sleep. Quiet activities like reading a story, having the child tell about the day's events, or singing a quiet song help a child relax and prepare for sleep. If the child does not feel ready to drop off to sleep, the child should still be in bed, looking at books or listening to quiet music while parents have some private time of their own. Sometimes naptime may have to be adjusted to allow the child to be ready for sleep at a time that fits with the rest of the child's and family's schedule.

3. Encourage your child to exercise in the fresh air.

   Exercise helps build the child's ability to cope with unexpected stress. Children enjoy exercise: skipping, hopping, jumping, running, throwing a ball, dancing. Many of these activities are fun for adults too!

4. Offer your child healthy foods and snacks.

   Children have small stomachs and need to eat small amounts of food often. Each snack should be a mini-meal of only good food, because the child may not be hungry at the regular meal time. Young children need to be offered food for breakfast, mid-morning snack, lunch, midafternoon snack, dinner, and before bed, but they may only want to eat at some of those times.

   Good snacks include unsweetened cereal, fruits, milkshakes made with fruit, raw vegetables with or without yogurt or cottage cheese dip, peanut butter on celery or bread, graham crackers with or without cream cheese, yogurt, cheese, unsalted pretzels, fruit juice popsicles, and popcorn (for older preschoolers). Wholesome leftovers from meals make good snacks as long as the child is not forced to eat something the child really doesn't like. Bad snacks are candy, cake, pies, cookies, chocolate syrup, sugary drinks, soda, potato chips, salted pretzels, doughnuts, sugared cereals, fudgesicles, and popsicles.

5. Be sure to keep your child up-to-date with checkups.

Checkups are visits scheduled in advance for routine well care, not short visits when the child is sick. When the child is sick, the problem gets attention, but routine tests and general assessment of the child's health are usually postponed to a visit scheduled just for that purpose. At checkup visits, special tests are often done to find disease problems when they are just starting and are easy to treat—sometimes before parents have noticed that anything is wrong. Younger children and children with special health problems need more frequent checkups than older children, but you should always know when the child's next checkup is due.

Checkups are usually scheduled for well children without special health problems at the following ages: at birth, by 1 month of age, at 2, 4, 6, 9, 12, 15, 18, and 24 months, and then 2½, 3, 4, 5, 6, 8, 10, and 12 years. Checkups are scheduled during adolescence every one or two years, depending on the recommendations of the child's physician.

Sample Handout for Parents:
Infectious Disease in Child Care Settings— What You Need to Know

Young children are more vulnerable to infectious diseases than older children and adults for several reasons. First, they have immature immune systems that do not respond to an infection as well as do the immune systems of adults. Second, young children are meeting many infections for the first time. Unlike older children and adults, whose bodies remember having fought off many similar infections, young children's bodies must fight off germs by building the defenses from no previous reserves. Therefore, young children become ill more often and may remain ill longer.

Even children who receive care only in their own homes with their own families have frequent illnesses. The average preschool-age child has about one respiratory infection a month in the wintertime. Infants and toddlers in child care centers seem to be ill somewhat more often than children of the same age in family day care homes or in their own homes. By age 3, children seem to have the same frequency of illness no matter where they are in care.

When children come together in group care, the opportunities for sharing infectious diseases are increased. Some of this increased risk can be controlled by good hygiene and healthful rest, exercise, and nutrition habits. Children who are in stable child care groups with the same caregivers have fewer illnesses than children who are in groups where new children and new caregivers are introduced from time to time. So, having the children and the caregivers stay together in the same group during the whole day and over the years that the child is in child care helps too.

PLANNING FOR ILLNESS

Your child will be sick sometimes. Some common signs of illness are fever, runny nose, cough, irritability, refusal to eat or drink, diarrhea, vomiting, and pulling at an ear. Because all children are sick sometimes, you need to have a plan for care of your child during illness.

See if your employer will let you use your sick leave to care for an ill child. Perhaps you can bring work home or share a workday with a spouse or other relative. Sometimes your child can come to work with you if there is a quiet place to rest and be near you. Perhaps you have a neighbor who knows your child well and will care for your child during a minor illness. Some communities have workers who can be called to come to your home to care for an ill child. Sometimes your child will be recovering from an illness and be able to participate in the regular child care program. As another option, check to see if there are special programs to care for ill children. Whatever you decide, remember that when your child feels sick, your love is good medicine that no one else can give as well as you can. If you can't take care of your child during some part of an illness, find the most familiar person and most familiar setting you can to care for your child.

WHAT TO DO WHEN YOUR CHILD IS SICK

Take stock of the child's symptoms and decide what part of your plan for illness you will use. If you are not sure what kind of care your child will need for the whole day, get medical advice from your child's usual source of health care. Be sure to let the child care program know about your child's illness. Your child's health problem could affect the other children or could provide a clue to a problem that is affecting more than one child in your child's group. Write down what the doctor tells you so you can give the correct information to the child care program staff. When you seek medical advice, be sure to tell the health professional that your child is in a child care program.

Do not be upset if your child's doctor implies that your child's illness is related to using child care. Because infections are more frequent in young children in group settings, doctors tend to make that connection, and you may feel it is your fault that your child is sick. Many of these illnesses are inevitable. If your child has a lot more trouble with illness than the average child, your doctor may suggest a smaller group setting for a while. Work together with the child care program and your child's physician to consider your options, but don't blame yourself.

When your child is ready to come back to the regular child care setting, be sure to let the caregivers know if any special care is still needed. Make plans for any medication to be given at home if possible, or follow the child care program policy for medication. If you tell the doctor the hours during which your child is in the child care program, the medication plan may be able to be changed so all doses of medication can be given at home.

Sample Letter for Parents of a
Child Exposed to an Infectious Disease

(Have a health professional help you fill in the blanks before you send the letter out to parents.)

Dear Parents:

A child in your child's group has been diagnosed with _____
(name of infectious disease). *We'd like you to know about this problem so that you can take good care of your child.*

What is (name of infectious disease)?

_____

Who can get (name of infectious disease)?

_____

How you can tell when someone has (name of infectious disease)?

_____

What problems can (name of infectious disease) *cause?*

_____

How (name of infectious disease) *is treated:*

_____

What the child care program is doing about this infectious disease:

_____

What you should do with this information:

_____

If any sign of this disease occurs in your child, call your doctor to find out what to do. Be sure to share this notice with your doctor and give your doctor permission to call us for further information. If you do not have a regular doctor who takes care of your child, ask us to help you find one. If you have any questions, contact:

(name) _____

at (telephone) _____ .

Sample Daily Log

	MON	TUES	WED	THURS	FRI
NAME OF CHILD _____ **WEEK OF** _____ **19**_____					

NOTES FROM CAREGIVERS TO PARENTS:

NOTES FROM PARENTS TO CAREGIVERS:

Growth Charts

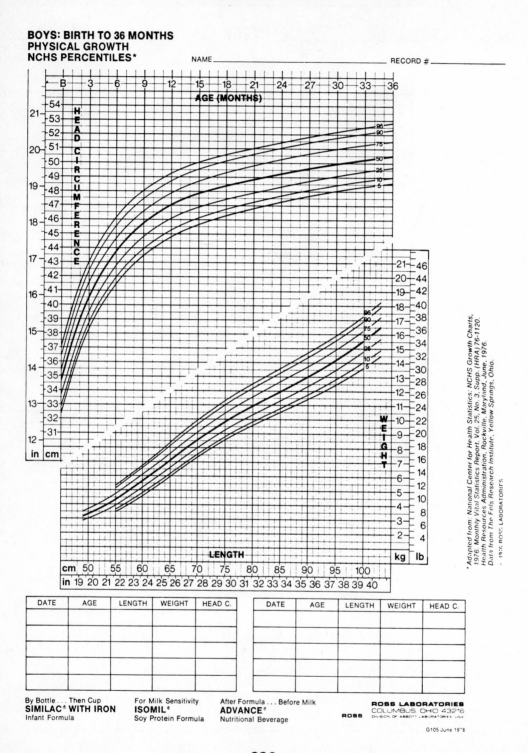

BOYS: BIRTH TO 36 MONTHS
PHYSICAL GROWTH
NCHS PERCENTILES*

NAME _____ RECORD # _____

DATE	AGE	LENGTH	WEIGHT	HEAD C.

DATE	AGE	LENGTH	WEIGHT	HEAD C.

*Adapted from: National Center for Health Statistics: NCHS Growth Charts, 1976. Monthly Vital Statistics Report. Vol. 25, No. 3, Supp. (HRA) 76-1120. Health Resources Administration, Rockville, Maryland, June, 1976. Data from The Fels Research Institute, Yellow Springs, Ohio.

© 1976 ROSS LABORATORIES

By Bottle . . . Then Cup
SIMILAC® WITH IRON
Infant Formula

For Milk Sensitivity
ISOMIL®
Soy Protein Formula

After Formula . . . Before Milk
ADVANCE®
Nutritional Beverage

ROSS LABORATORIES
COLUMBUS, OHIO 43216
DIVISION OF ABBOTT LABORATORIES USA

ROSS

G105 June 1978

Growth Charts

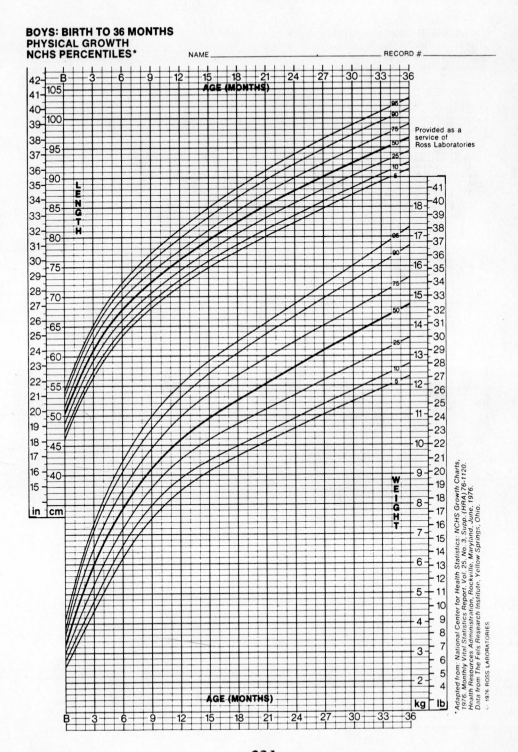

BOYS: BIRTH TO 36 MONTHS
PHYSICAL GROWTH
NCHS PERCENTILES*

NAME _____ RECORD # _____

Provided as a
service of
Ross Laboratories

*Adapted from: National Center for Health Statistics: NCHS Growth Charts, 1976. Monthly Vital Statistics Report, Vol. 25, No. 3, Supp. (HRA) 76-1120. Health Resources Administration, Rockville, Maryland, June, 1976. Data from The Fels Research Institute, Yellow Springs, Ohio.

© 1976 ROSS LABORATORIES

Growth Charts

GIRLS: BIRTH TO 36 MONTHS
PHYSICAL GROWTH
NCHS PERCENTILES*

NAME _____ RECORD # _____

DATE	AGE	LENGTH	WEIGHT	HEAD CIRC.	COMMENT

*Adapted from: Hamill PVV, Drizd TA, Johnson CL, Reed RB, Roche AF, Moore WM. Physical growth: National Center for Health Statistics percentiles. AM J CLIN NUTR 32:607-629, 1979. Data from the Fels Research Institute, Wright State University School of Medicine, Yellow Springs, Ohio.

© 1982 ROSS LABORATORIES

Recommend the formulation you prefer with the name you trust

SIMILAC*
SIMILAC* WITH IRON
SIMILAC* WITH WHEY + IRON
Infant Formulas

The ISOMIL* System of Soy Protein Formulas

ADVANCE*
Nutritional Beverage

ROSS LABORATORIES
COLUMBUS, OHIO 43216
Division of Abbott Laboratories, USA

G106 DECEMBER 1983   LITHO IN USA

232

Growth Charts

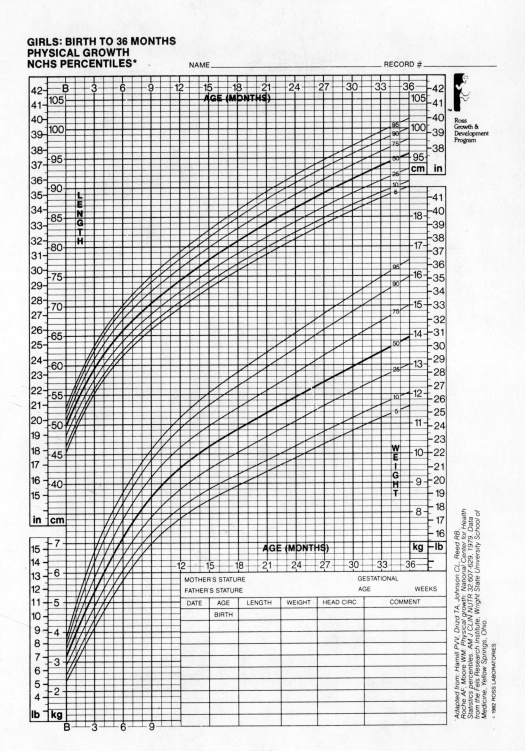

GIRLS: BIRTH TO 36 MONTHS
PHYSICAL GROWTH
NCHS PERCENTILES*

NAME _____ RECORD # _____

Ross
Growth &
Development
Program

AGE (MONTHS)

LENGTH

WEIGHT

AGE (MONTHS)

MOTHER'S STATURE			GESTATIONAL			
FATHER'S STATURE			AGE		WEEKS	
DATE	AGE	LENGTH	WEIGHT	HEAD CIRC.	COMMENT	
	BIRTH					

*Adapted from: Hamill PVV, Dnzd TA, Johnson CL, Reed RB, Roche AF, Moore WM. Physical growth: National Center for Health Statistics percentiles. AM J CLIN NUTR 32:607-629, 1979. Data from the Fels Research Institute, Wright State University School of Medicine, Yellow Springs, Ohio.

© 1982 ROSS LABORATORIES

Growth Charts

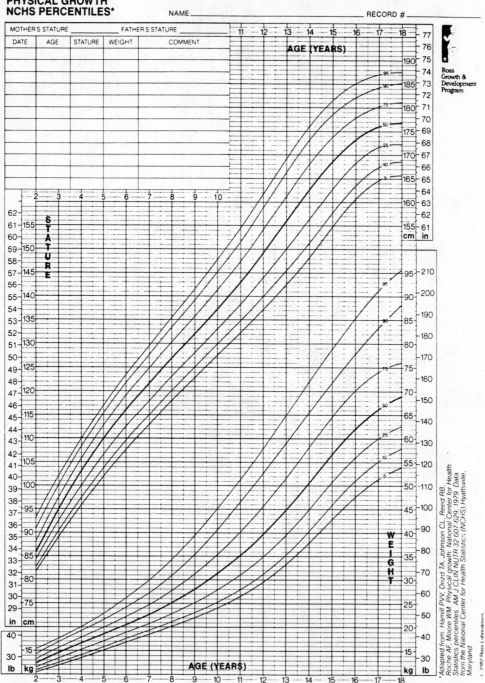

BOYS: 2 TO 18 YEARS
PHYSICAL GROWTH
NCHS PERCENTILES*

NAME _____ RECORD # _____

Ross
Growth &
Development
Program

MOTHER'S STATURE		FATHER'S STATURE		
DATE	AGE	STATURE	WEIGHT	COMMENT

AGE (YEARS)

STATURE

WEIGHT

AGE (YEARS)

*Adapted from: Hamill PVV, Drizd TA, Johnson CL, Reed RB, Roche AF, Moore WM. Physical growth: National Center for Health Statistics percentiles. AM J CLIN NUTR 32:607-629, 1979. Data from the National Center for Health Statistics (NCHS), Hyattsville, Maryland.

© 1982 Ross Laboratories

Growth Charts

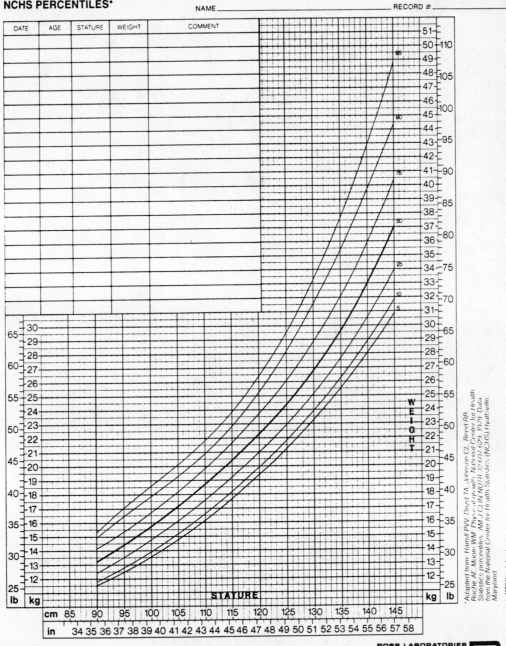

**BOYS: PREPUBESCENT
PHYSICAL GROWTH
NCHS PERCENTILES***

NAME _____ RECORD # _____

*Adapted from Hamill PVV, Drizd TA, Johnson CL, Reed RR, Roche AF, Moore WM: Physical growth: National Center for Health Statistics percentiles, AM J CLIN NUTR 32:607-629, 1979. Data from the National Center for Health Statistics (NCHS), Hyattsville, Maryland

© 1982 Ross Laboratories

235

Growth Charts

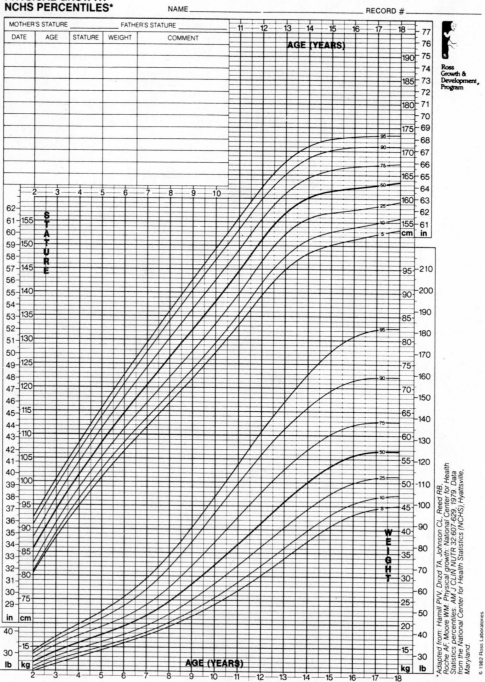

GIRLS: 2 TO 18 YEARS
PHYSICAL GROWTH
NCHS PERCENTILES*

NAME _____ RECORD # _____

Ross
Growth &
Development
Program

DATE	AGE	STATURE	WEIGHT	COMMENT

MOTHER'S STATURE _____ FATHER'S STATURE _____

AGE (YEARS)

STATURE

WEIGHT

AGE (YEARS)

*Adapted from: Hamill PVV, Drizd TA, Johnson CL, Reed RB, Roche AF, Moore WM. Physical growth: National Center for Health Statistics percentiles. AM J CLIN NUTR 32:607-629, 1979. Data from the National Center for Health Statistics (NCHS), Hyattsville, Maryland.

Growth Charts

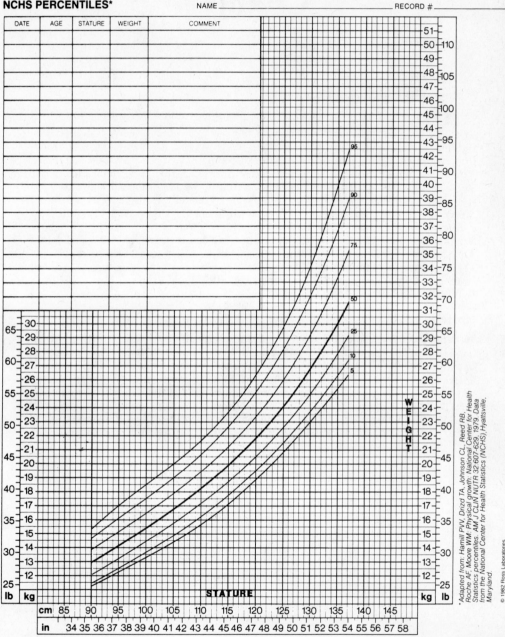

GIRLS: PREPUBESCENT PHYSICAL GROWTH NCHS PERCENTILES*

NAME _____ RECORD # _____

DATE	AGE	STATURE	WEIGHT	COMMENT

STATURE

WEIGHT

*Adapted from: Hamill PVV, Drizd TA, Johnson CL, Reed RB, Roche AF, Moore WM: Physical growth: National Center for Health Statistics percentiles. AM J CLIN NUTR 32:607-629, 1979. Data from the National Center for Health Statistics (NCHS), Hyattsville, Maryland.

© 1982 Ross Laboratories

ROSS LABORATORIES
COLUMBUS, OHIO 43216
DIVISION OF ABBOTT LABORATORIES USA

G108(0.05) JANUARY 1986   LITHO IN USA

Credits

Index

Illness management, 153, 160–181. *See also* Infectious diseases
for chronic illnesses, 168, 171–175
exclusion guidelines in. *See* Exclusion guidelines
medication and, 178–179
policies on, 198, 199
for short-term illnesses, 161–171. *See also* Short-term illnesses
written policies and procedures for, 179–180
Immune system diseases, 173. *See also specific types*
Immunizations, 2, 64, 130, 137, 148–150, 158, 198, 214
for adults, 54, 58
adverse reactions to, 150, 164, 169
for AIDS patients, 144
for caregivers, 198
health consultants and, 204
infections preventable by, 140
records of, 202
Impetigo, 135, 139, 155, 156
Implementation of the health component, 195–211
Individualized education plans (IEPs), 172
Individualized family service plans (IFSPs), 172
Indoor safety, 76, 106–124
Indoor space, 67–68
Infant formula, 33, 34, 35
Infants
chronic illness in, 172
common causes of injuries in, 81
defined, 4
emergency evacuation of, 123
exercise needs of, 11
feeding of, 30–36, 40, 72
infectious diseases in, 136, 148
motor vehicle safety for, 87
obesity in, 45
playground safety for, 94
safety measures for, 106–108, 110, 113
sleep problems in, 23
space requirements of, 67, 68
water safety for, 79
Infant walkers, 107
Infectious diseases, 69–70, 126–145, 147–158, 208. *See also specific types*
activities for patients with, 171
humidity and, 9–10, 73
overcrowding and, 67
risk management for, 3
sample handouts on, 225–226, 227–228
Influenza, 135, 170
Injuries. *See also* Indoor safety; Outdoor safety
common causes of, 81–83
facility design and, 75, 76
policies on management of, 198, 200
risk management and, 3
Inspections, 158

Insurance
health, 175
liability, 190
motor vehicle, 91
Integrated pest management, 118
Iron, 33, 34, 36, 40
Isolation, 157, 168, 171

Juvenile rheumatoid arthritis, 164

Kitchens. *See* Food preparation

Landings, 74–76
Laryngitis, 136
Laundry areas, 72
Lead poisoning, 173
Learning difficulties, 115
Legal liability, 210
caregiver health and, 51, 56
child abuse and, 188, 191
Leukemia, 173
Lice, 135, 139–140, 155, 156
Lighting, 77–78, 112, 200
Literacy Council, 209
Lung disease, 116. *See also specific types*

Maintenance, 8–10
Measles, 135
exclusion guidelines on, 156
vaccine for, 64, 140, 150
Medicaid, 175
Medical home, 16, 53, 204
Medication
administration of, 163, 178–179, 198, 200, 208
disease prevention with, 150
drawbacks of, 129
hazards of, 107, 113
Meningitis, 135, 137, 150
Mental health, 2, 20–22, 55
Mental health professionals, 21–22
Mental retardation, 172
Menu planning, 28, 42–43
Microwave ovens, 35, 72, 108
Milk, 33, 35–36, 39
Mononucleosis, 141
Mortality
from child abuse, 183
from drowning, 102
from guns, 119
from injuries, 81
from motor vehicle accidents, 83–84, 85, 89, 91
from pedestrian accidents, 103
Motor skill development, 94–95
Motor vehicle safety, 2–3, 82, 83–94, 174, 198, 201, 208

486 DX 33
4 meg
130 Meg Hard disk
14 in SVGA
2123 printer (fast & quiet)
$1,500
til 7PM M-F
Sat til 5PM